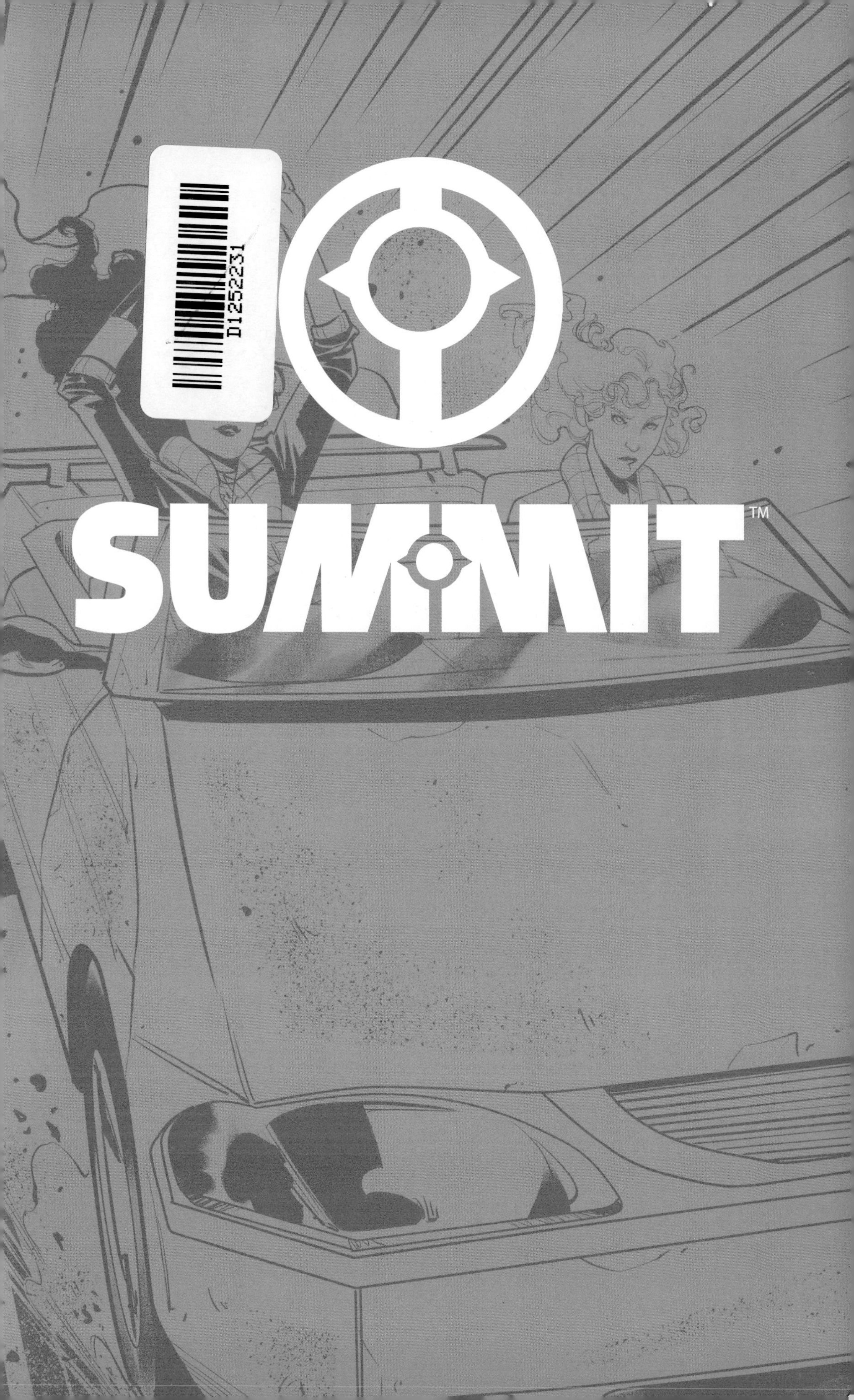
SUMMIT™

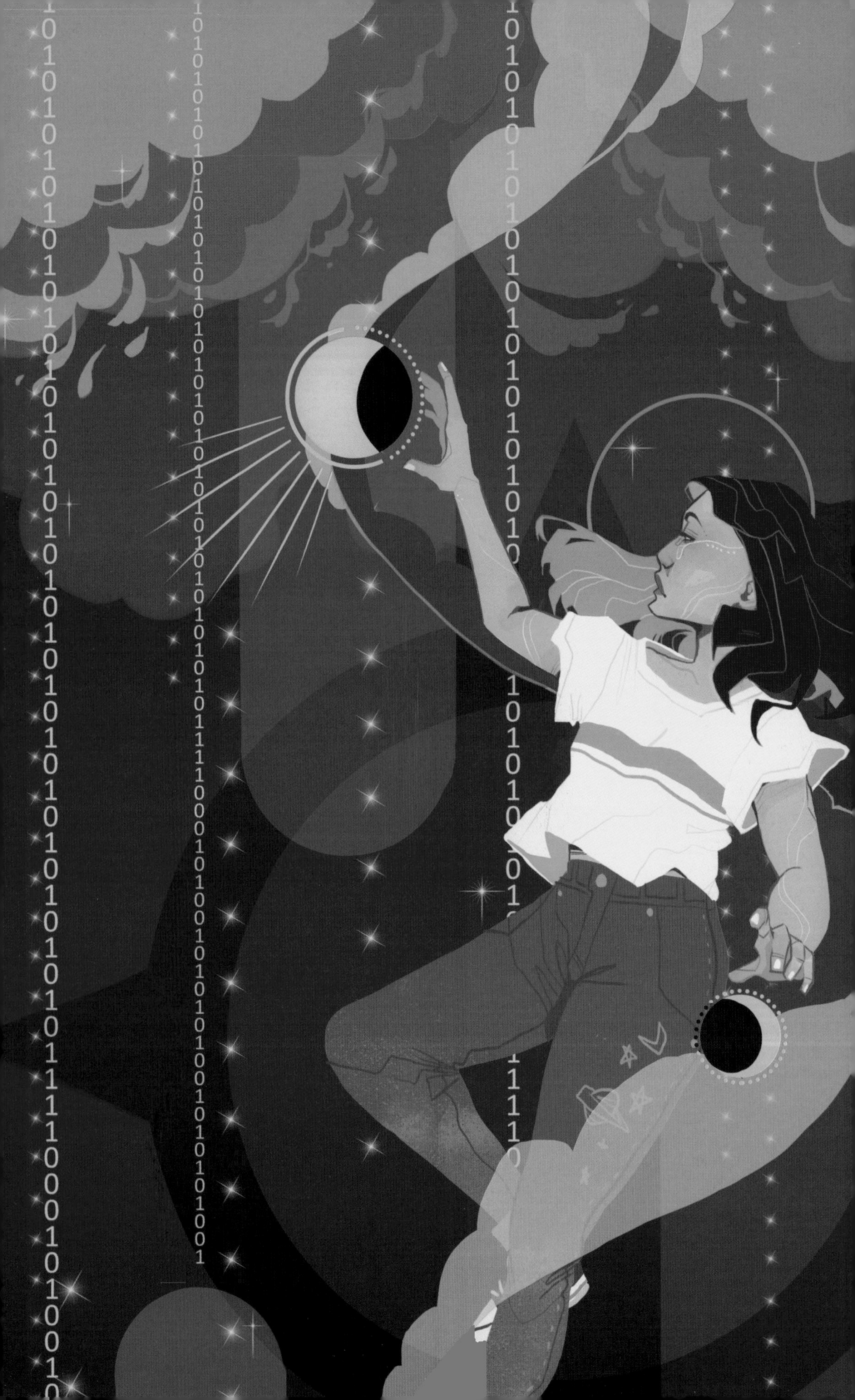

SUMMIT™

TRUTH OR CONSEQUENCES

written by **AMY CHU**
illustrated by **MARIKA CRESTA**
colored by **JESSICA KHOLINNE,**
BRYAN VALENZA, AND SNAKEBITE CORTEZ
lettered by **AW'S DC HOPKINS**
cover by: **ROBERTA INGRANATA**
AND WARNIA SAHADEWA

DESIREE RODRIGUEZ • editor
KAT VENDETTI • editorial assistant
cover by **ROBERTA INGRANATA**
colored by **WARNIA SAHADEWA**

ISBN: 978-1-5493-0286-2

LCCN: 2018941616

Summit Vol. 3, published 2019, by The Lion Forge, LLC. Copyright 2019 The Lion Forge, LLC. Portions of this book were previously published in Summit, Vol. 3 Issues 10-14. All Rights Reserved. SUMMIT™, LION FORGE™, CATALYST PRIME™, and their associated distinctive designs, as well as all characters featured in this book and the distinctive names and likenesses thereof, and all related indicia, are trademarks of The Lion Forge, LLC. No similarity between any of the names, characters, persons, or institutions in this issue with those of any living or dead person or institution is intended, and any such similarity which may exist is purely coincidental. Printed in Korea.

CHAPTER ONE

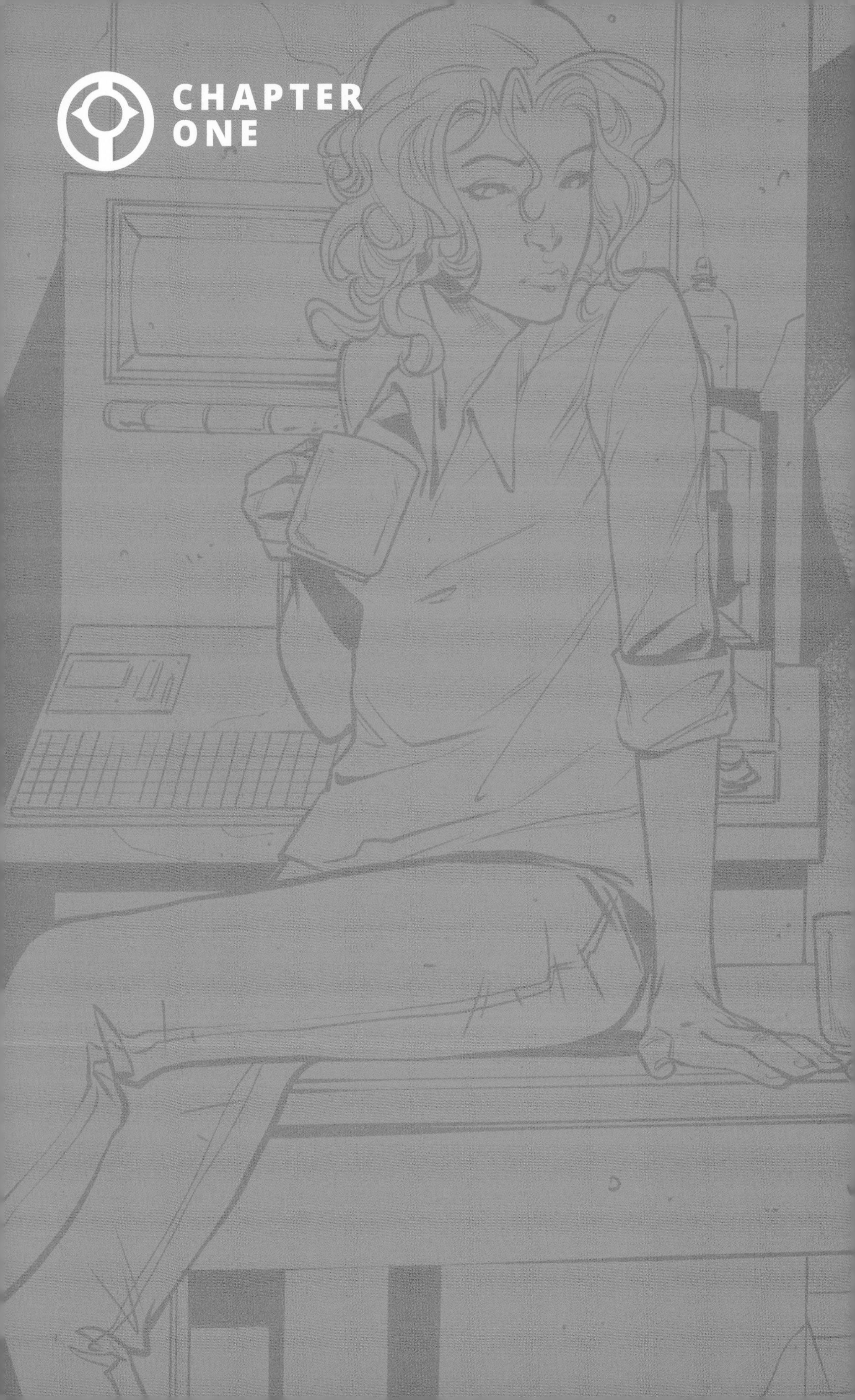

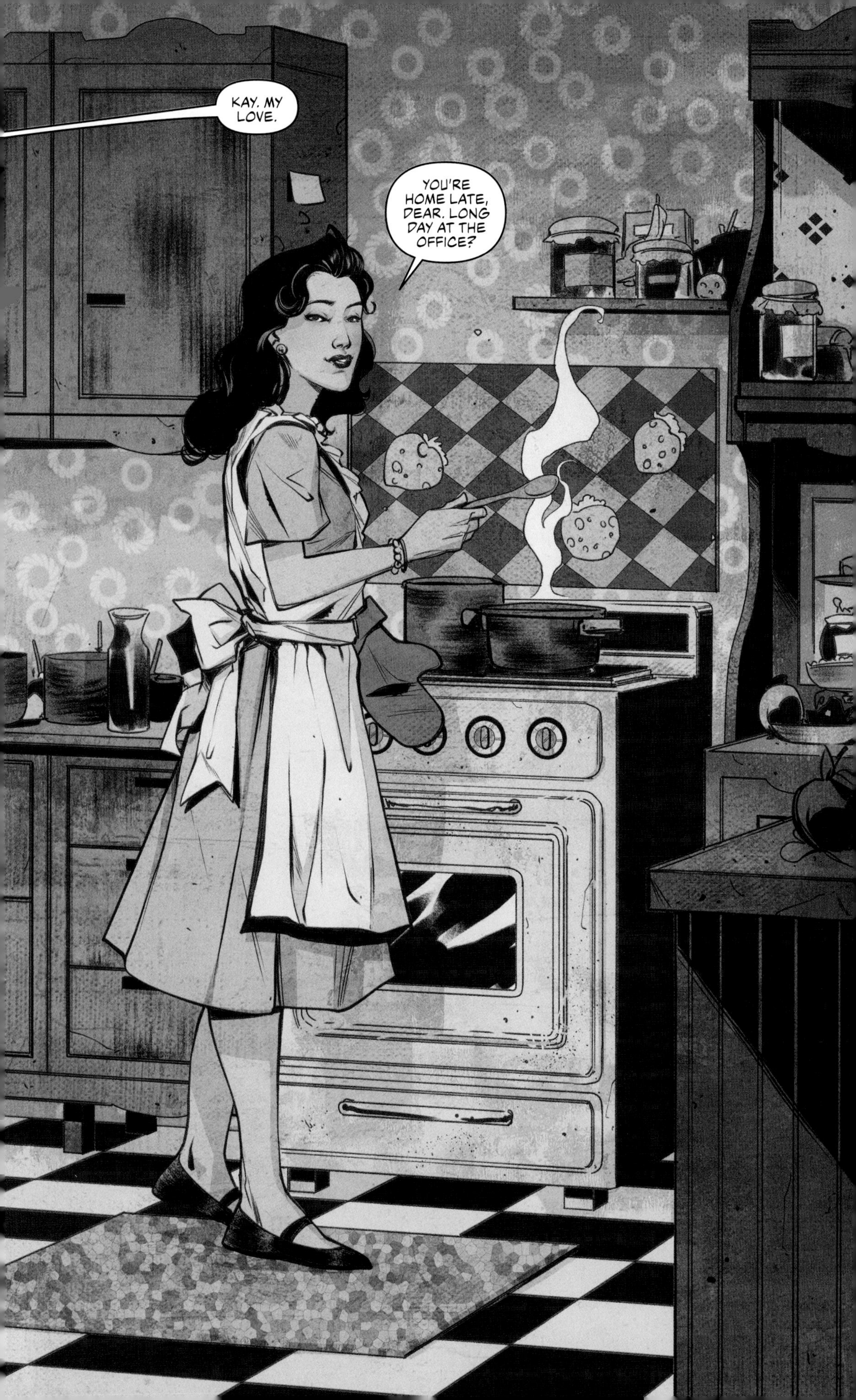
KAY. MY LOVE.
YOU'RE HOME LATE, DEAR. LONG DAY AT THE OFFICE?

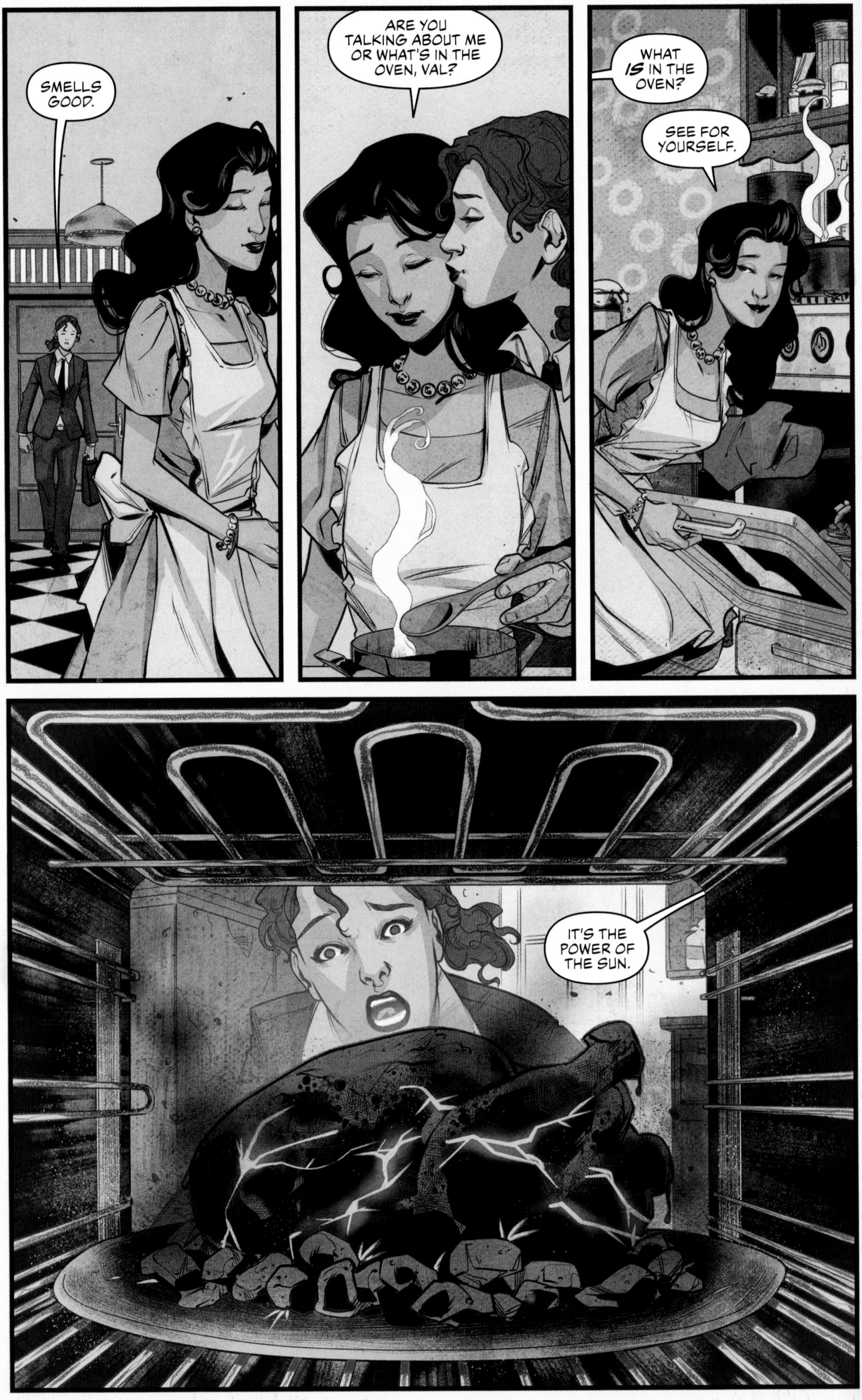
SMELLS GOOD.
ARE YOU TALKING ABOUT ME OR WHAT'S IN THE OVEN, VAL?
WHAT *IS* IN THE OVEN?
SEE FOR YOURSELF.
IT'S THE POWER OF THE SUN.

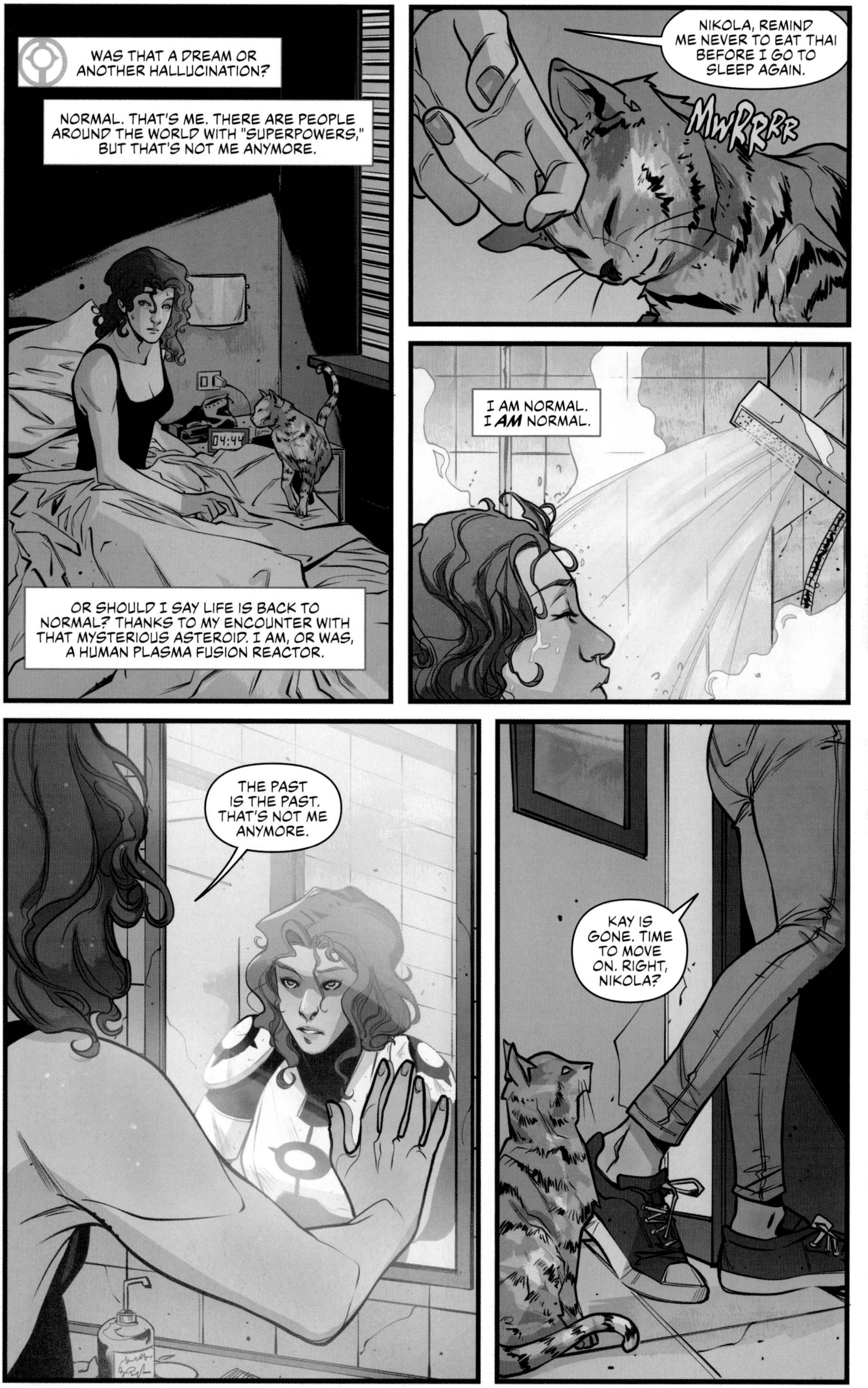
WAS THAT A DREAM OR ANOTHER HALLUCINATION?
NORMAL. THAT'S ME. THERE ARE PEOPLE AROUND THE WORLD WITH "SUPERPOWERS," BUT THAT'S NOT ME ANYMORE.
04:44
OR SHOULD I SAY LIFE IS BACK TO NORMAL? THANKS TO MY ENCOUNTER WITH THAT MYSTERIOUS ASTEROID. I AM, OR WAS, A HUMAN PLASMA FUSION REACTOR.
NIKOLA, REMIND ME NEVER TO EAT THAI BEFORE I GO TO SLEEP AGAIN.
MWRRRR
I AM NORMAL. I *AM* NORMAL.
THE PAST IS THE PAST. THAT'S NOT ME ANYMORE.
KAY IS GONE. TIME TO MOVE ON. RIGHT, NIKOLA?

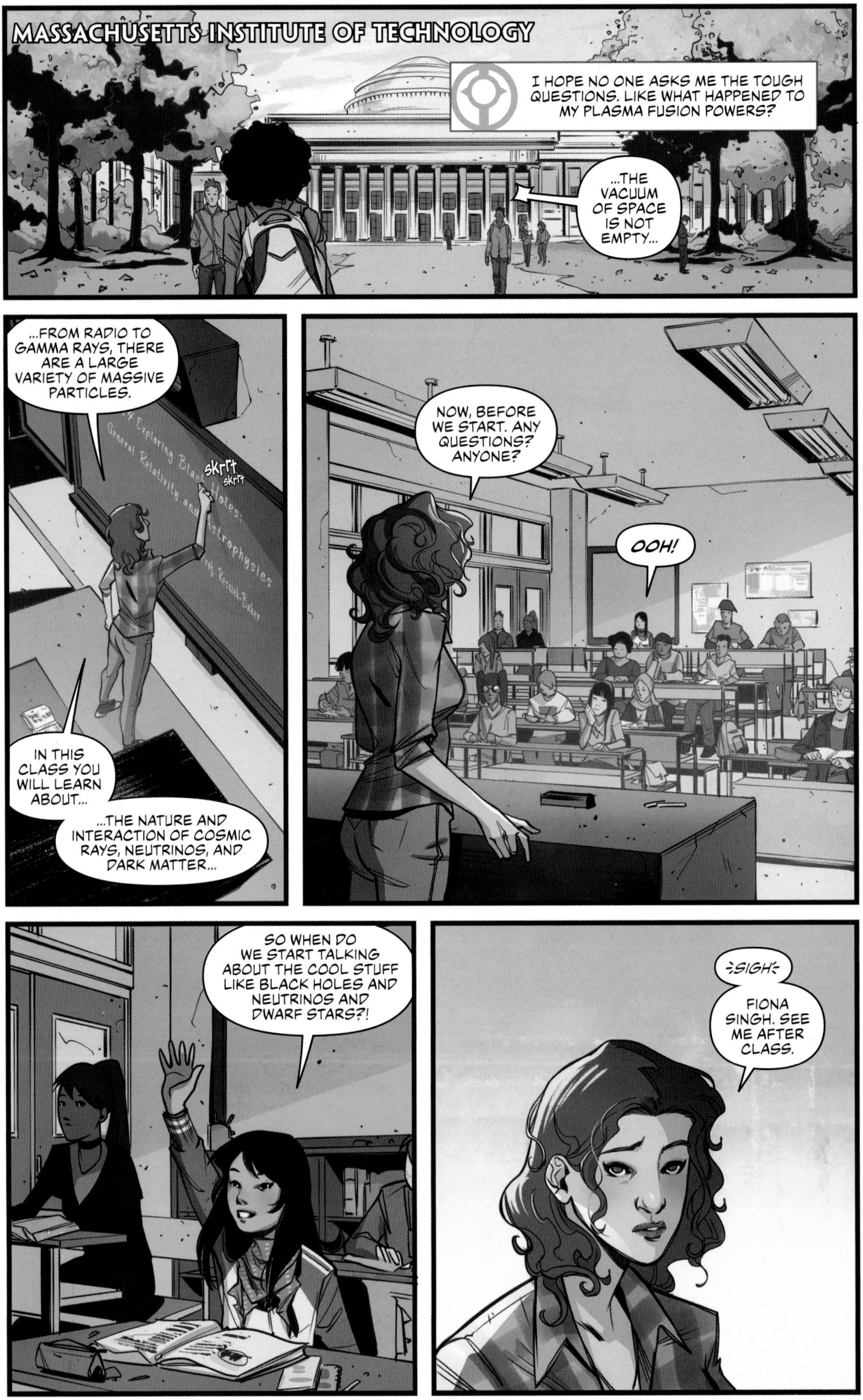
MASSACHUSETTS INSTITUTE OF TECHNOLOGY
I HOPE NO ONE ASKS ME THE TOUGH QUESTIONS. LIKE WHAT HAPPENED TO MY PLASMA FUSION POWERS?
...THE VACUUM OF SPACE IS NOT EMPTY...
...FROM RADIO TO GAMMA RAYS, THERE ARE A LARGE VARIETY OF MASSIVE PARTICLES.
SKRT SKRT
IN THIS CLASS YOU WILL LEARN ABOUT...
...THE NATURE AND INTERACTION OF COSMIC RAYS, NEUTRINOS, AND DARK MATTER...
NOW, BEFORE WE START. ANY QUESTIONS? ANYONE?
OOH!
SO WHEN DO WE START TALKING ABOUT THE COOL STUFF LIKE BLACK HOLES AND NEUTRINOS AND DWARF STARS?!
SIGH
FIONA SINGH. SEE ME AFTER CLASS.

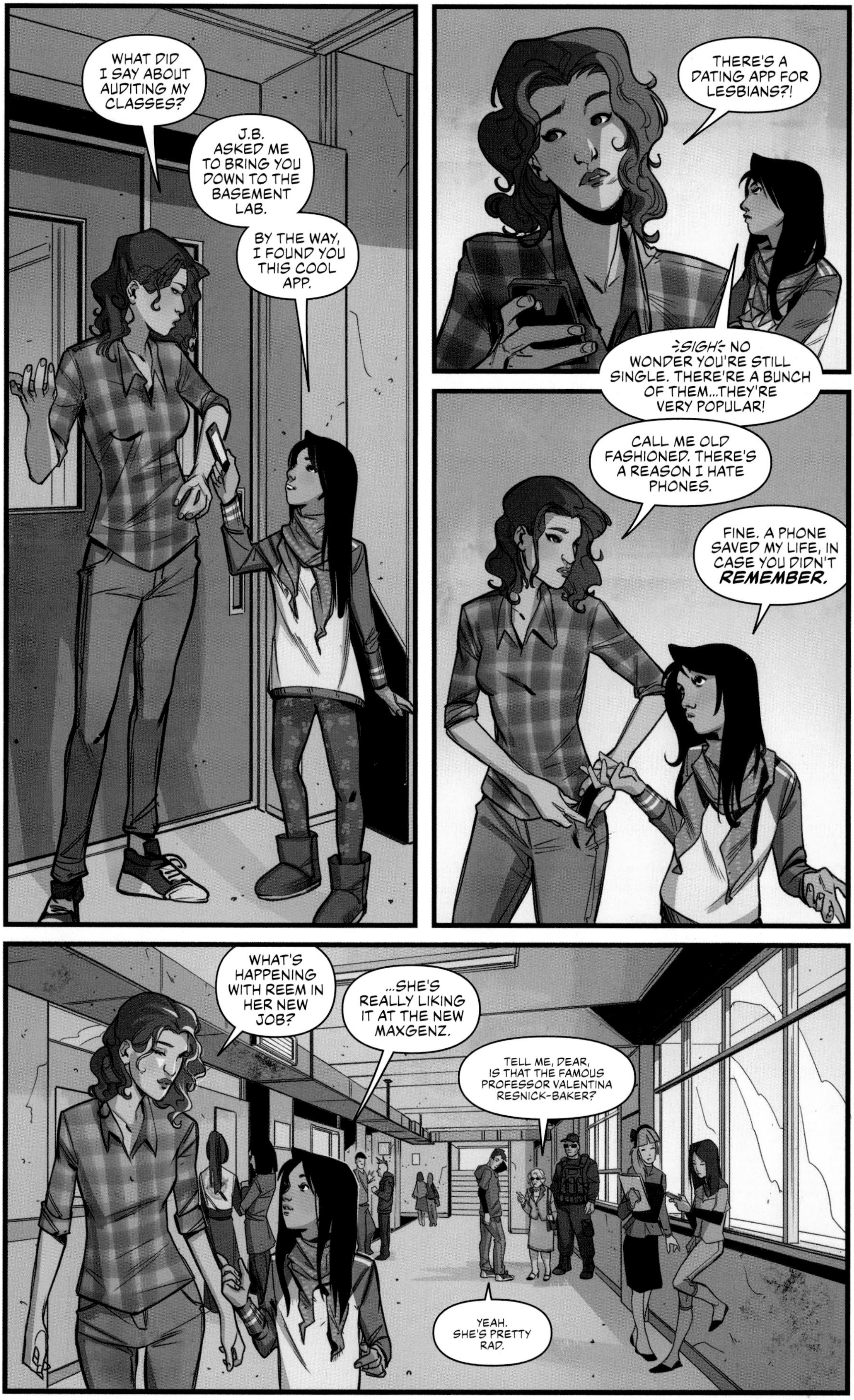
WHAT DID I SAY ABOUT AUDITING MY CLASSES?
J.B. ASKED ME TO BRING YOU DOWN TO THE BASEMENT LAB.
BY THE WAY, I FOUND YOU THIS COOL APP.
THERE'S A DATING APP FOR LESBIANS?!
-SIGH- NO WONDER YOU'RE STILL SINGLE. THERE'RE A BUNCH OF THEM...THEY'RE VERY POPULAR!
CALL ME OLD FASHIONED. THERE'S A REASON I HATE PHONES.
FINE. A PHONE SAVED MY LIFE, IN CASE YOU DIDN'T REMEMBER.
WHAT'S HAPPENING WITH REEM IN HER NEW JOB?
...SHE'S REALLY LIKING IT AT THE NEW MAXGENZ.
TELL ME, DEAR, IS THAT THE FAMOUS PROFESSOR VALENTINA RESNICK-BAKER?
YEAH. SHE'S PRETTY RAD.

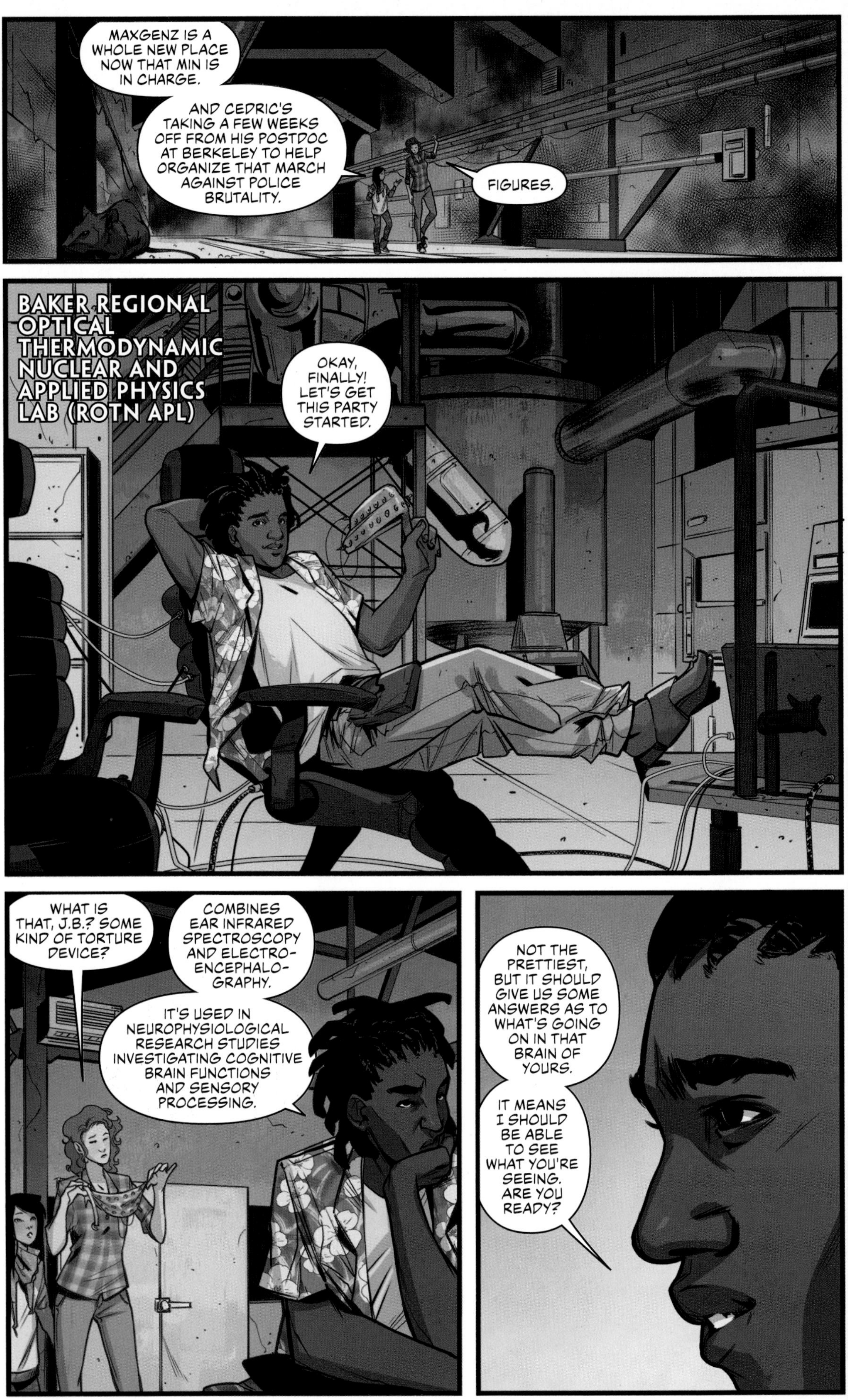
MAXGENZ IS A WHOLE NEW PLACE NOW THAT MIN IS IN CHARGE.
AND CEDRIC'S TAKING A FEW WEEKS OFF FROM HIS POSTDOC AT BERKELEY TO HELP ORGANIZE THAT MARCH AGAINST POLICE BRUTALITY.
FIGURES.
BAKER REGIONAL OPTICAL THERMODYNAMIC NUCLEAR AND APPLIED PHYSICS LAB (ROTN APL)
OKAY, FINALLY! LET'S GET THIS PARTY STARTED.
WHAT IS THAT, J.B.? SOME KIND OF TORTURE DEVICE?
COMBINES EAR INFRARED SPECTROSCOPY AND ELECTRO-ENCEPHALO-GRAPHY.
IT'S USED IN NEUROPHYSIOLOGICAL RESEARCH STUDIES INVESTIGATING COGNITIVE BRAIN FUNCTIONS AND SENSORY PROCESSING.
NOT THE PRETTIEST, BUT IT SHOULD GIVE US SOME ANSWERS AS TO WHAT'S GOING ON IN THAT BRAIN OF YOURS.
IT MEANS I SHOULD BE ABLE TO SEE WHAT YOU'RE SEEING. ARE YOU READY?

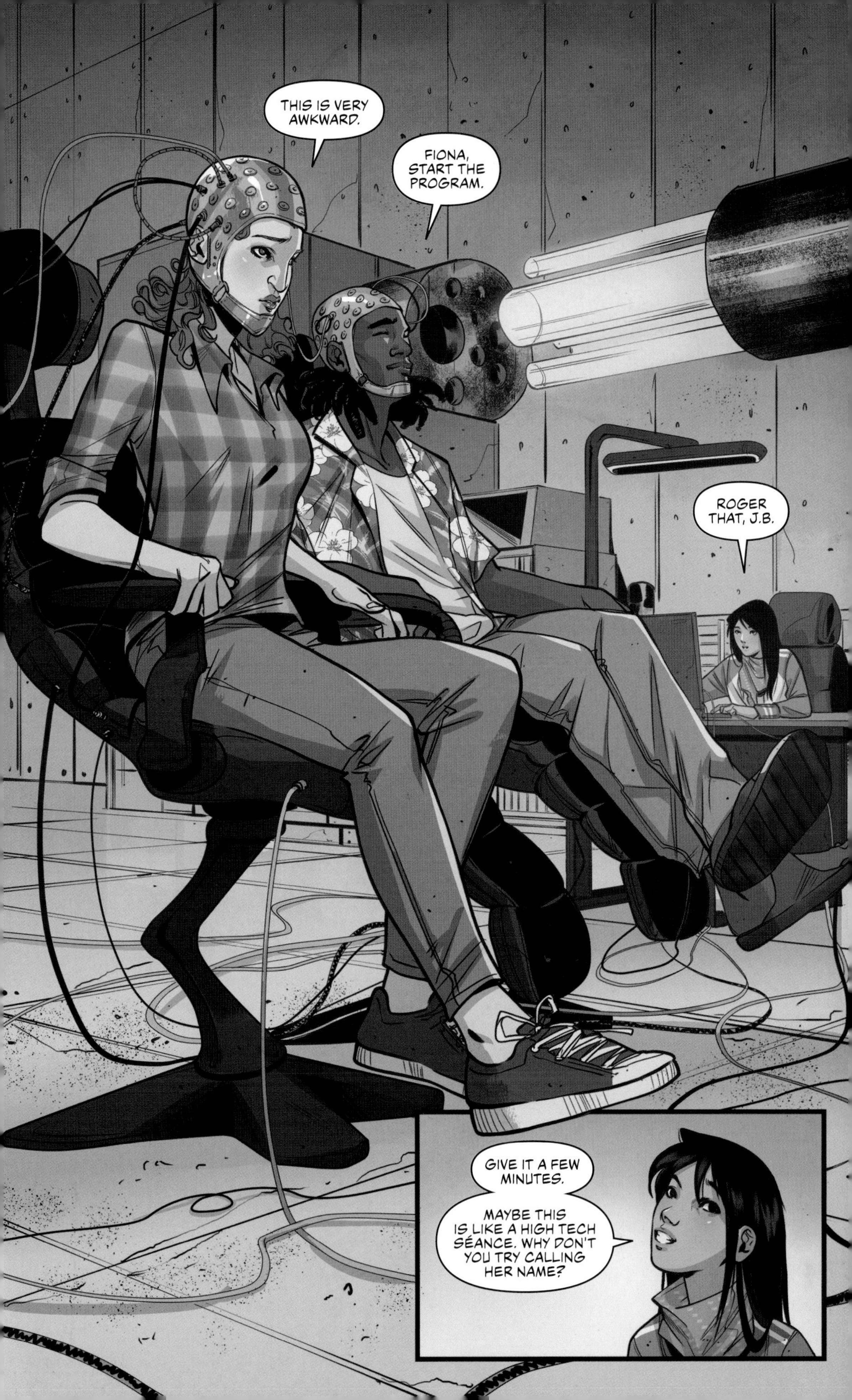
THIS IS VERY AWKWARD.
FIONA, START THE PROGRAM.
ROGER THAT, J.B.
GIVE IT A FEW MINUTES.
MAYBE THIS IS LIKE A HIGH TECH SÉANCE. WHY DON'T YOU TRY CALLING HER NAME?

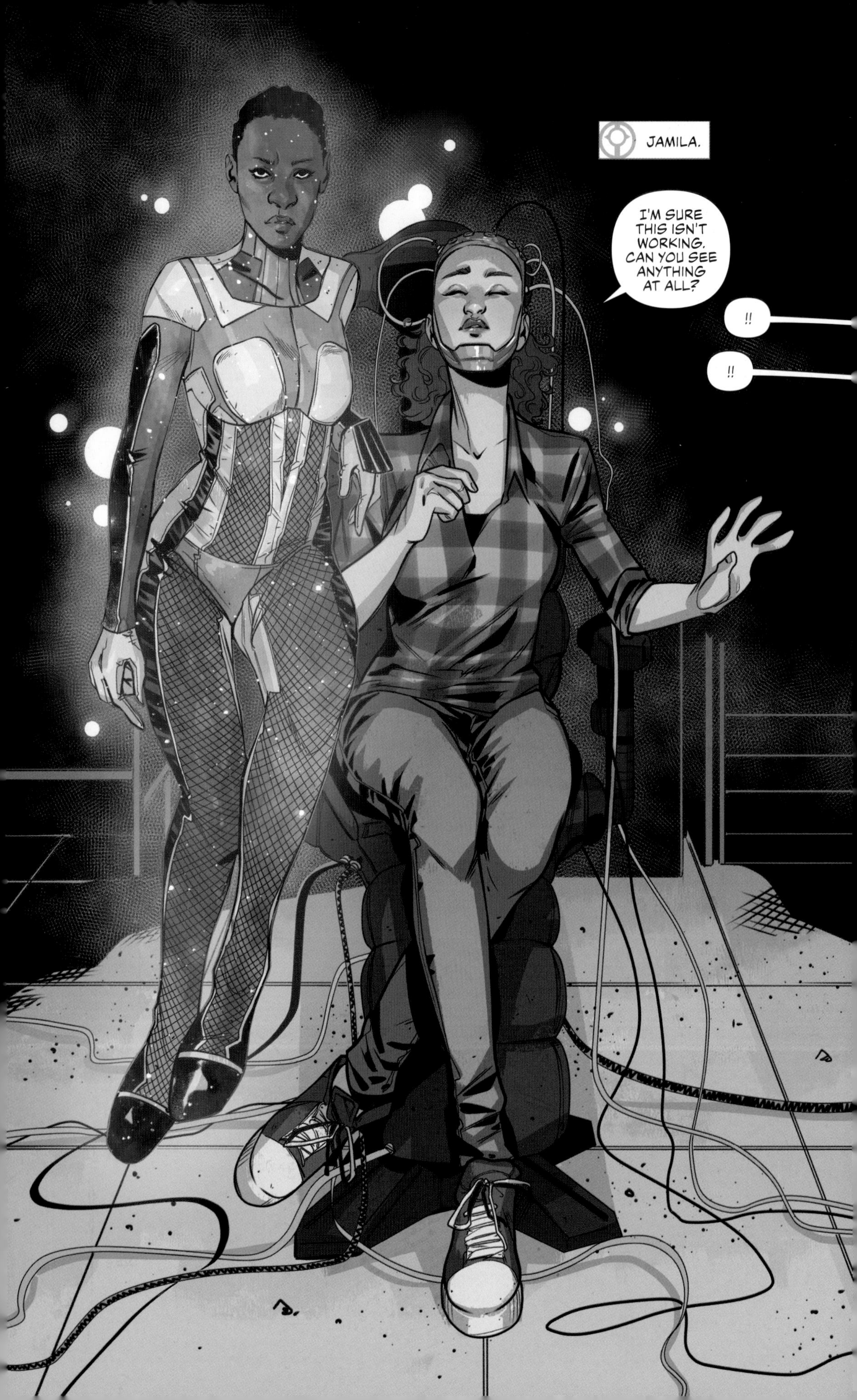
JAMILA.
I'M SURE THIS ISN'T WORKING. CAN YOU SEE ANYTHING AT ALL?
!!
!!

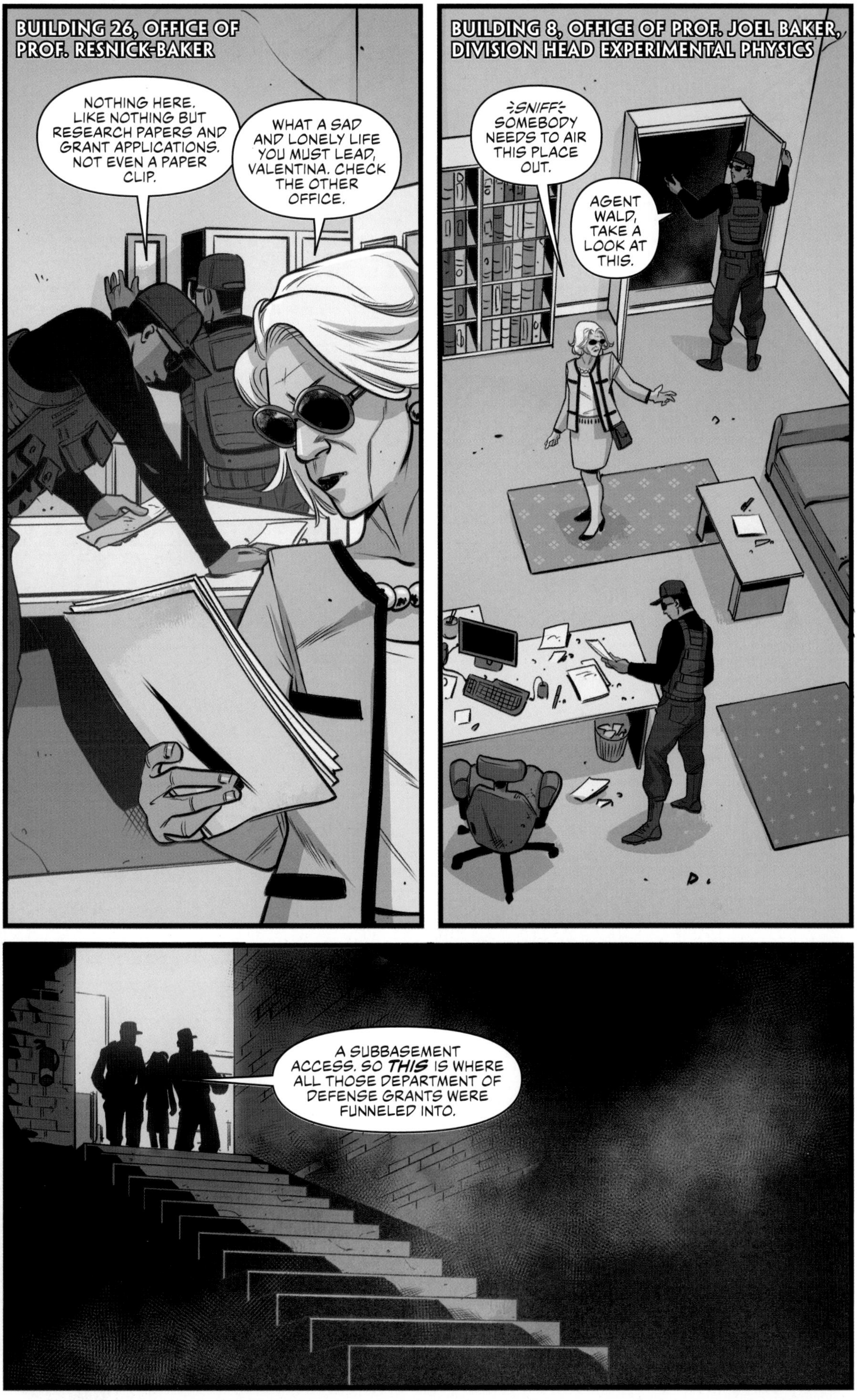
BUILDING 26, OFFICE OF PROF. RESNICK-BAKER
NOTHING HERE. LIKE NOTHING BUT RESEARCH PAPERS AND GRANT APPLICATIONS. NOT EVEN A PAPER CLIP.
WHAT A SAD AND LONELY LIFE YOU MUST LEAD, VALENTINA. CHECK THE OTHER OFFICE.
BUILDING 8, OFFICE OF PROF. JOEL BAKER, DIVISION HEAD EXPERIMENTAL PHYSICS
SNIFF SOMEBODY NEEDS TO AIR THIS PLACE OUT.
AGENT WALD, TAKE A LOOK AT THIS.
A SUBBASEMENT ACCESS. SO THIS IS WHERE ALL THOSE DEPARTMENT OF DEFENSE GRANTS WERE FUNNELED INTO.

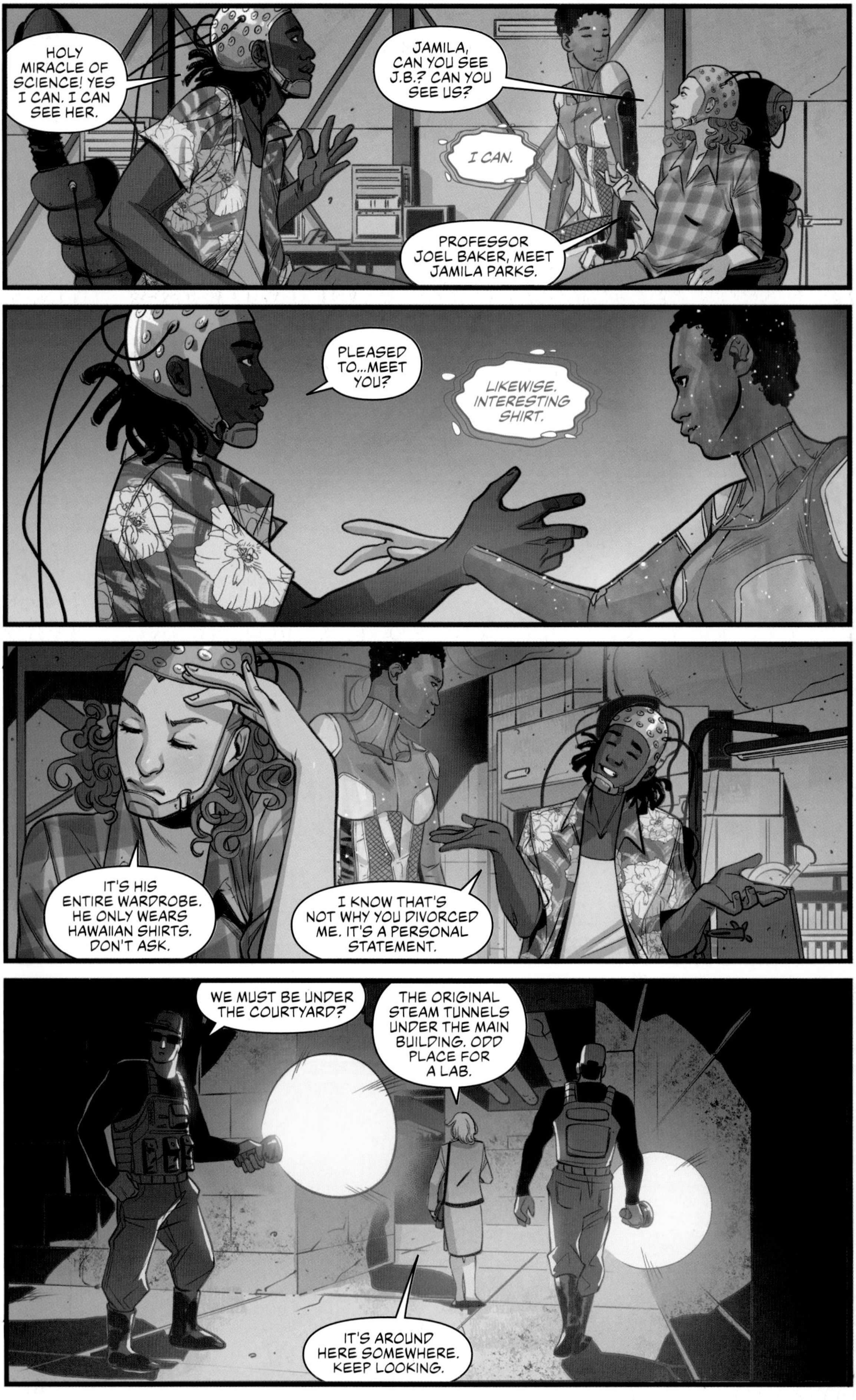
HOLY MIRACLE OF SCIENCE! YES I CAN. I CAN SEE HER.
JAMILA, CAN YOU SEE J.B.? CAN YOU SEE US?
I CAN.
PROFESSOR JOEL BAKER, MEET JAMILA PARKS.
PLEASED TO...MEET YOU?
LIKEWISE. INTERESTING SHIRT.
IT'S HIS ENTIRE WARDROBE. HE ONLY WEARS HAWAIIAN SHIRTS. DON'T ASK.
I KNOW THAT'S NOT WHY YOU DIVORCED ME. IT'S A PERSONAL STATEMENT.
WE MUST BE UNDER THE COURTYARD?
THE ORIGINAL STEAM TUNNELS UNDER THE MAIN BUILDING. ODD PLACE FOR A LAB.
IT'S AROUND HERE SOMEWHERE. KEEP LOOKING.

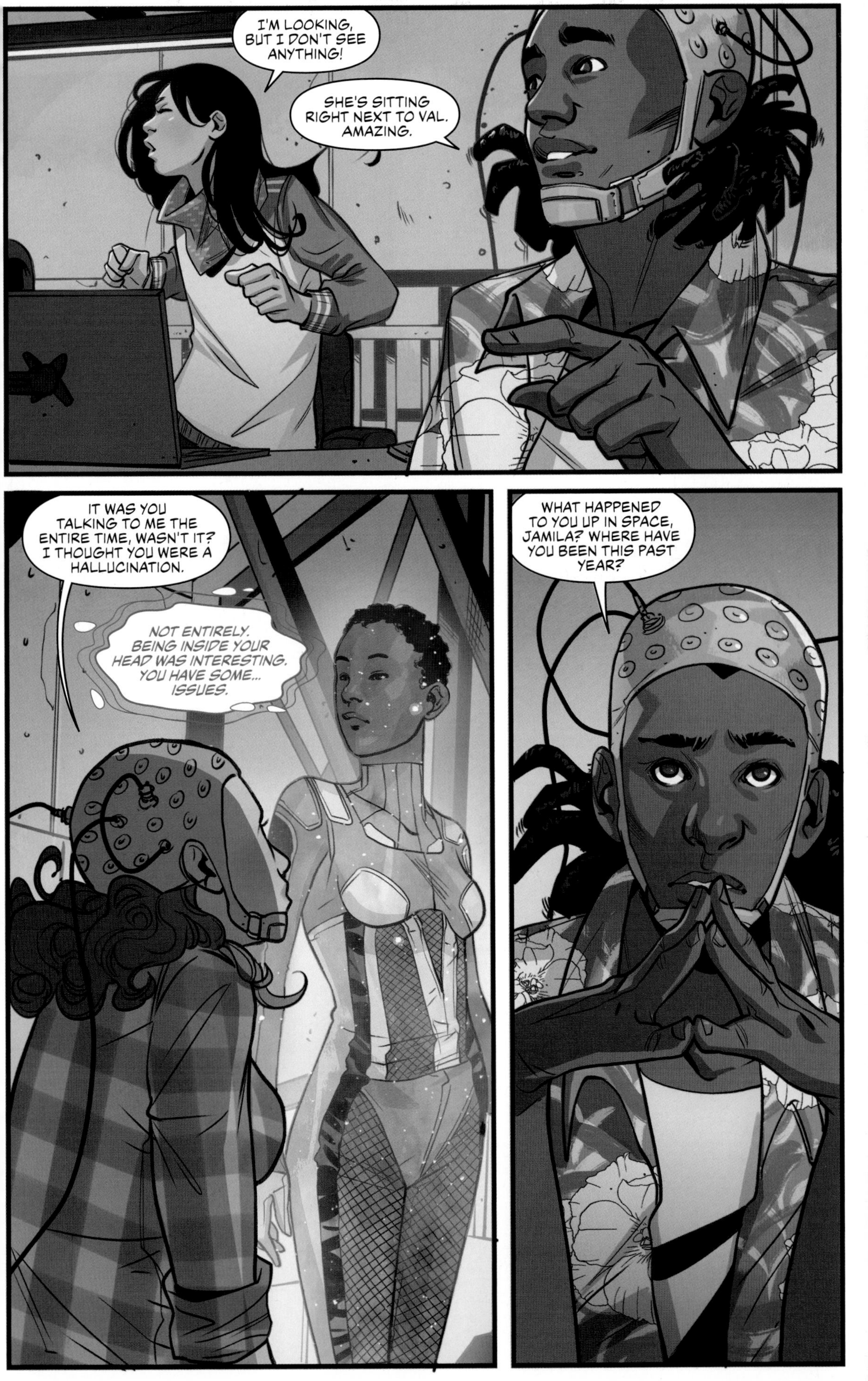
I'M LOOKING, BUT I DON'T SEE ANYTHING!
SHE'S SITTING RIGHT NEXT TO VAL. AMAZING.
IT WAS YOU TALKING TO ME THE ENTIRE TIME, WASN'T IT? I THOUGHT YOU WERE A HALLUCINATION.
NOT ENTIRELY. BEING INSIDE YOUR HEAD WAS INTERESTING. YOU HAVE SOME... ISSUES.
WHAT HAPPENED TO YOU UP IN SPACE, JAMILA? WHERE HAVE YOU BEEN THIS PAST YEAR?

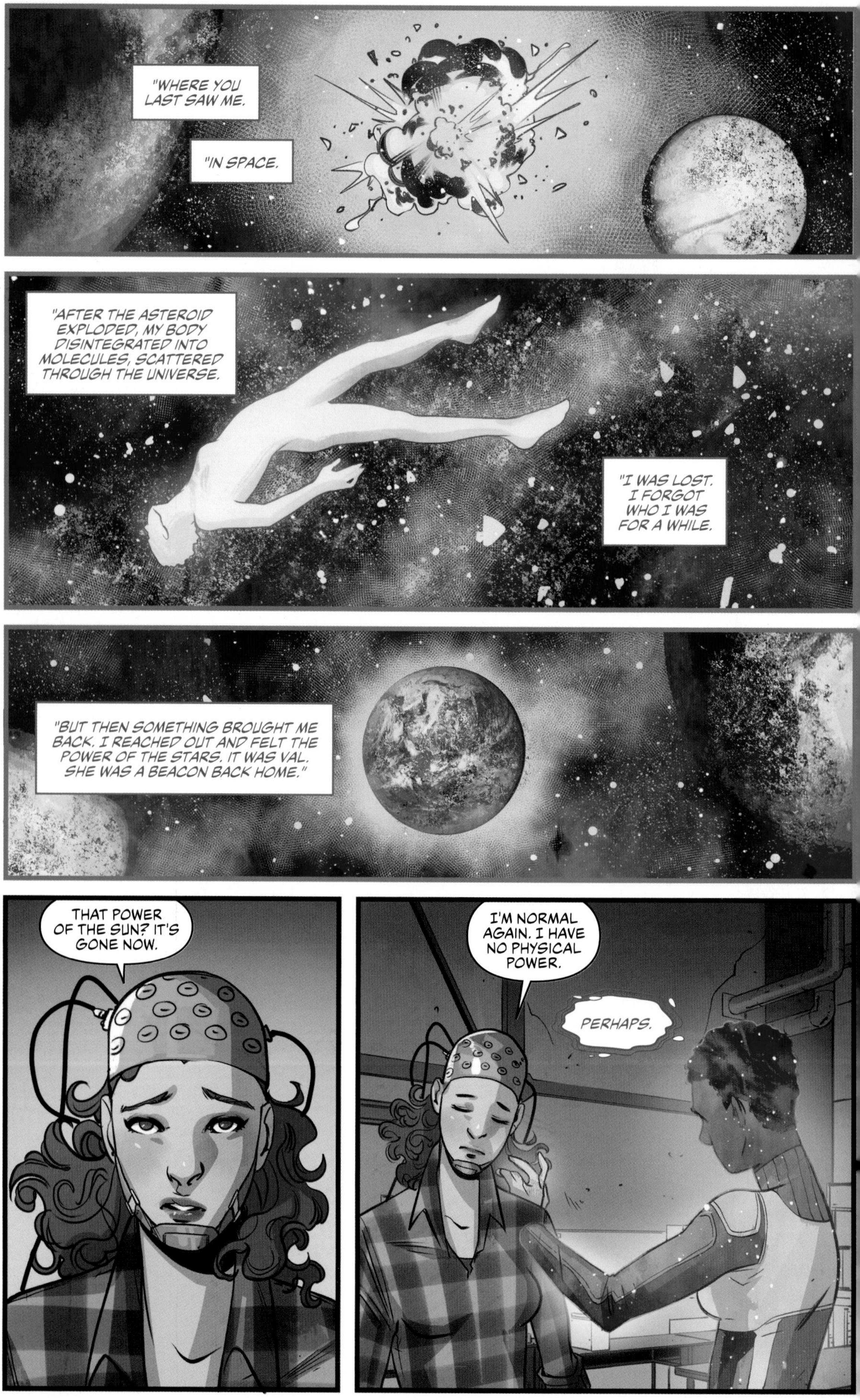
"WHERE YOU LAST SAW ME.
"IN SPACE.
"AFTER THE ASTEROID EXPLODED, MY BODY DISINTEGRATED INTO MOLECULES, SCATTERED THROUGH THE UNIVERSE.
"I WAS LOST. I FORGOT WHO I WAS FOR A WHILE.
"BUT THEN SOMETHING BROUGHT ME BACK. I REACHED OUT AND FELT THE POWER OF THE STARS. IT WAS VAL. SHE WAS A BEACON BACK HOME."
THAT POWER OF THE SUN? IT'S GONE NOW.
I'M NORMAL AGAIN. I HAVE NO PHYSICAL POWER.
PERHAPS.

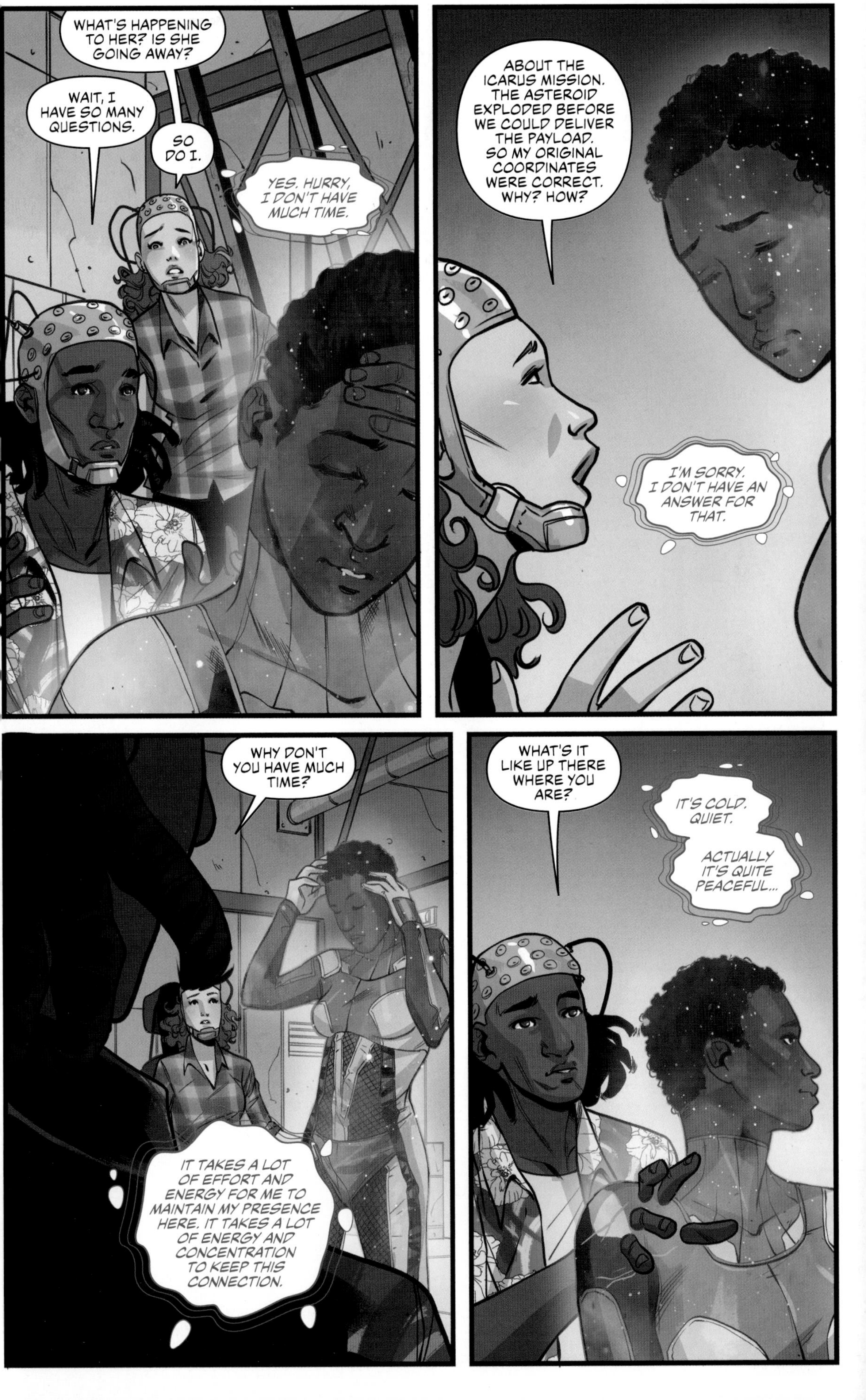
WHAT'S HAPPENING TO HER? IS SHE GOING AWAY?
WAIT, I HAVE SO MANY QUESTIONS.
SO DO I.
YES. HURRY, I DON'T HAVE MUCH TIME.
ABOUT THE ICARUS MISSION. THE ASTEROID EXPLODED BEFORE WE COULD DELIVER THE PAYLOAD. SO MY ORIGINAL COORDINATES WERE CORRECT. WHY? HOW?
I'M SORRY. I DON'T HAVE AN ANSWER FOR THAT.
WHY DON'T YOU HAVE MUCH TIME?
IT TAKES A LOT OF EFFORT AND ENERGY FOR ME TO MAINTAIN MY PRESENCE HERE. IT TAKES A LOT OF ENERGY AND CONCENTRATION TO KEEP THIS CONNECTION.
WHAT'S IT LIKE UP THERE WHERE YOU ARE?
IT'S COLD. QUIET.
ACTUALLY IT'S QUITE PEACEFUL...

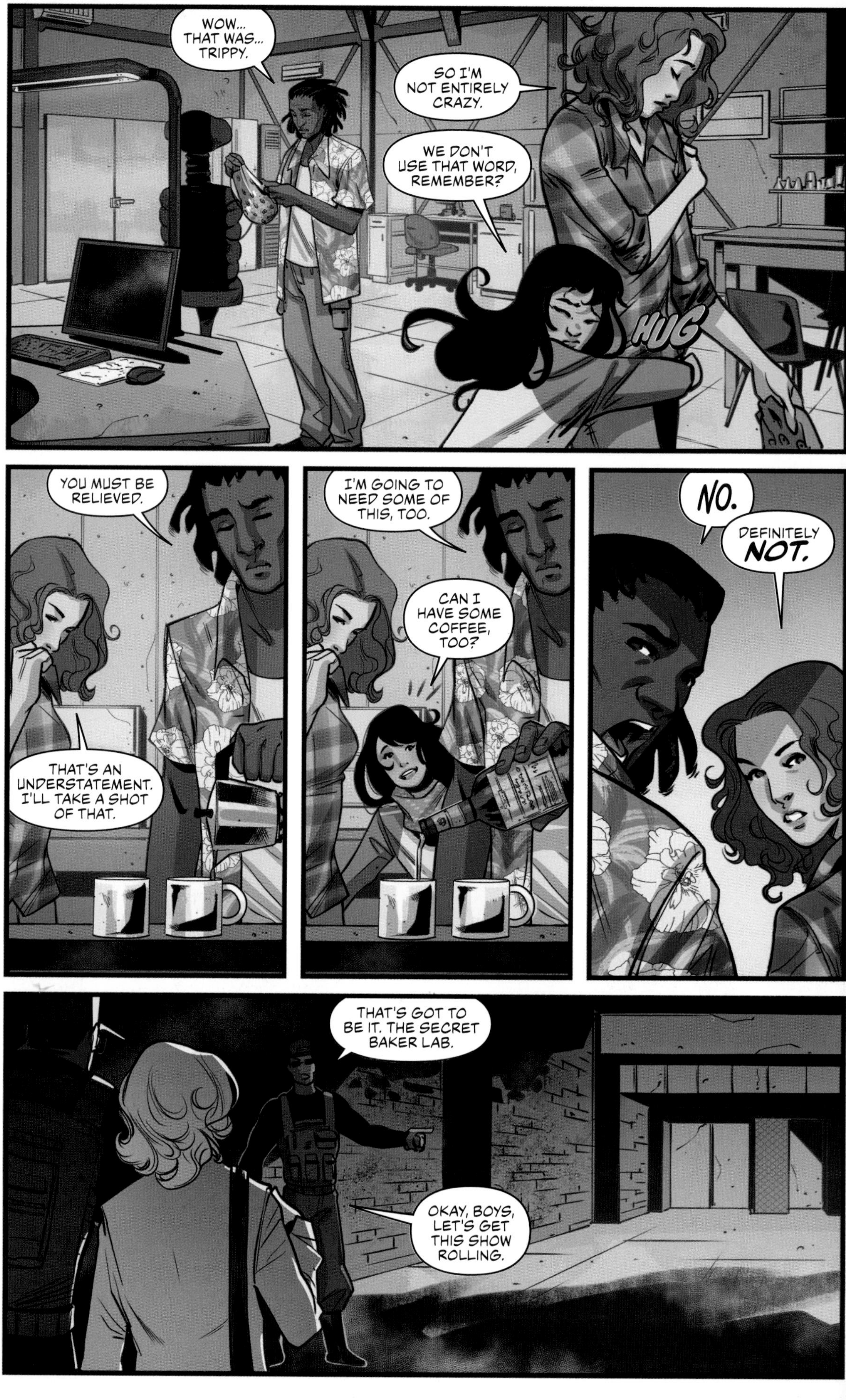
WOW... THAT WAS... TRIPPY.
SO I'M NOT ENTIRELY CRAZY.
WE DON'T USE THAT WORD, REMEMBER?
HUG
YOU MUST BE RELIEVED.
THAT'S AN UNDERSTATEMENT. I'LL TAKE A SHOT OF THAT.
I'M GOING TO NEED SOME OF THIS, TOO.
CAN I HAVE SOME COFFEE, TOO?
NO.
DEFINITELY NOT.
THAT'S GOT TO BE IT. THE SECRET BAKER LAB.
OKAY, BOYS, LET'S GET THIS SHOW ROLLING.

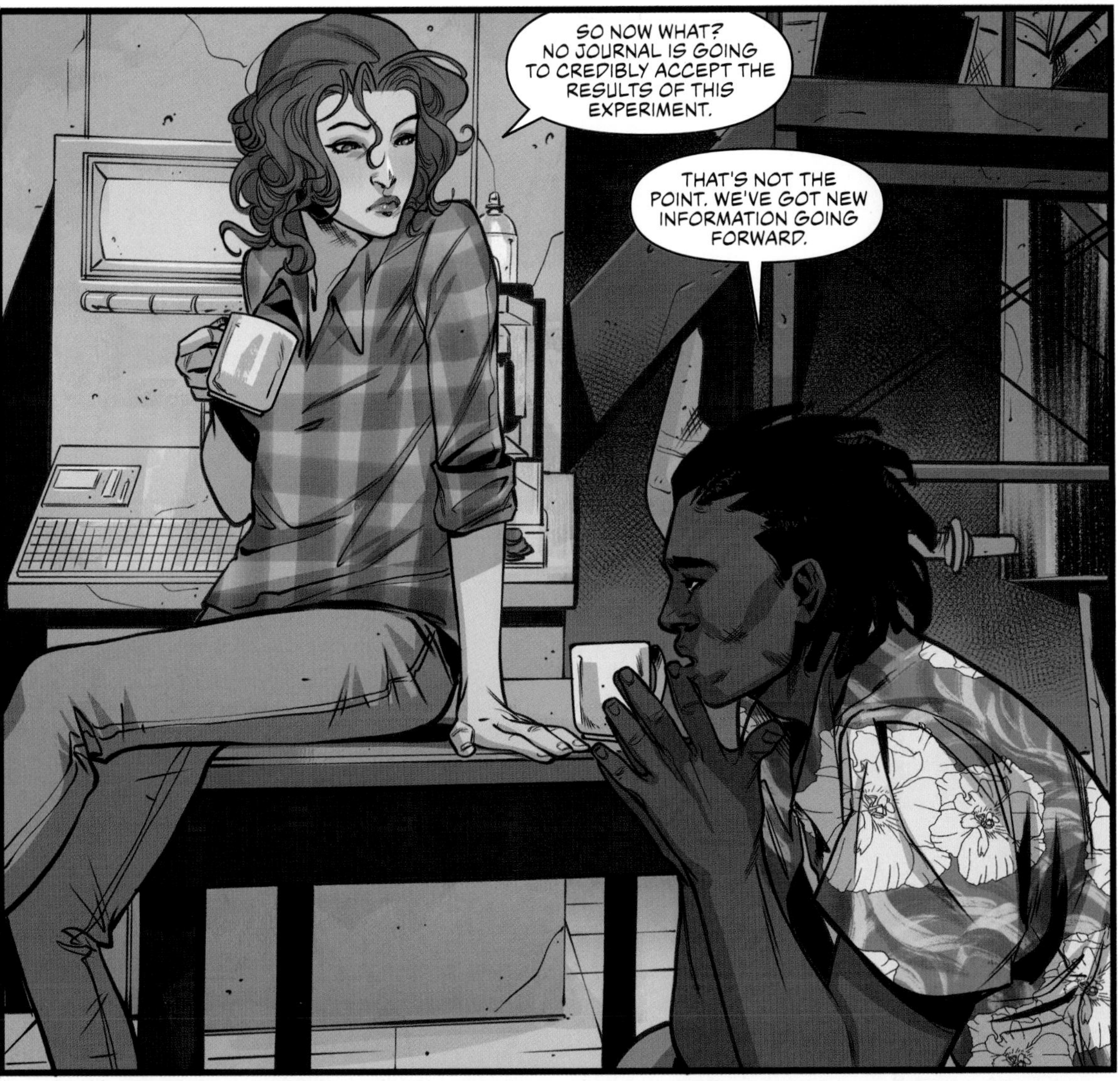
SO NOW WHAT? NO JOURNAL IS GOING TO CREDIBLY ACCEPT THE RESULTS OF THIS EXPERIMENT.
THAT'S NOT THE POINT. WE'VE GOT NEW INFORMATION GOING FORWARD.
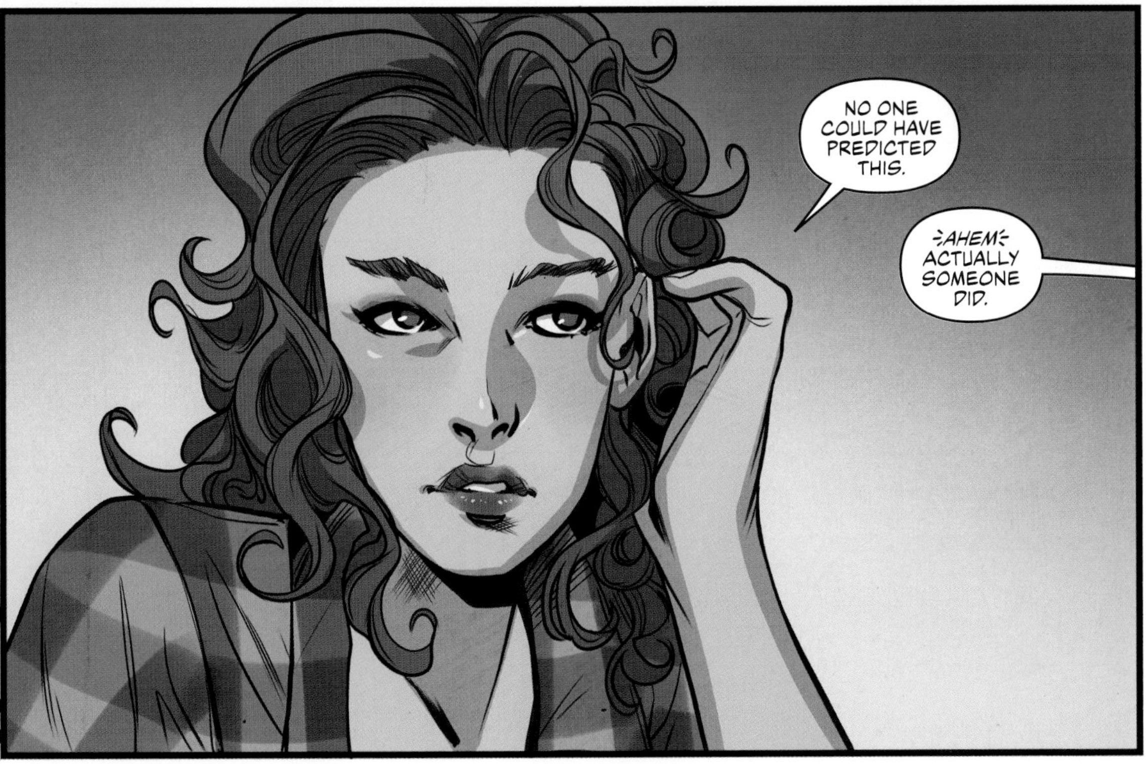
NO ONE COULD HAVE PREDICTED THIS.
AHEM ACTUALLY SOMEONE DID.

CEDRIC JUST SENT ME THIS FILE. HIS ONLINE NAME IS "MAJOR TOM."

AS FAR AS I CAN TELL, HE GOT ALMOST EVERYTHING RIGHT. FROM THE ASTEROID TO FORESIGHT AND LORENA.

HOW IS THAT POSSIBLE AND NO ONE NOTICED?

HE'S GOT A BAJILLION ALIEN CONSPIRACY THEORIES ON YOUTUBE. GUESSING NO ONE TAKES HIM SERIOUSLY.

THAT'LL DO IT.

Aliens are taking over the world!

HE'S EITHER GOT AN INSIDE WITH FORESIGHT OR MILITARY INTELLIGENCE.

OR SOMEHOW HE PIECED IT ALL TOGETHER.

OR HE'S AN ALIEN HIMSELF! LOOK--

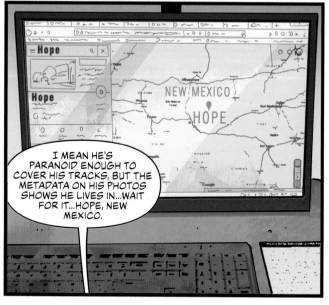

Hope

Hope

NEW MEXICO

HOPE

I MEAN HE'S PARANOID ENOUGH TO COVER HIS TRACKS, BUT THE METADATA ON HIS PHOTOS SHOWS HE LIVES IN...WAIT FOR IT...HOPE, NEW MEXICO.

SO?

THAT'S RIGHT BY ROSWELL!

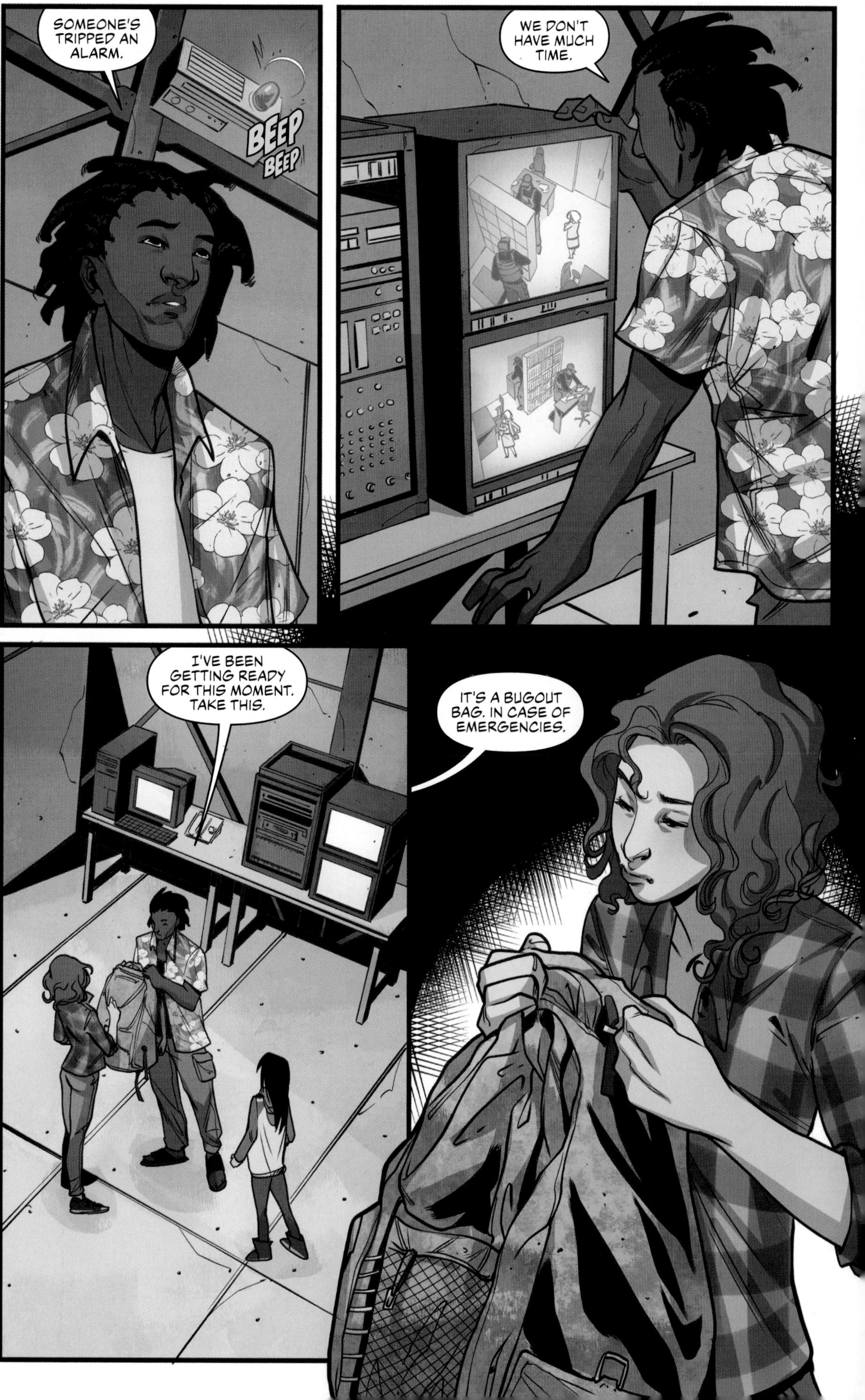
SOMEONE'S TRIPPED AN ALARM.
BEEP
BEEP
WE DON'T HAVE MUCH TIME.
I'VE BEEN GETTING READY FOR THIS MOMENT. TAKE THIS.
IT'S A BUGOUT BAG. IN CASE OF EMERGENCIES.

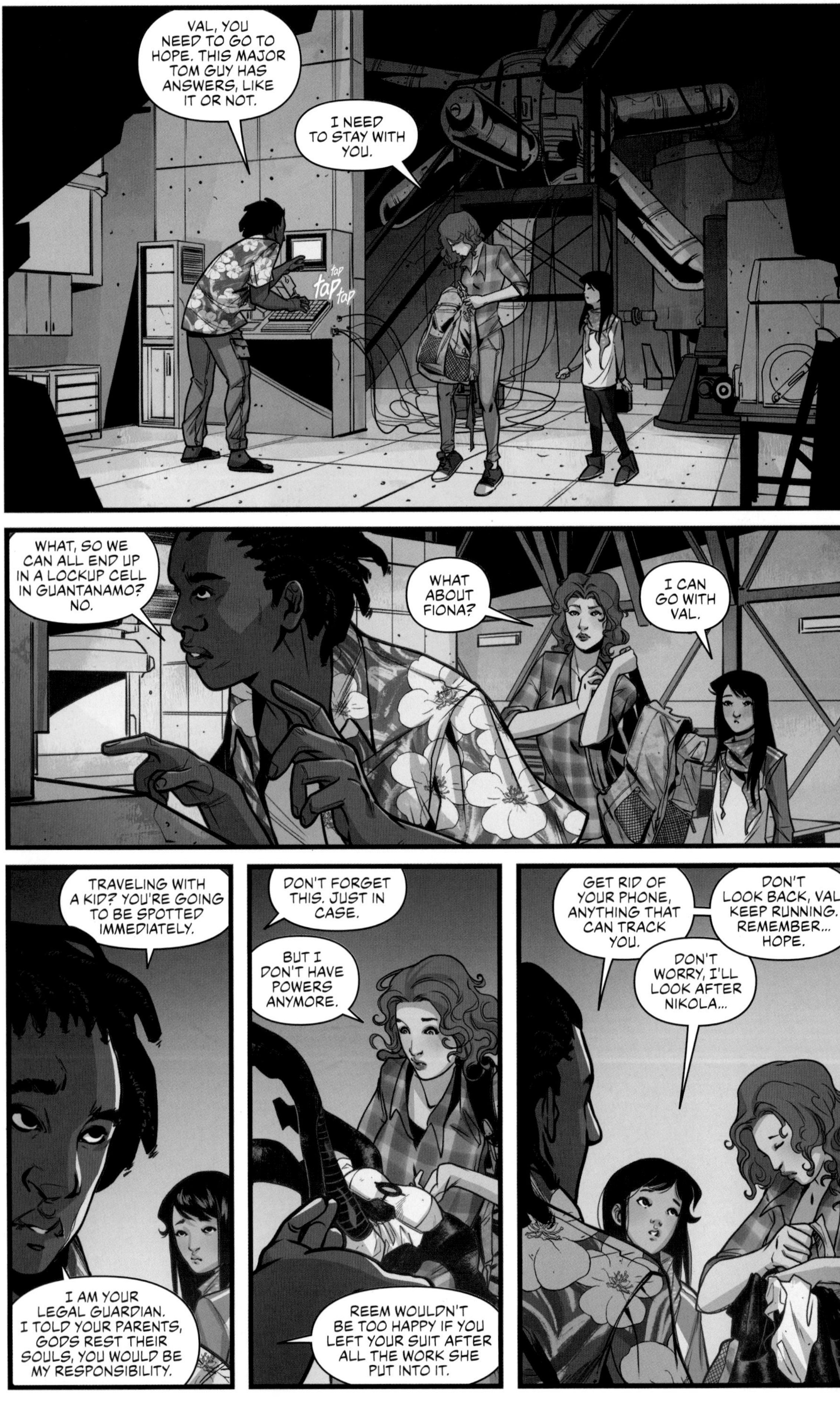
VAL, YOU NEED TO GO TO HOPE. THIS MAJOR TOM GUY HAS ANSWERS, LIKE IT OR NOT.
I NEED TO STAY WITH YOU.
tap tap tap
WHAT, SO WE CAN ALL END UP IN A LOCKUP CELL IN GUANTANAMO? NO.
WHAT ABOUT FIONA?
I CAN GO WITH VAL.
TRAVELING WITH A KID? YOU'RE GOING TO BE SPOTTED IMMEDIATELY.
I AM YOUR LEGAL GUARDIAN. I TOLD YOUR PARENTS, GODS REST THEIR SOULS, YOU WOULD BE MY RESPONSIBILITY.
DON'T FORGET THIS. JUST IN CASE.
BUT I DON'T HAVE POWERS ANYMORE.
REEM WOULDN'T BE TOO HAPPY IF YOU LEFT YOUR SUIT AFTER ALL THE WORK SHE PUT INTO IT.
GET RID OF YOUR PHONE, ANYTHING THAT CAN TRACK YOU.
DON'T LOOK BACK, VAL. KEEP RUNNING. REMEMBER... HOPE.
DON'T WORRY, I'LL LOOK AFTER NIKOLA...

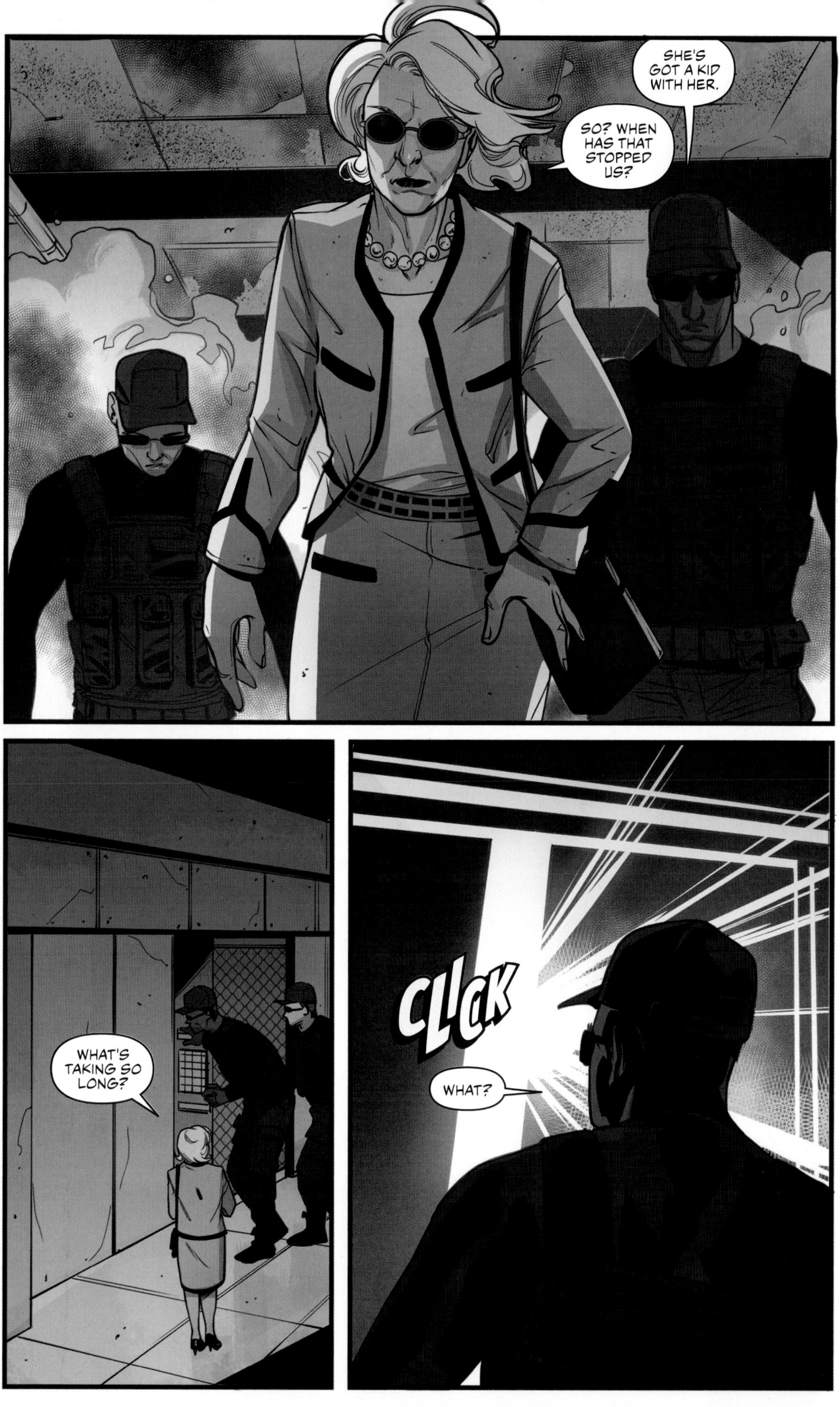
SHE'S GOT A KID WITH HER.
SO? WHEN HAS THAT STOPPED US?
WHAT'S TAKING SO LONG?
CLICK
WHAT?

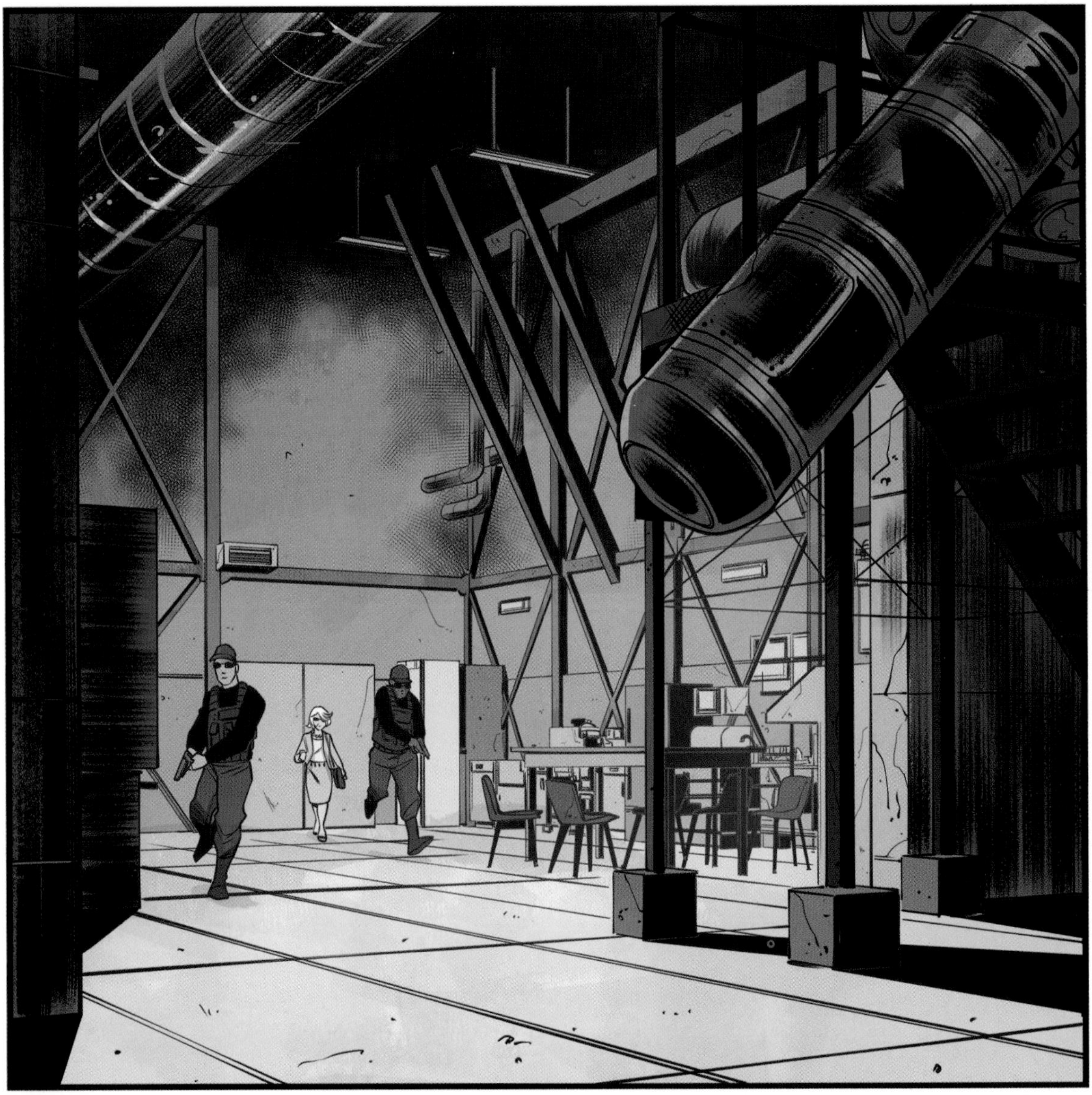

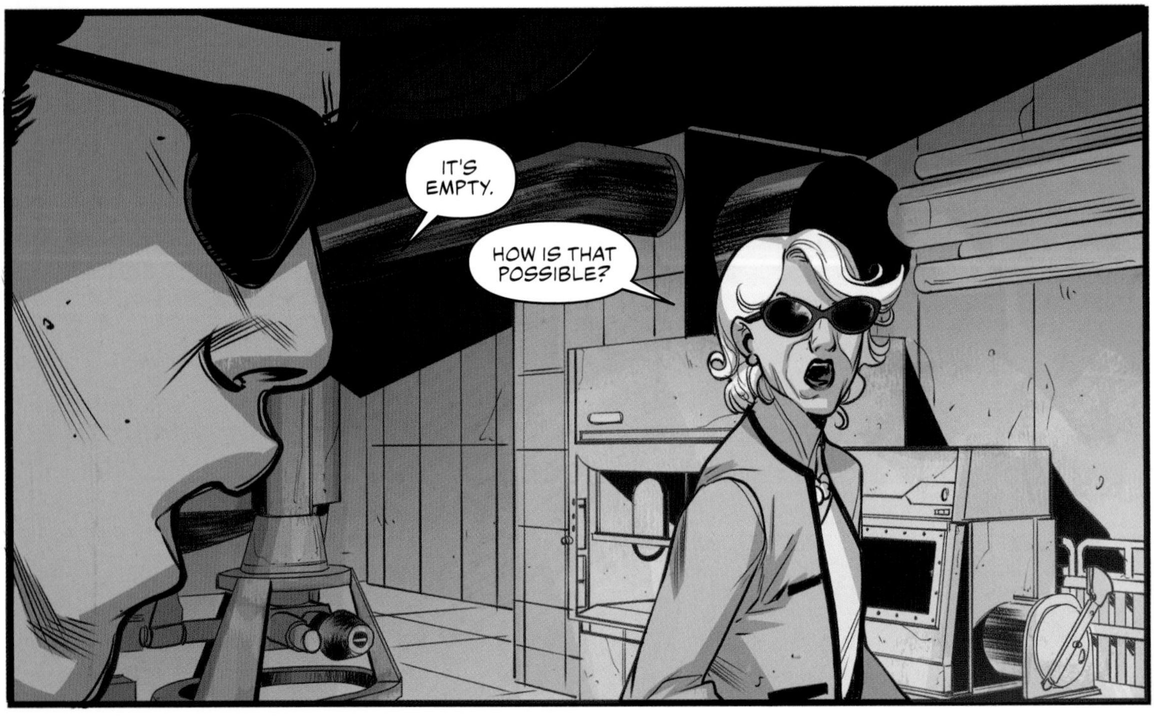
IT'S EMPTY.
HOW IS THAT POSSIBLE?

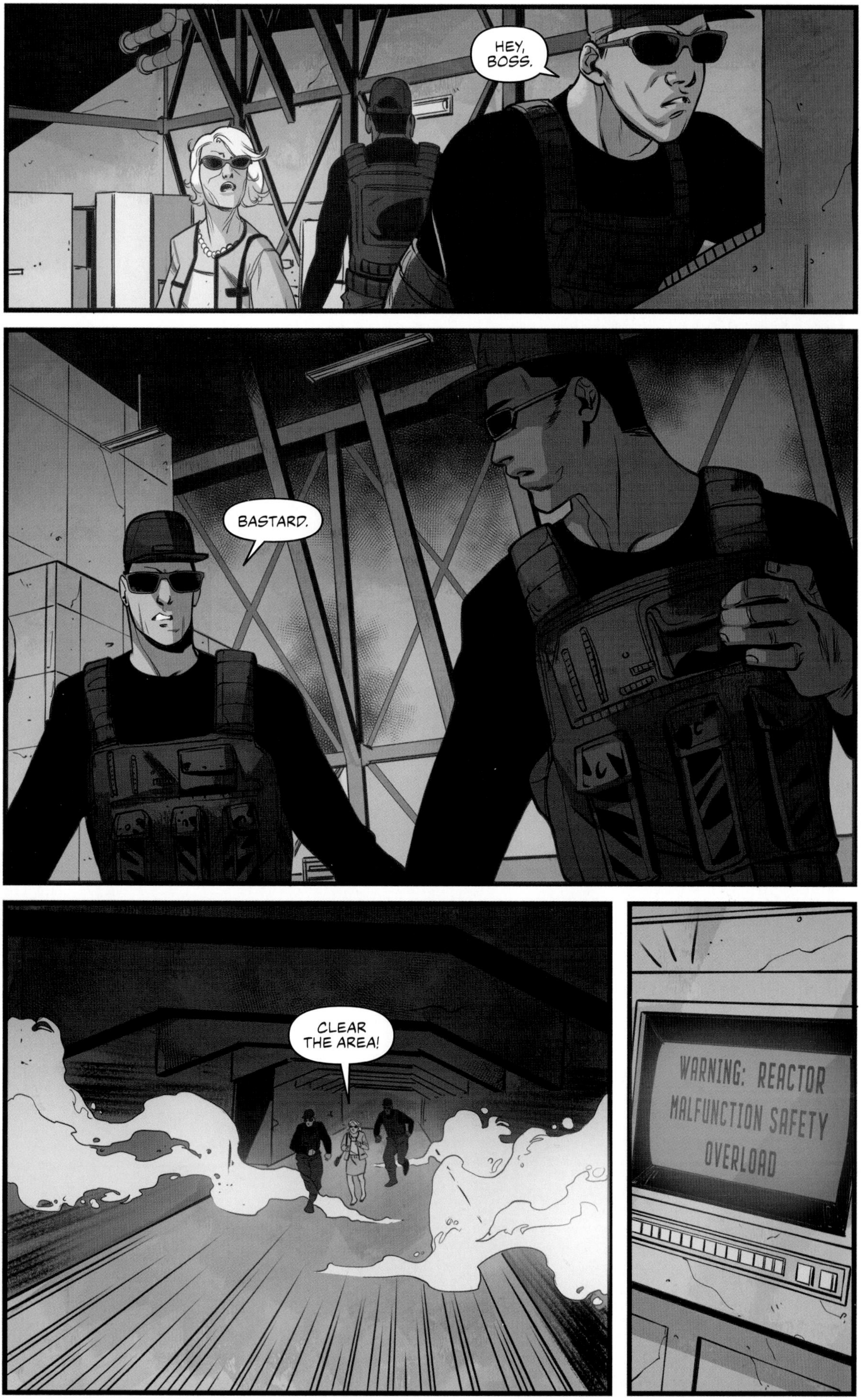
HEY, BOSS.
BASTARD.
CLEAR THE AREA!
WARNING: REACTOR MALFUNCTION SAFETY OVERLOAD

THERE ARE STILL TOO MANY STUDENTS AROUND!

I KNOW.

FIONA, WHAT ARE YOU DOING?

REPORTING AN ACTIVE SHOOTER IN BUILDING 8.

AND JUST TO BE SURE.

FIRE

KLAAANG KLAAANG KLAAANG

HOW'S THAT?

AN EMERGENCY HAS BEEN REPORTED. PLEASE FIND THE NEAREST EXIT.

YOU SCARE ME SOMETIMES.

KLAAANG KLAAANG KLAAANG

CLEAR THE AREA!

KEEP OUT   KEEP OUT

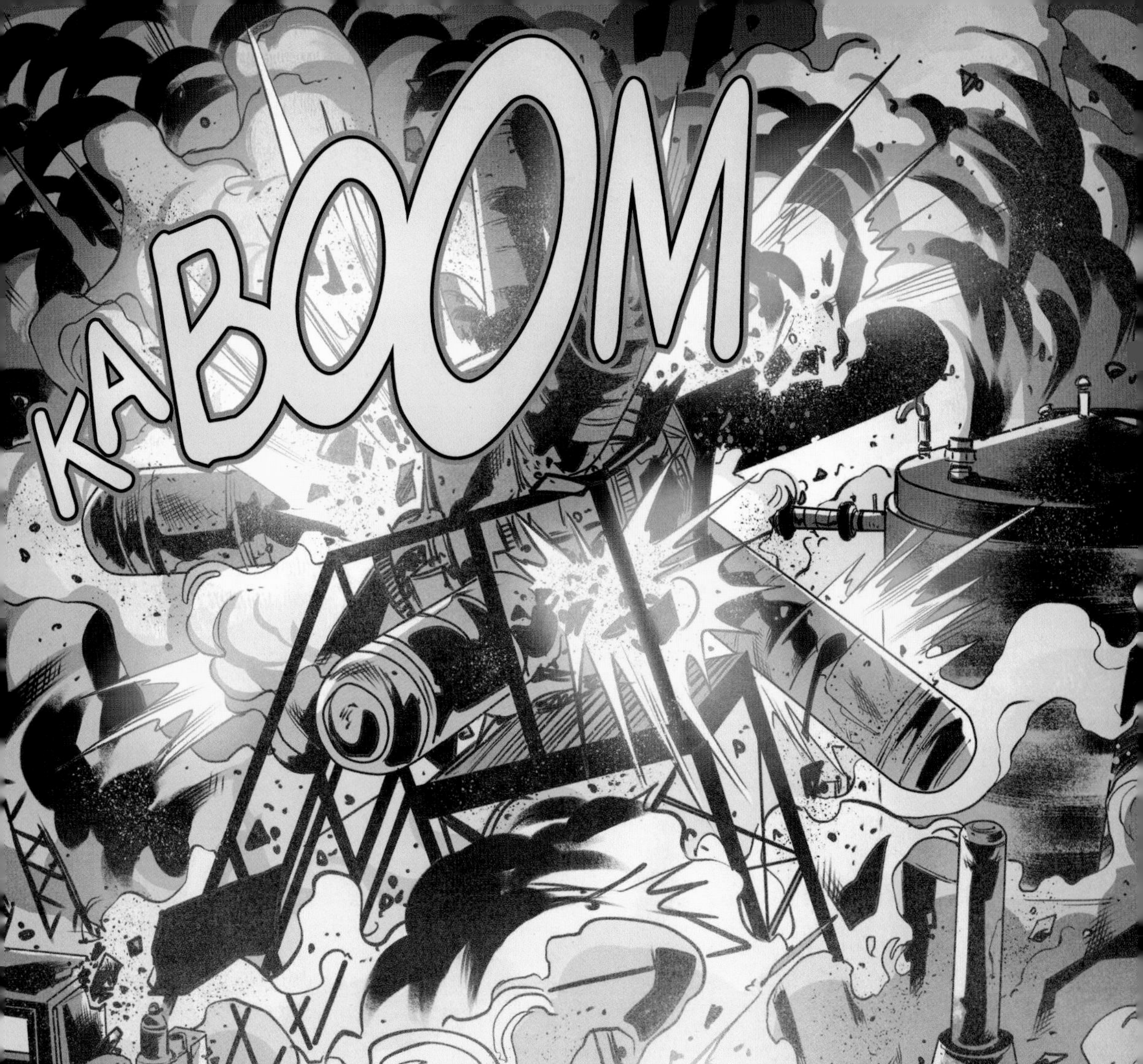
KABOOM

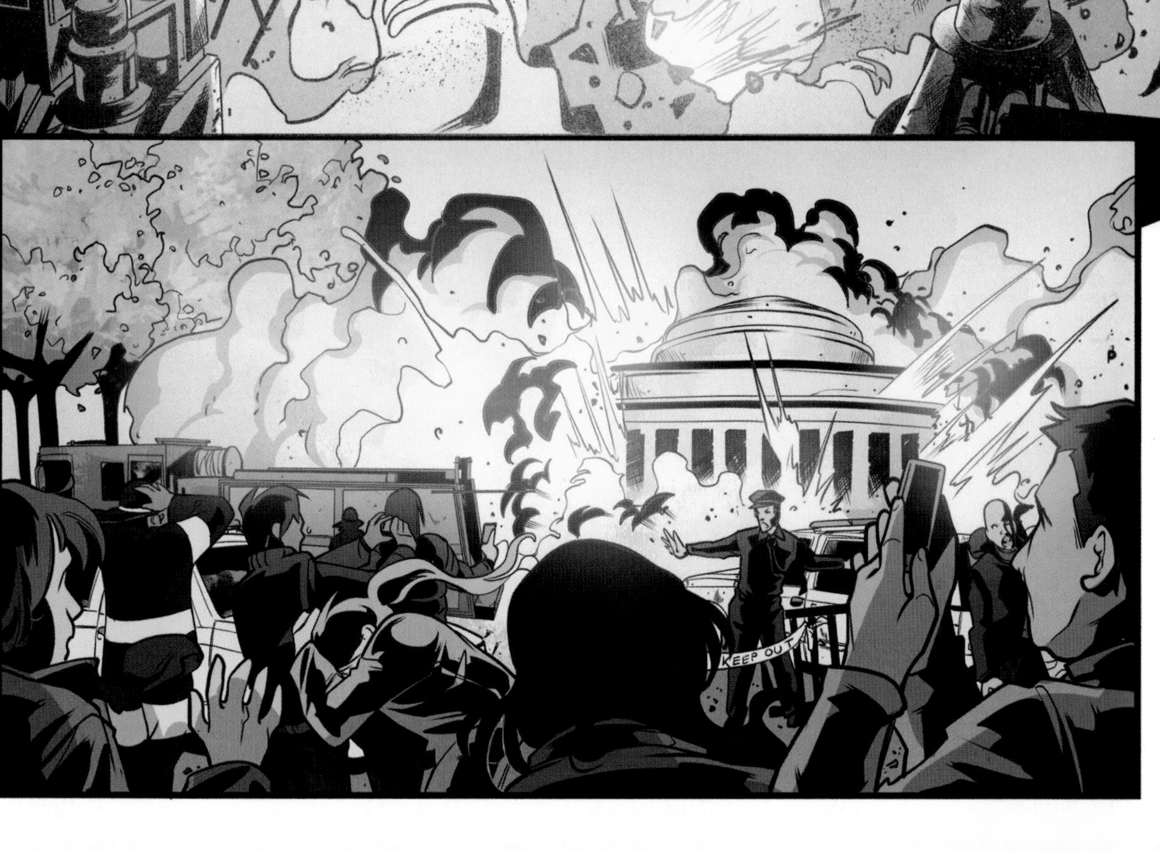
KEEP OUT

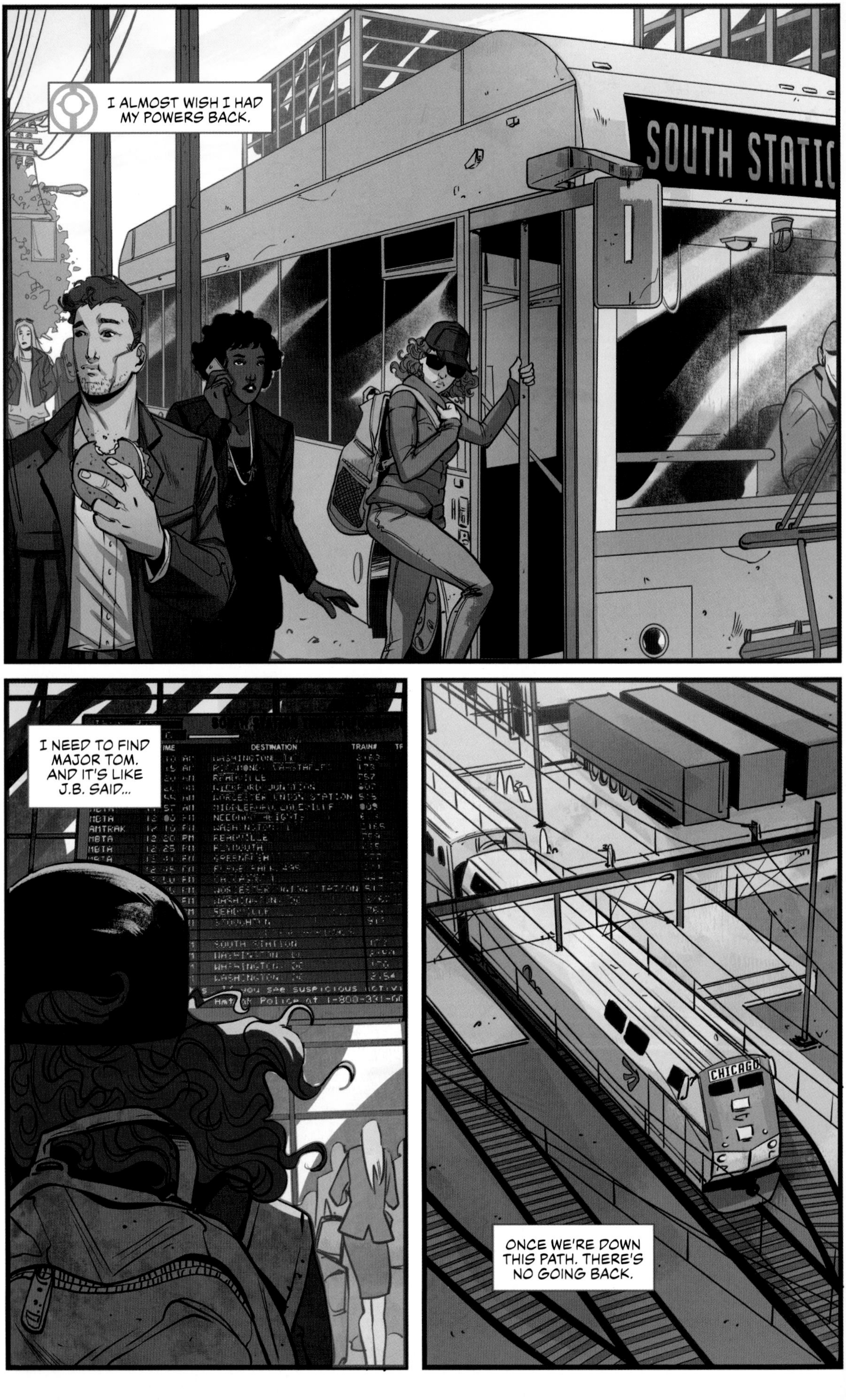
I ALMOST WISH I HAD MY POWERS BACK.
SOUTH STATIO
I NEED TO FIND MAJOR TOM. AND IT'S LIKE J.B. SAID...
DESTINATION
TRAIN#
CHICAGO
ONCE WE'RE DOWN THIS PATH. THERE'S NO GOING BACK.

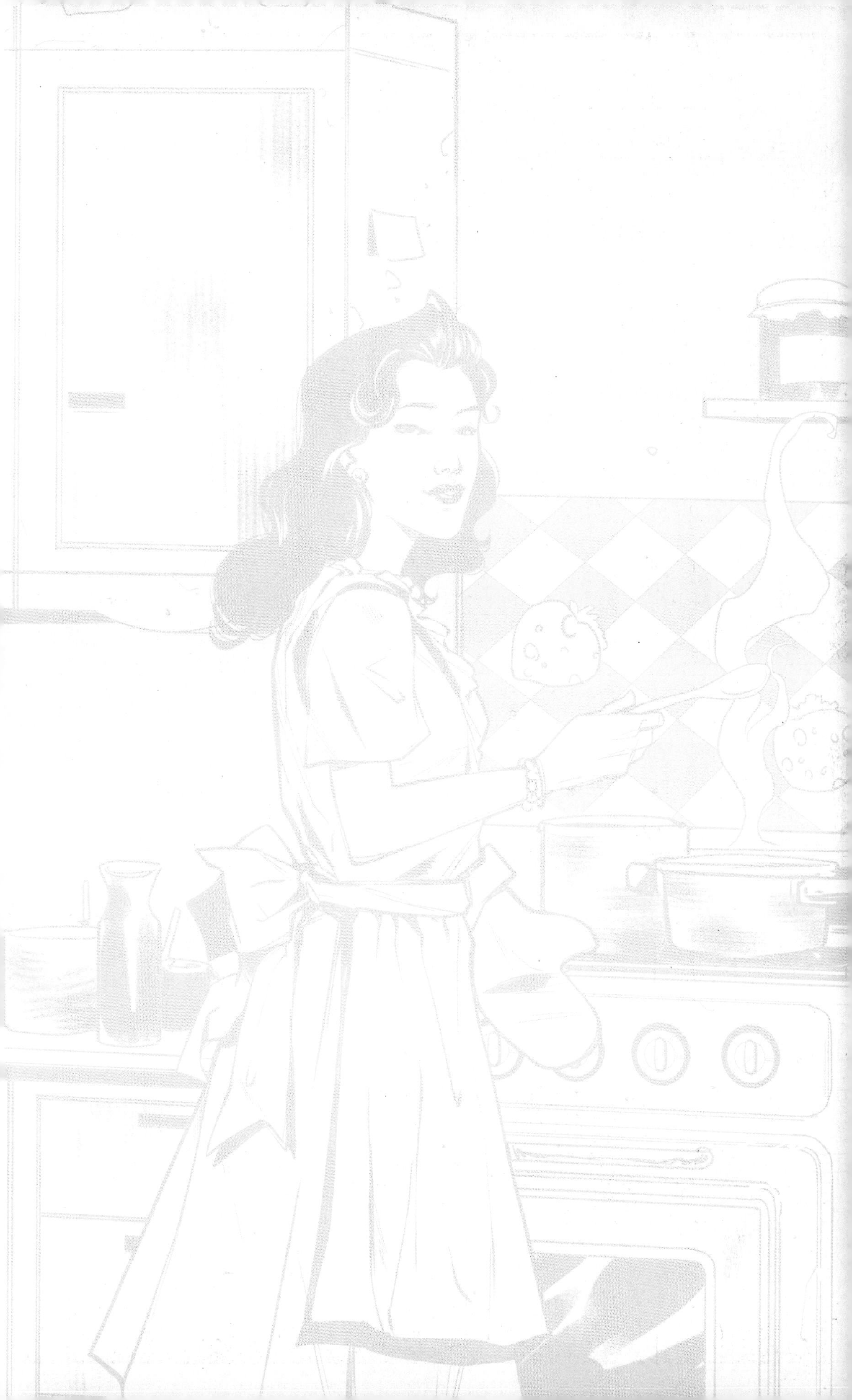

CHAPTER TWO

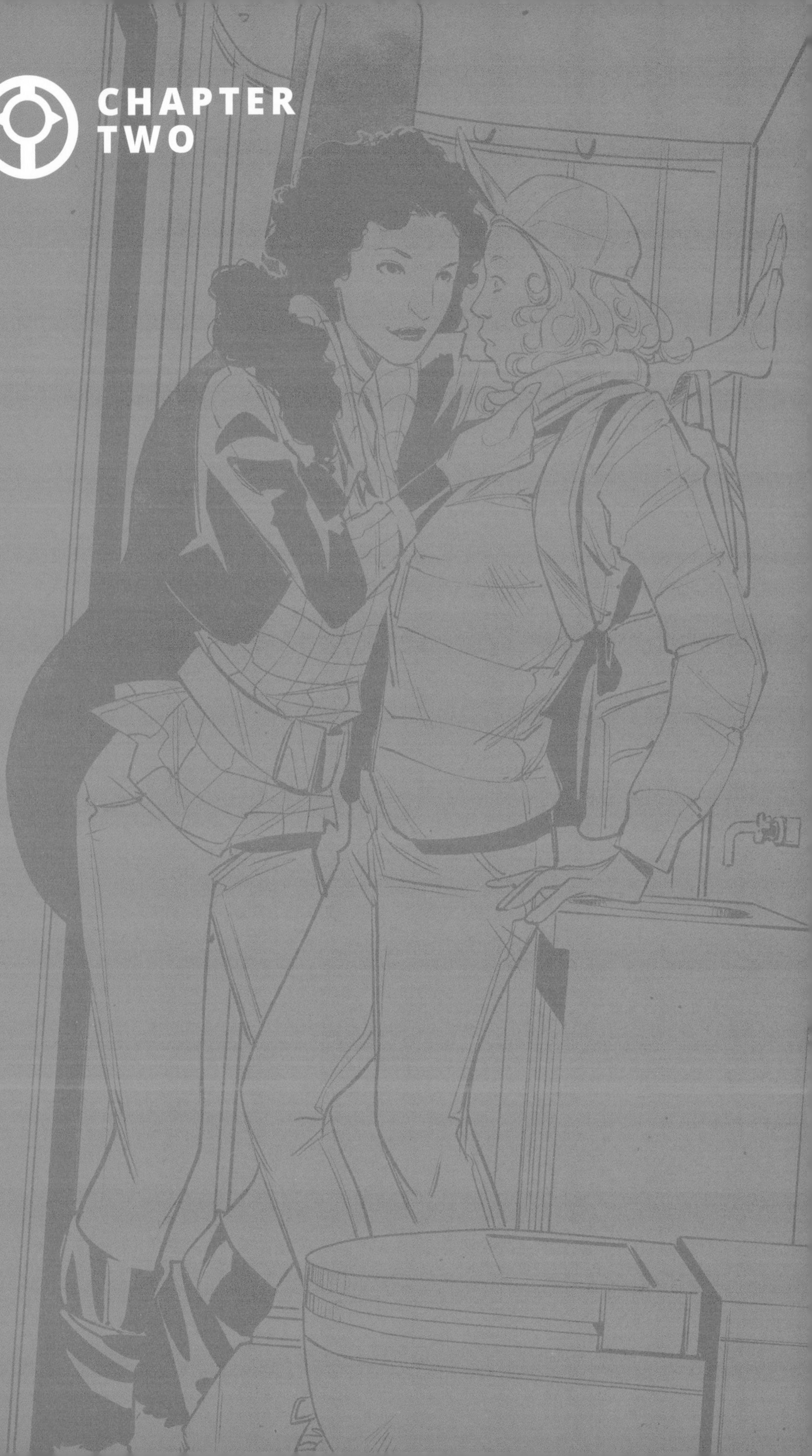

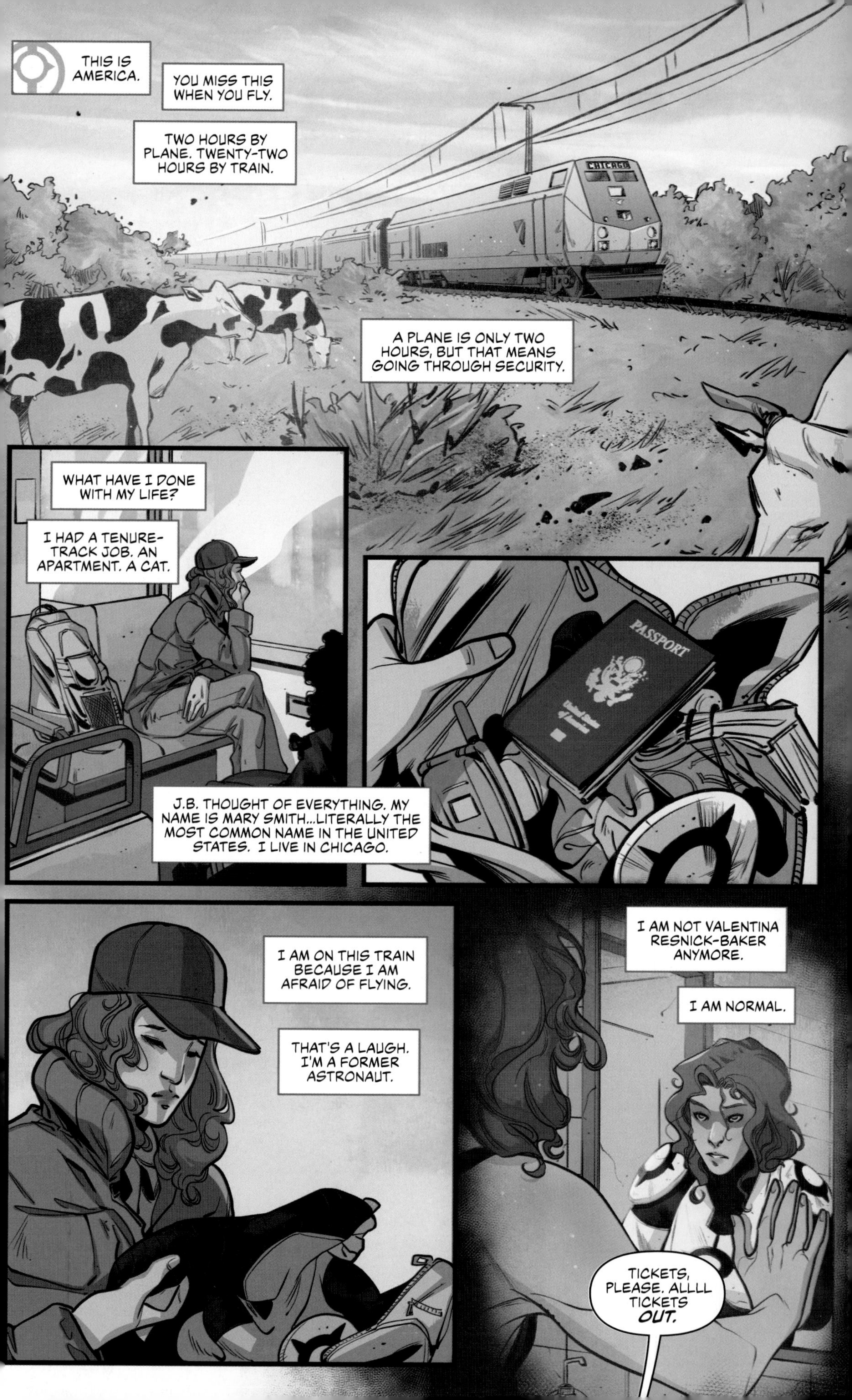
THIS IS AMERICA.
YOU MISS THIS WHEN YOU FLY.
TWO HOURS BY PLANE. TWENTY-TWO HOURS BY TRAIN.
CHICAGO
A PLANE IS ONLY TWO HOURS, BUT THAT MEANS GOING THROUGH SECURITY.
WHAT HAVE I DONE WITH MY LIFE?
I HAD A TENURE-TRACK JOB. AN APARTMENT. A CAT.
PASSPORT
J.B. THOUGHT OF EVERYTHING. MY NAME IS MARY SMITH...LITERALLY THE MOST COMMON NAME IN THE UNITED STATES. I LIVE IN CHICAGO.
I AM ON THIS TRAIN BECAUSE I AM AFRAID OF FLYING.
THAT'S A LAUGH. I'M A FORMER ASTRONAUT.
I AM NOT VALENTINA RESNICK-BAKER ANYMORE.
I AM NORMAL.
TICKETS, PLEASE. ALLLL TICKETS OUT.

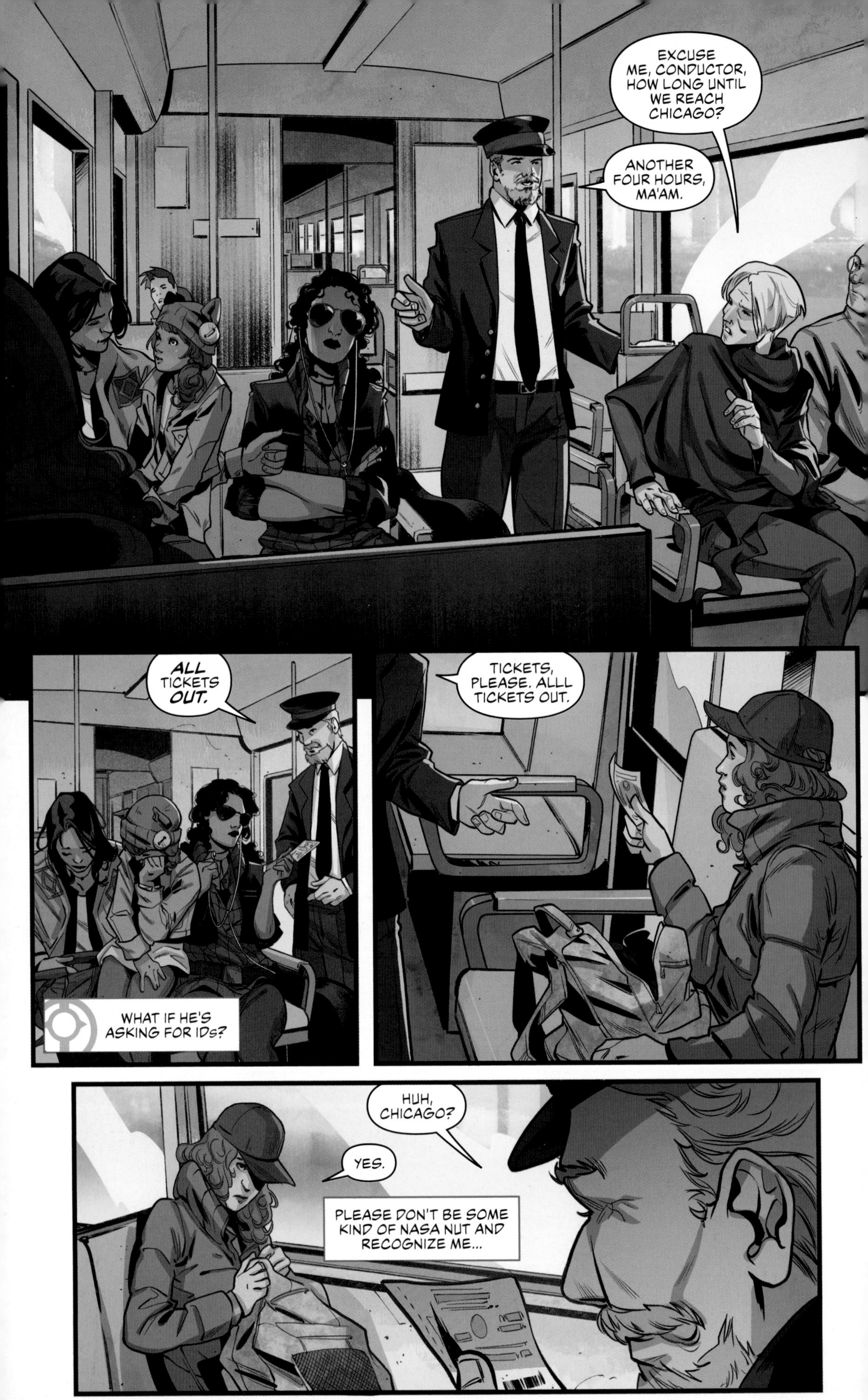

EXCUSE ME, CONDUCTOR, HOW LONG UNTIL WE REACH CHICAGO?
ANOTHER FOUR HOURS, MA'AM.
ALL TICKETS OUT.
WHAT IF HE'S ASKING FOR IDs?
TICKETS, PLEASE. ALLL TICKETS OUT.
HUH, CHICAGO?
YES.
PLEASE DON'T BE SOME KIND OF NASA NUT AND RECOGNIZE ME...

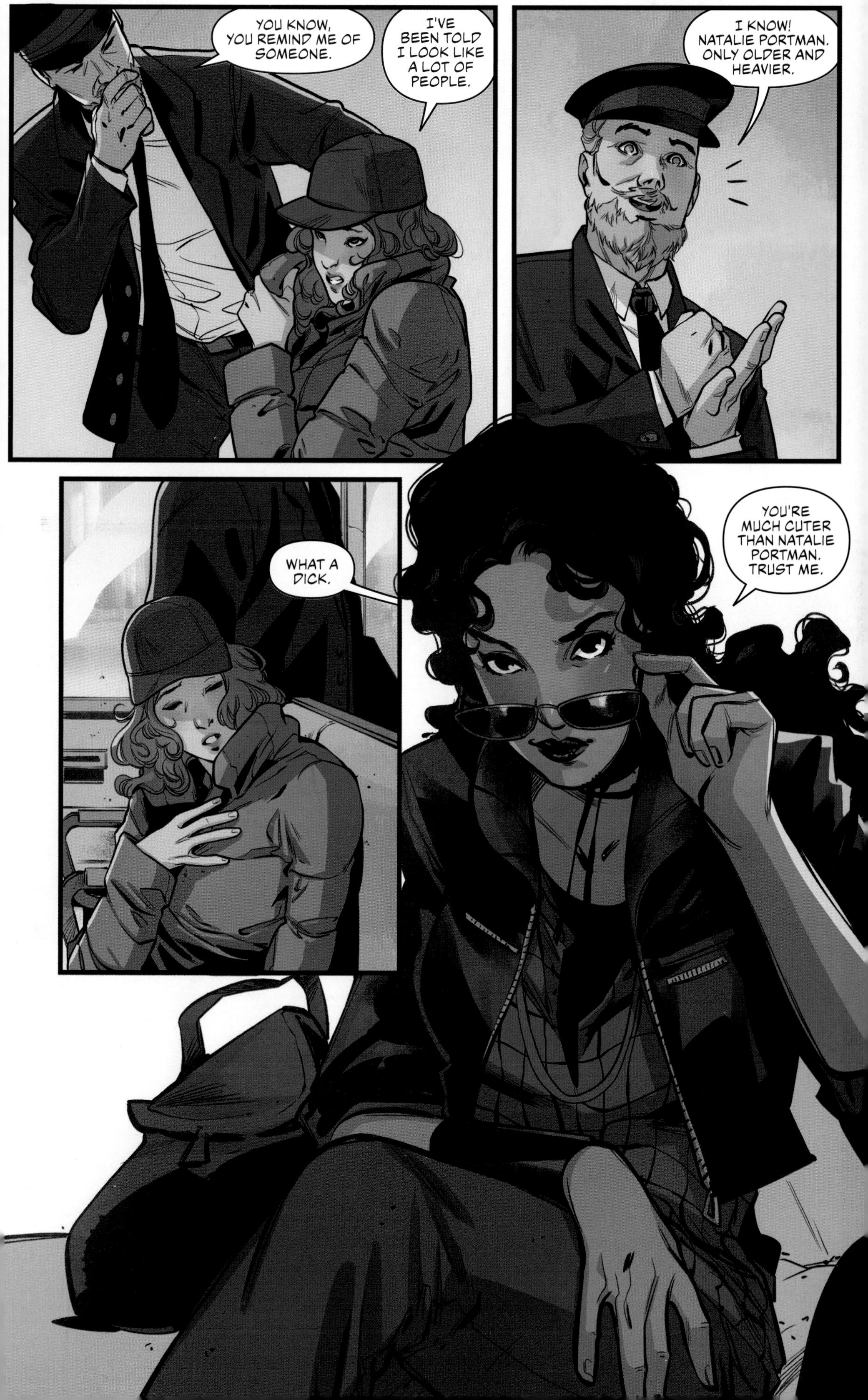
YOU KNOW, YOU REMIND ME OF SOMEONE.
I'VE BEEN TOLD I LOOK LIKE A LOT OF PEOPLE.
I KNOW! NATALIE PORTMAN. ONLY OLDER AND HEAVIER.
WHAT A DICK.
YOU'RE MUCH CUTER THAN NATALIE PORTMAN. TRUST ME.

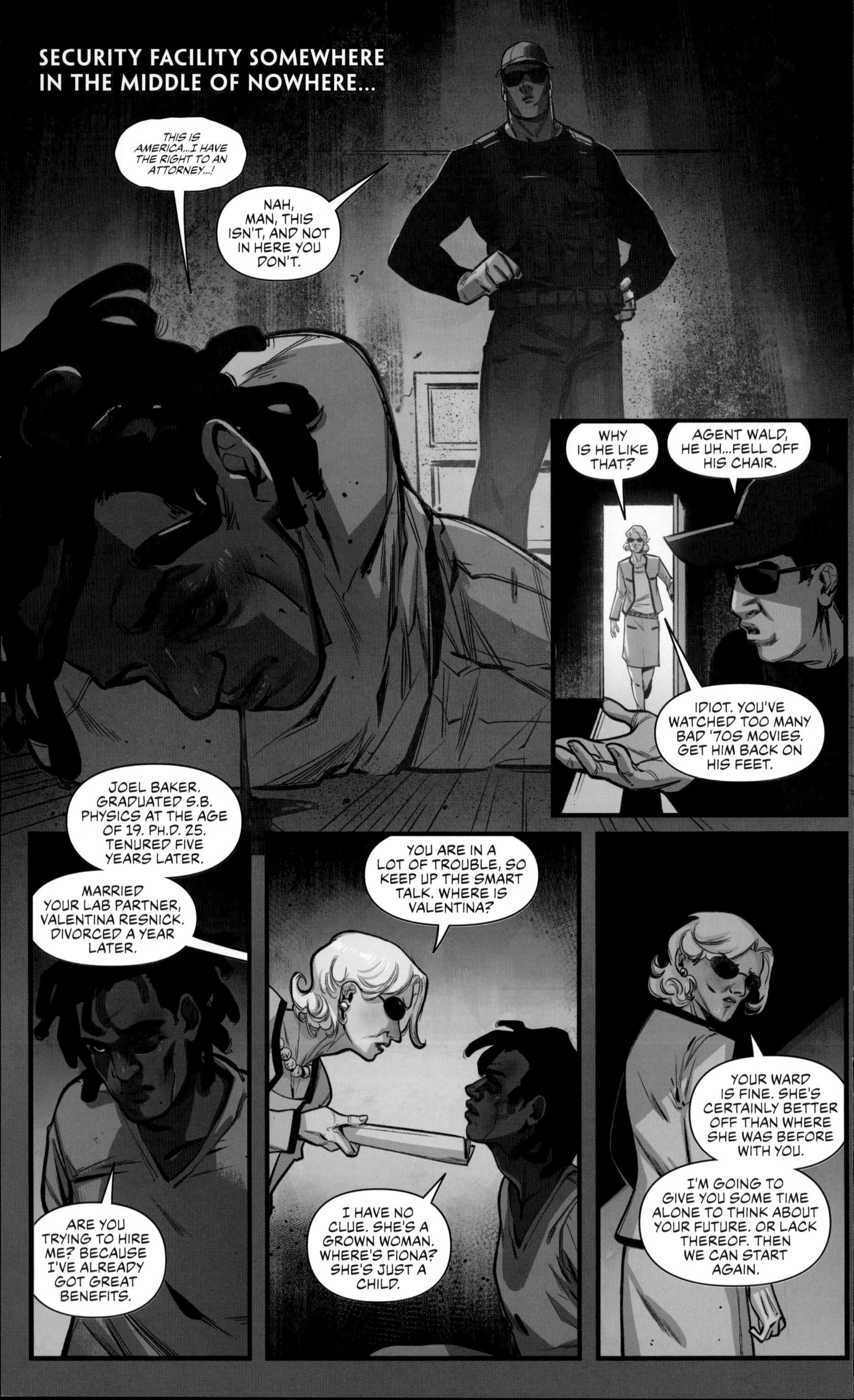
SECURITY FACILITY SOMEWHERE IN THE MIDDLE OF NOWHERE...
THIS IS AMERICA...I HAVE THE RIGHT TO AN ATTORNEY...!
NAH, MAN, THIS ISN'T, AND NOT IN HERE YOU DON'T.
WHY IS HE LIKE THAT?
AGENT WALD, HE UH...FELL OFF HIS CHAIR.
IDIOT. YOU'VE WATCHED TOO MANY BAD '70S MOVIES. GET HIM BACK ON HIS FEET.
JOEL BAKER. GRADUATED S.B. PHYSICS AT THE AGE OF 19. PH.D. 25. TENURED FIVE YEARS LATER.
MARRIED YOUR LAB PARTNER, VALENTINA RESNICK. DIVORCED A YEAR LATER.
ARE YOU TRYING TO HIRE ME? BECAUSE I'VE ALREADY GOT GREAT BENEFITS.
YOU ARE IN A LOT OF TROUBLE, SO KEEP UP THE SMART TALK. WHERE IS VALENTINA?
I HAVE NO CLUE. SHE'S A GROWN WOMAN. WHERE'S FIONA? SHE'S JUST A CHILD.
YOUR WARD IS FINE. SHE'S CERTAINLY BETTER OFF THAN WHERE SHE WAS BEFORE WITH YOU.
I'M GOING TO GIVE YOU SOME TIME ALONE TO THINK ABOUT YOUR FUTURE. OR LACK THEREOF. THEN WE CAN START AGAIN.

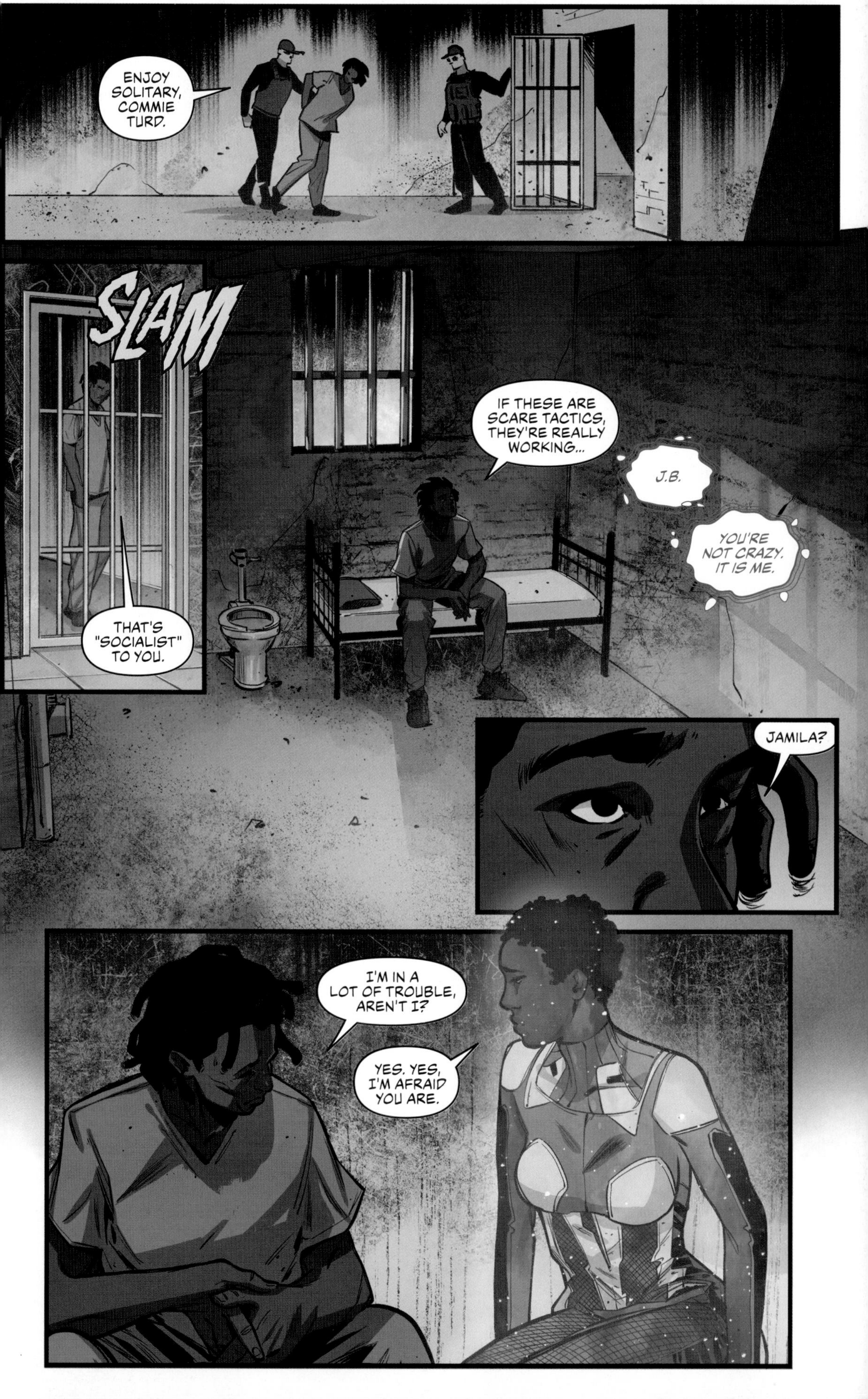
ENJOY SOLITARY, COMMIE TURD.
SLAM
THAT'S "SOCIALIST" TO YOU.
IF THESE ARE SCARE TACTICS, THEY'RE REALLY WORKING...
J.B.
YOU'RE NOT CRAZY. IT IS ME.
JAMILA?
I'M IN A LOT OF TROUBLE, AREN'T I?
YES. YES, I'M AFRAID YOU ARE.

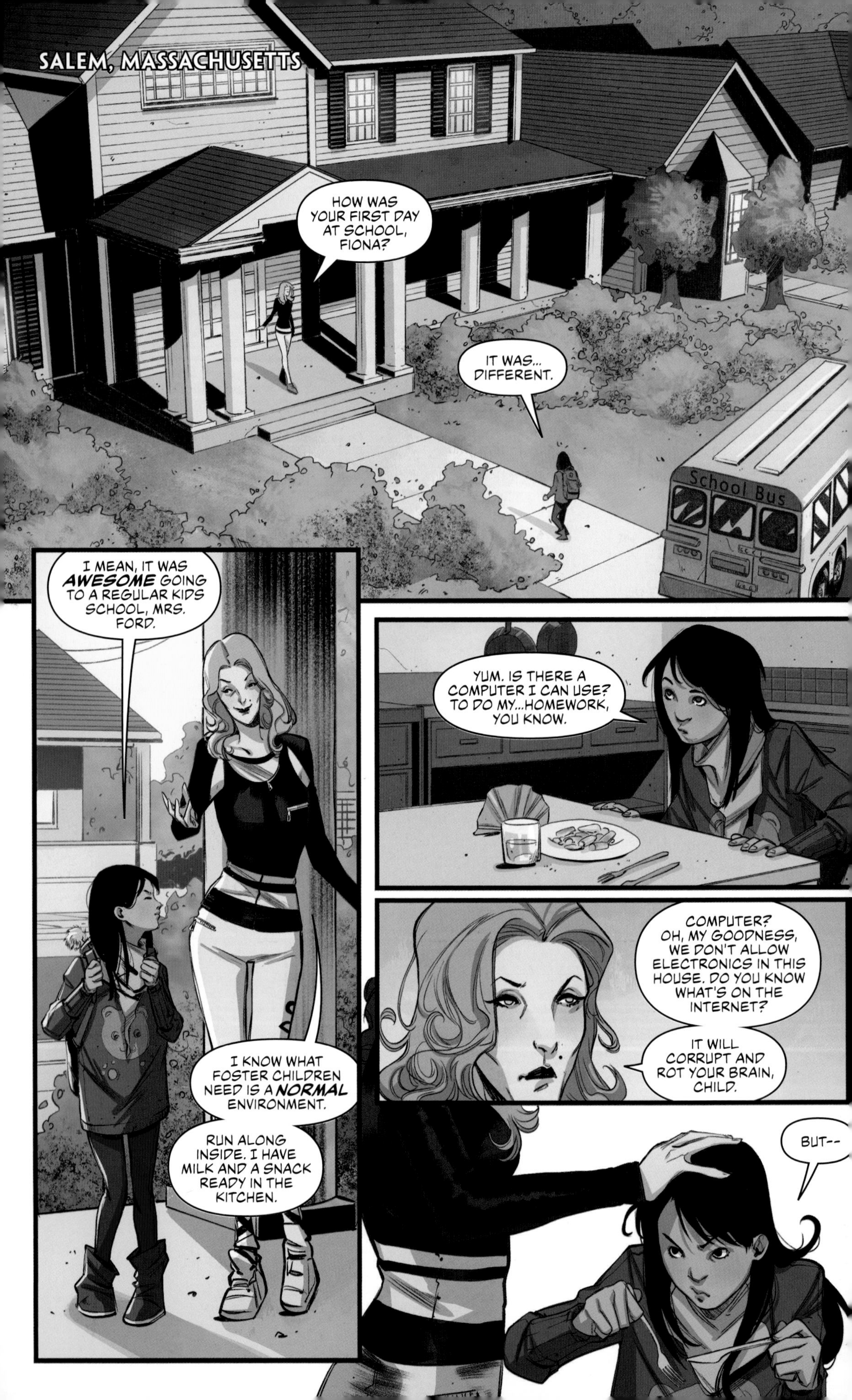
SALEM, MASSACHUSETTS
HOW WAS YOUR FIRST DAY AT SCHOOL, FIONA?
IT WAS... DIFFERENT.
School Bus
I MEAN, IT WAS AWESOME GOING TO A REGULAR KIDS SCHOOL, MRS. FORD.
I KNOW WHAT FOSTER CHILDREN NEED IS A NORMAL ENVIRONMENT.
RUN ALONG INSIDE. I HAVE MILK AND A SNACK READY IN THE KITCHEN.
YUM. IS THERE A COMPUTER I CAN USE? TO DO MY...HOMEWORK, YOU KNOW.
COMPUTER? OH, MY GOODNESS, WE DON'T ALLOW ELECTRONICS IN THIS HOUSE. DO YOU KNOW WHAT'S ON THE INTERNET?
IT WILL CORRUPT AND ROT YOUR BRAIN, CHILD.
BUT--

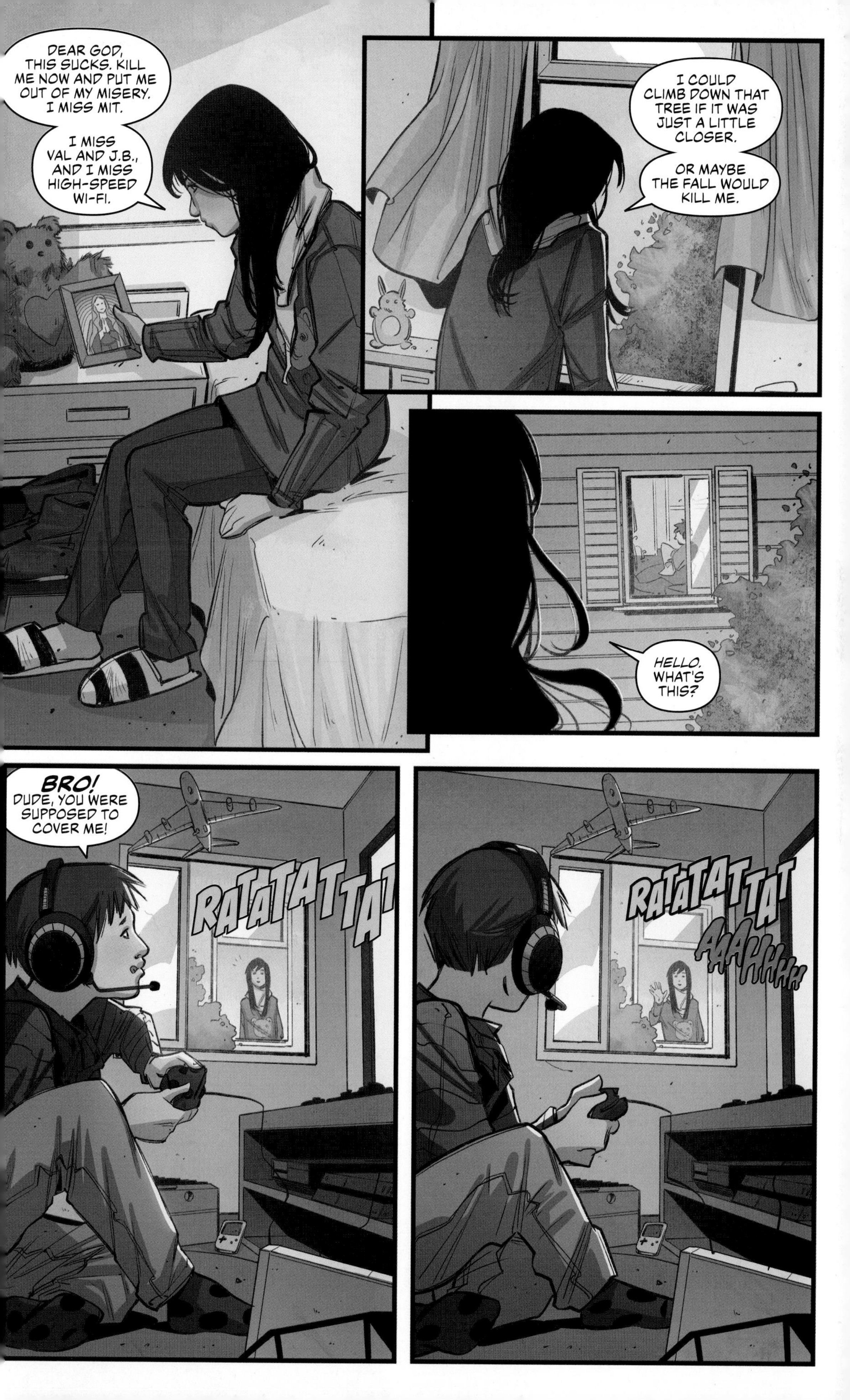
DEAR GOD, THIS SUCKS. KILL ME NOW AND PUT ME OUT OF MY MISERY. I MISS MIT.
I MISS VAL AND J.B., AND I MISS HIGH-SPEED WI-FI.
I COULD CLIMB DOWN THAT TREE IF IT WAS JUST A LITTLE CLOSER.
OR MAYBE THE FALL WOULD KILL ME.
HELLO. WHAT'S THIS?
BRO! DUDE, YOU WERE SUPPOSED TO COVER ME!
RATATATTAT
RATATATTAT
AAAHHHH

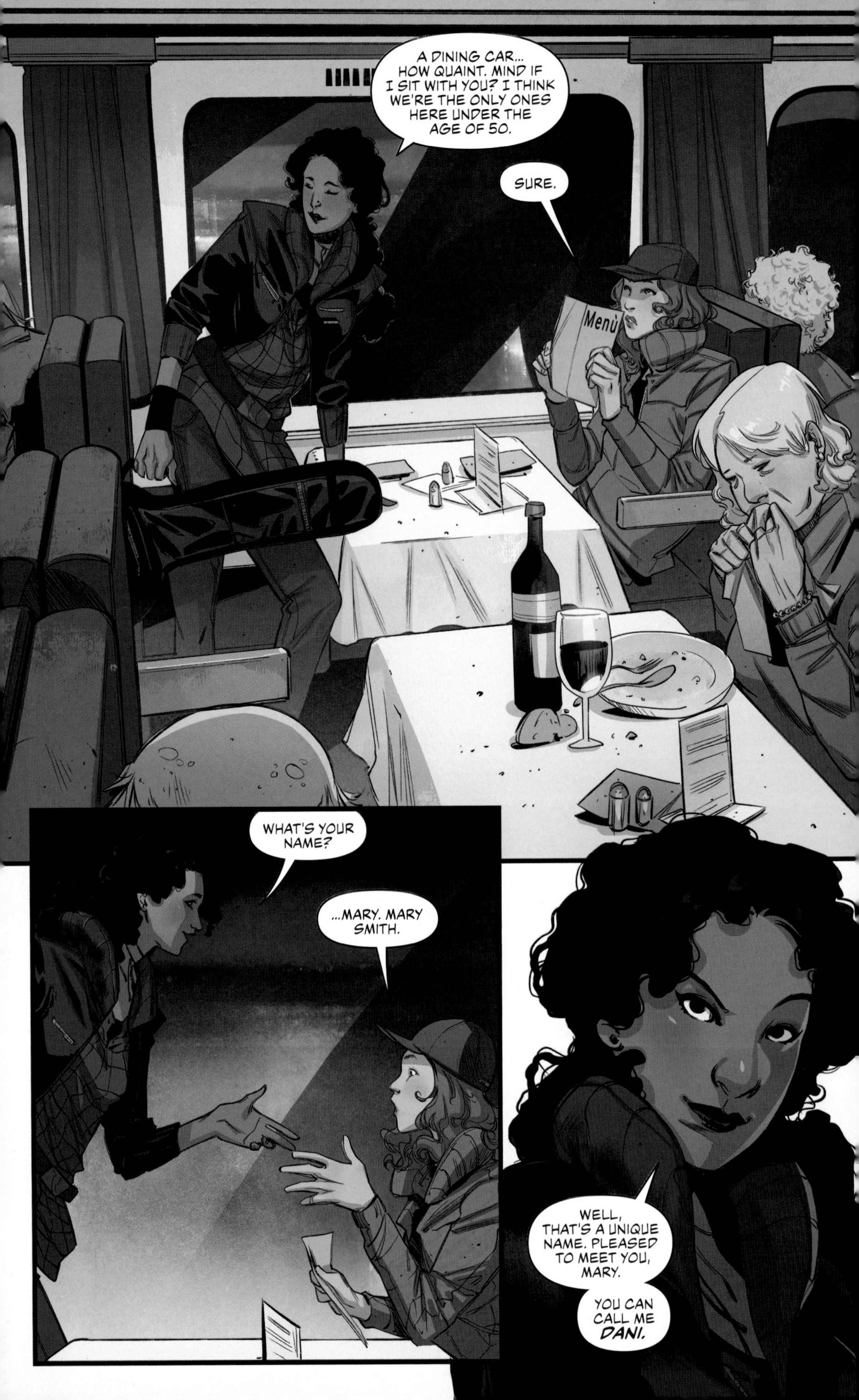
A DINING CAR... HOW QUAINT. MIND IF I SIT WITH YOU? I THINK WE'RE THE ONLY ONES HERE UNDER THE AGE OF 50.
SURE.
Menù
WHAT'S YOUR NAME?
...MARY. MARY SMITH.
WELL, THAT'S A UNIQUE NAME. PLEASED TO MEET YOU, MARY.
YOU CAN CALL ME *DANI.*

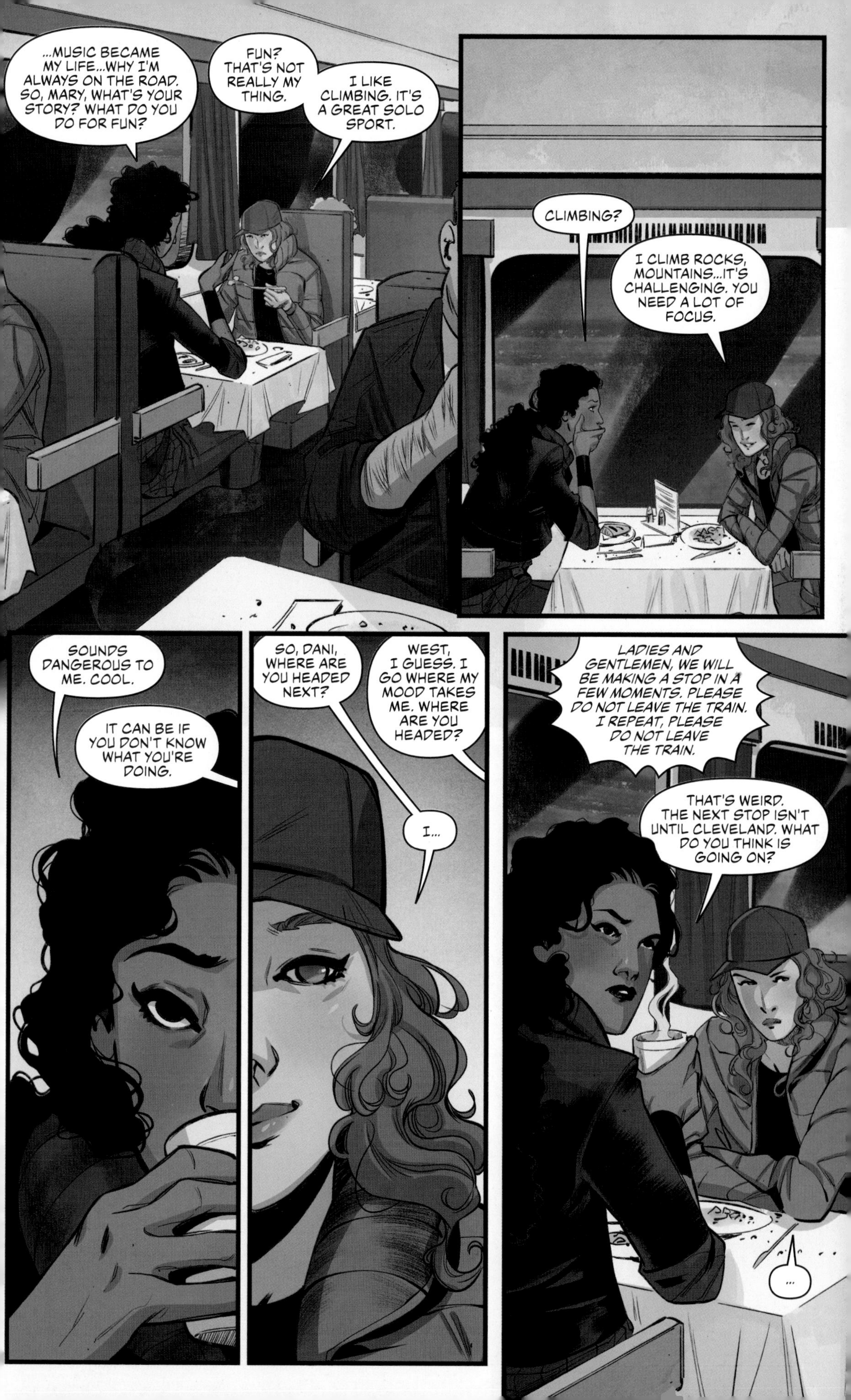
...MUSIC BECAME MY LIFE...WHY I'M ALWAYS ON THE ROAD. SO, MARY, WHAT'S YOUR STORY? WHAT DO YOU DO FOR FUN?
FUN? THAT'S NOT REALLY MY THING.
I LIKE CLIMBING. IT'S A GREAT SOLO SPORT.
CLIMBING?
I CLIMB ROCKS, MOUNTAINS...IT'S CHALLENGING. YOU NEED A LOT OF FOCUS.
SOUNDS DANGEROUS TO ME. COOL.
IT CAN BE IF YOU DON'T KNOW WHAT YOU'RE DOING.
SO, DANI, WHERE ARE YOU HEADED NEXT?
WEST, I GUESS. I GO WHERE MY MOOD TAKES ME. WHERE ARE YOU HEADED?
I...
LADIES AND GENTLEMEN, WE WILL BE MAKING A STOP IN A FEW MOMENTS. PLEASE DO NOT LEAVE THE TRAIN. I REPEAT, PLEASE DO NOT LEAVE THE TRAIN.
THAT'S WEIRD. THE NEXT STOP ISN'T UNTIL CLEVELAND. WHAT DO YOU THINK IS GOING ON?
...

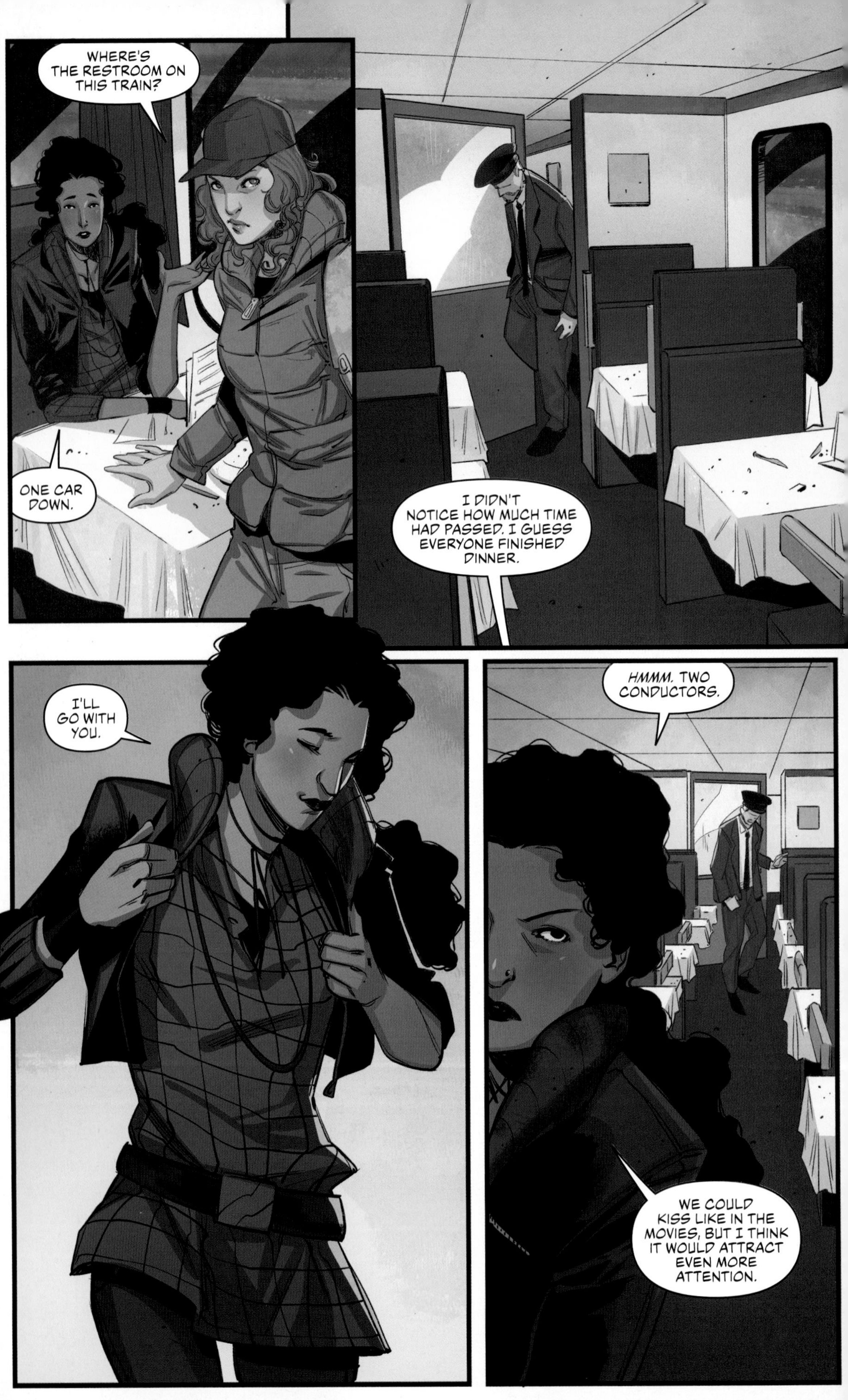
WHERE'S THE RESTROOM ON THIS TRAIN?
ONE CAR DOWN.
I DIDN'T NOTICE HOW MUCH TIME HAD PASSED. I GUESS EVERYONE FINISHED DINNER.
I'LL GO WITH YOU.
HMMM. TWO CONDUCTORS.
WE COULD KISS LIKE IN THE MOVIES, BUT I THINK IT WOULD ATTRACT EVEN MORE ATTENTION.

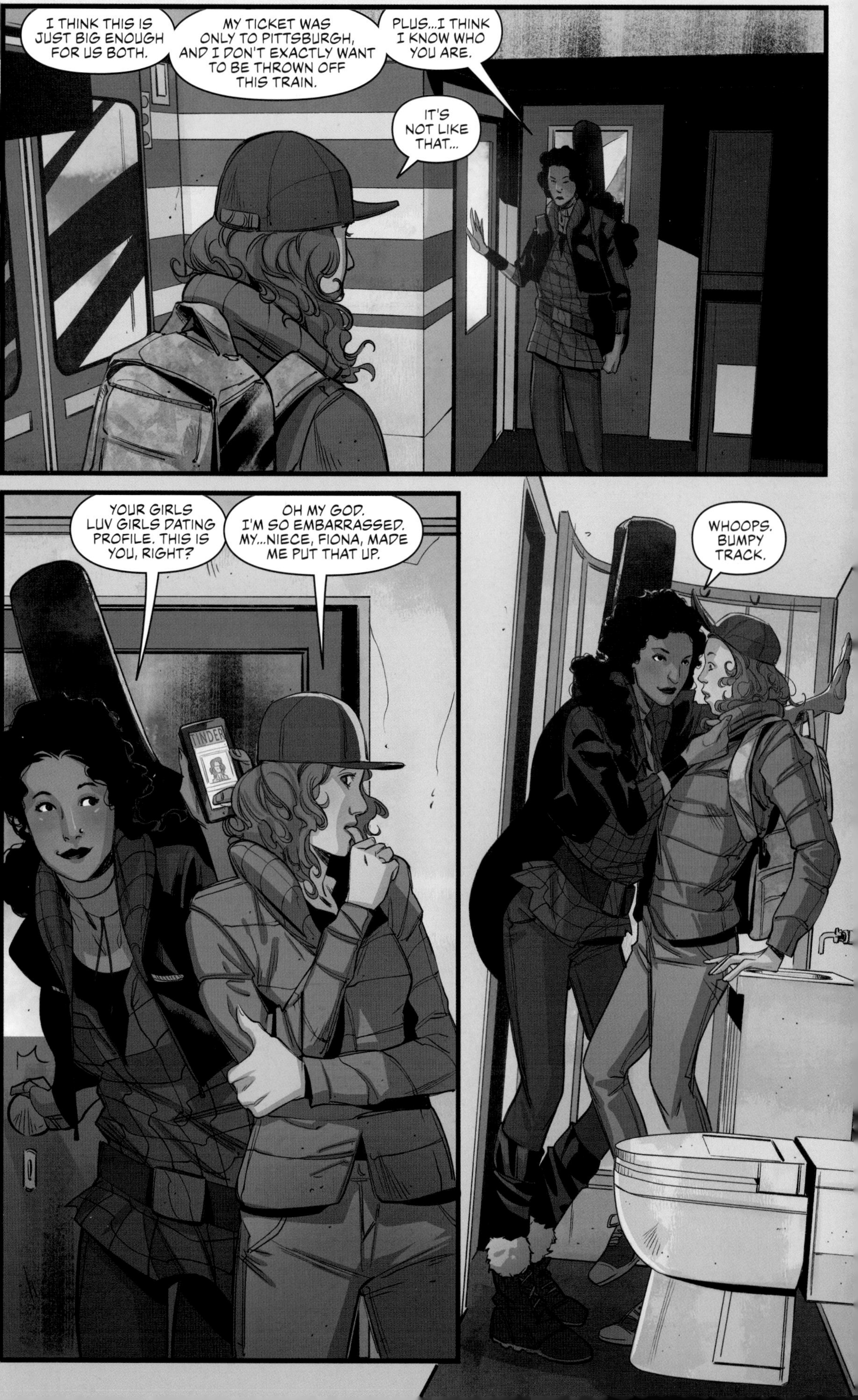
I THINK THIS IS JUST BIG ENOUGH FOR US BOTH.
MY TICKET WAS ONLY TO PITTSBURGH, AND I DON'T EXACTLY WANT TO BE THROWN OFF THIS TRAIN.
PLUS...I THINK I KNOW WHO YOU ARE.
IT'S NOT LIKE THAT...
YOUR GIRLS LUV GIRLS DATING PROFILE. THIS IS YOU, RIGHT?
OH MY GOD. I'M SO EMBARRASSED. MY...NIECE, FIONA, MADE ME PUT THAT UP.
TINDER
WHOOPS. BUMPY TRACK.

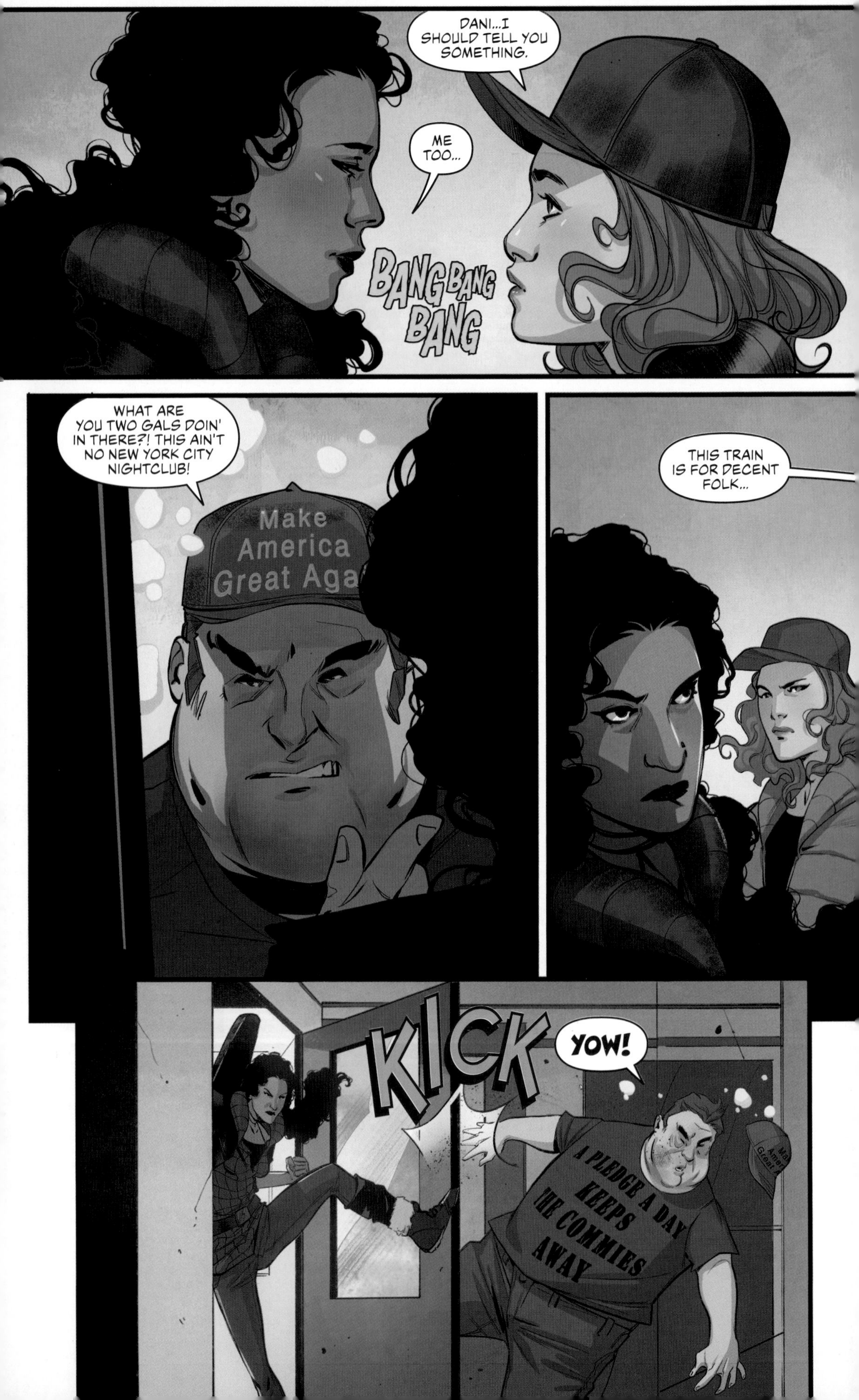
DANI...I SHOULD TELL YOU SOMETHING.
ME TOO...
BANG BANG BANG
WHAT ARE YOU TWO GALS DOIN' IN THERE?! THIS AIN'T NO NEW YORK CITY NIGHTCLUB!
Make America Great Aga
THIS TRAIN IS FOR DECENT FOLK...
KICK
YOW!
A PLEDGE A DAY KEEPS THE COMMIES AWAY

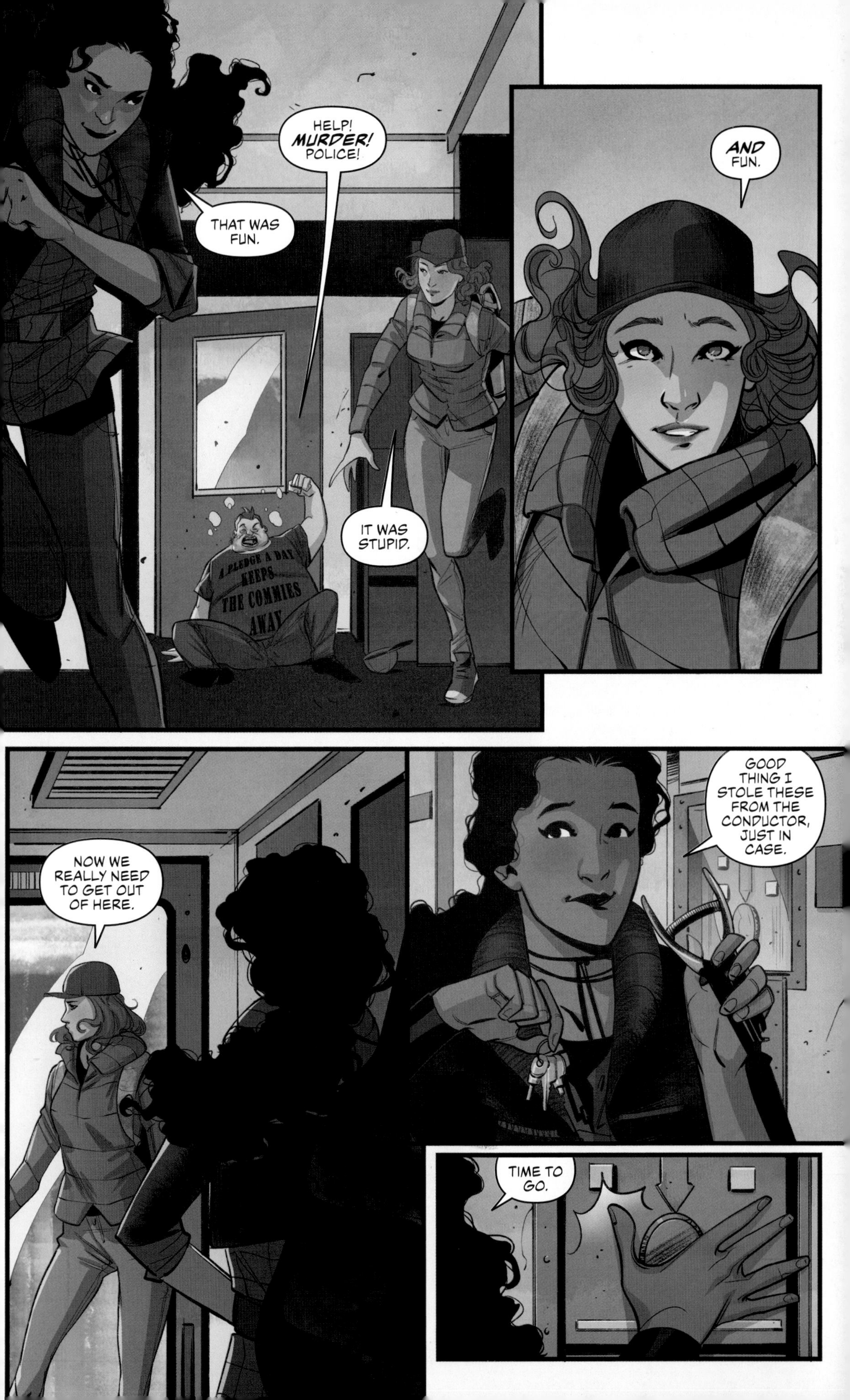
HELP! MURDER! POLICE!
THAT WAS FUN.
IT WAS STUPID.
A PLEDGE A DAY KEEPS THE COMMIES AWAY
AND FUN.
NOW WE REALLY NEED TO GET OUT OF HERE.
GOOD THING I STOLE THESE FROM THE CONDUCTOR, JUST IN CASE.
TIME TO GO.

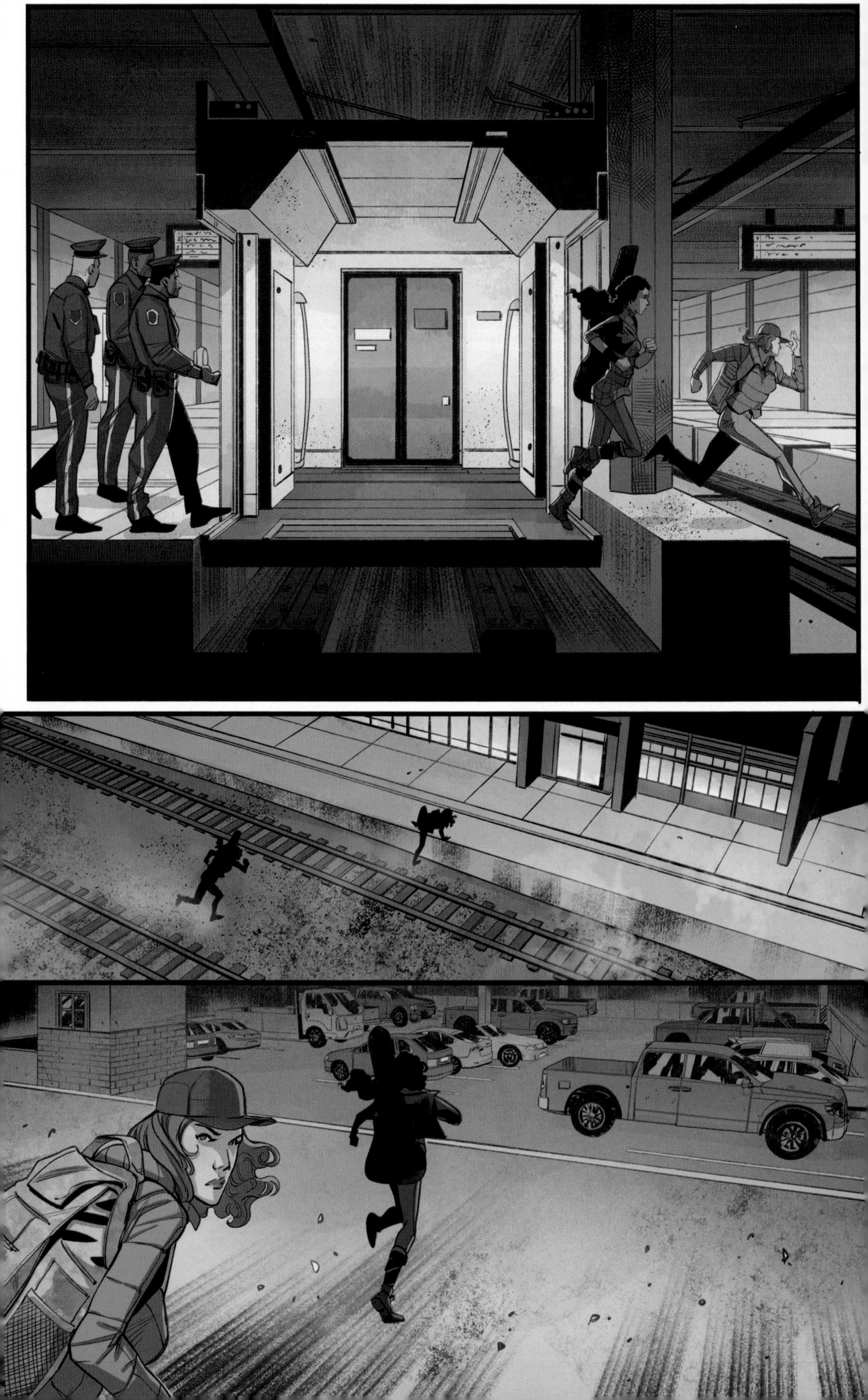

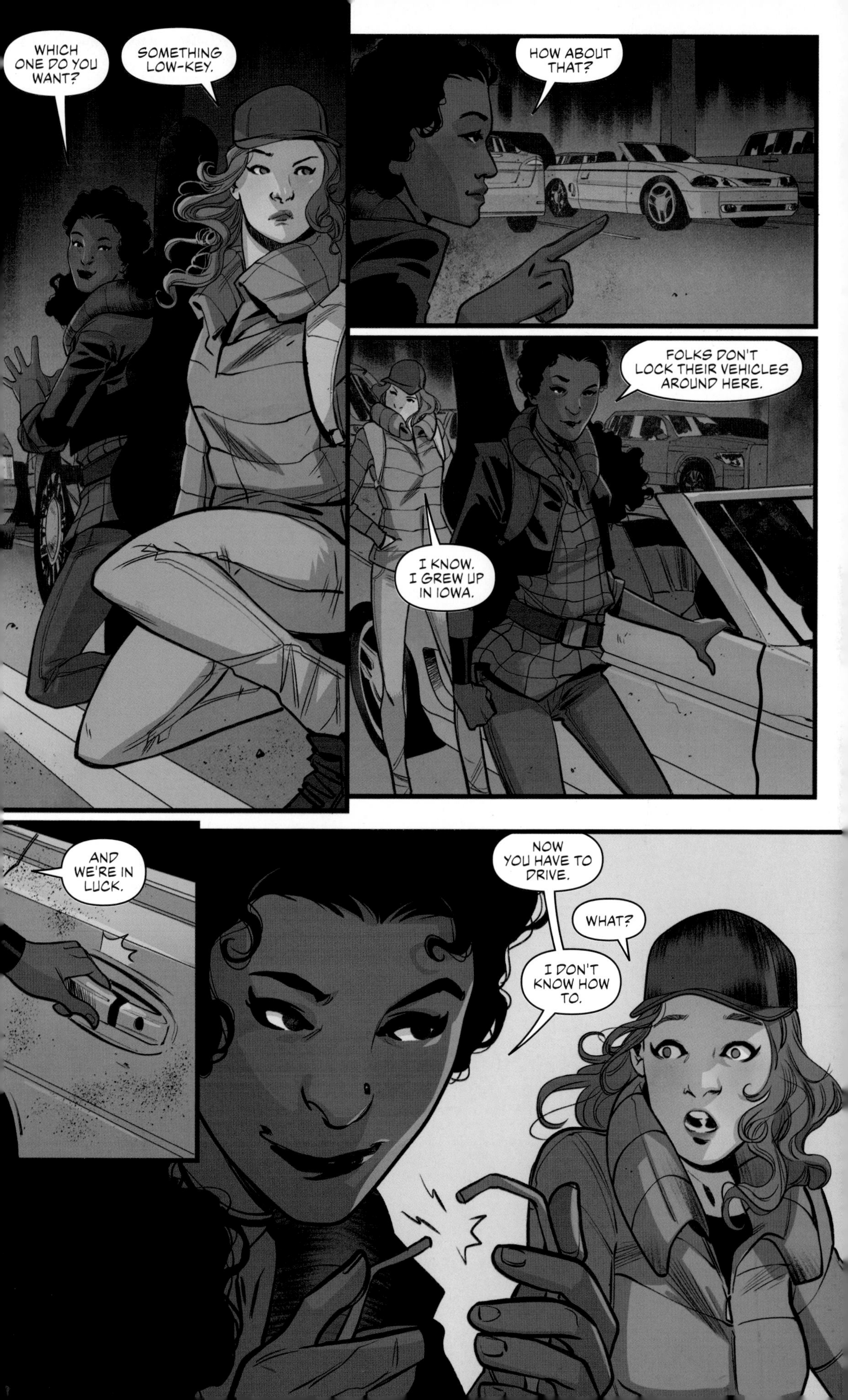
WHICH ONE DO YOU WANT?
SOMETHING LOW-KEY.
HOW ABOUT THAT?
FOLKS DON'T LOCK THEIR VEHICLES AROUND HERE.
I KNOW. I GREW UP IN IOWA.
AND WE'RE IN LUCK.
NOW YOU HAVE TO DRIVE.
WHAT?
I DON'T KNOW HOW TO.

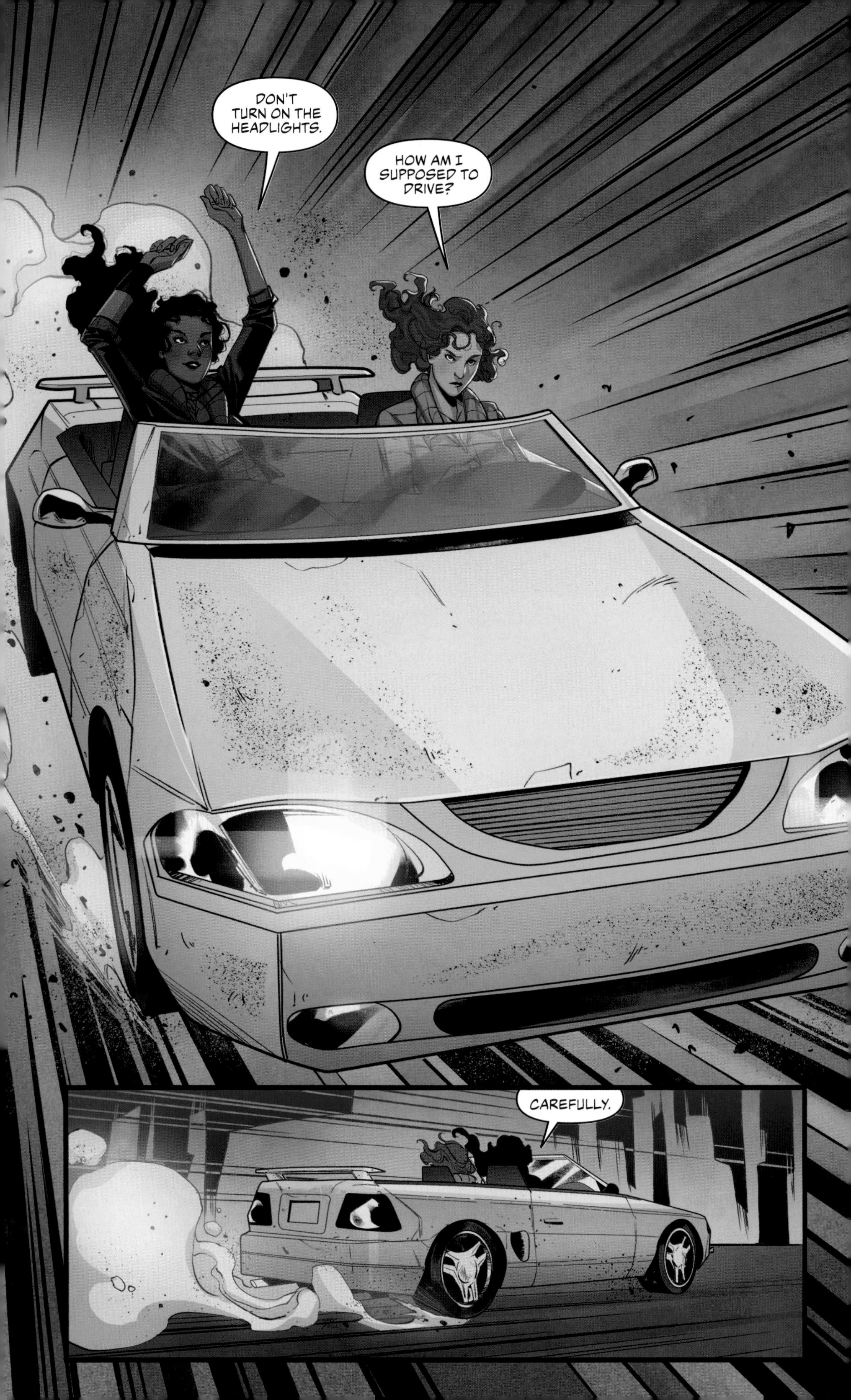
DON'T TURN ON THE HEADLIGHTS.
HOW AM I SUPPOSED TO DRIVE?
CAREFULLY.

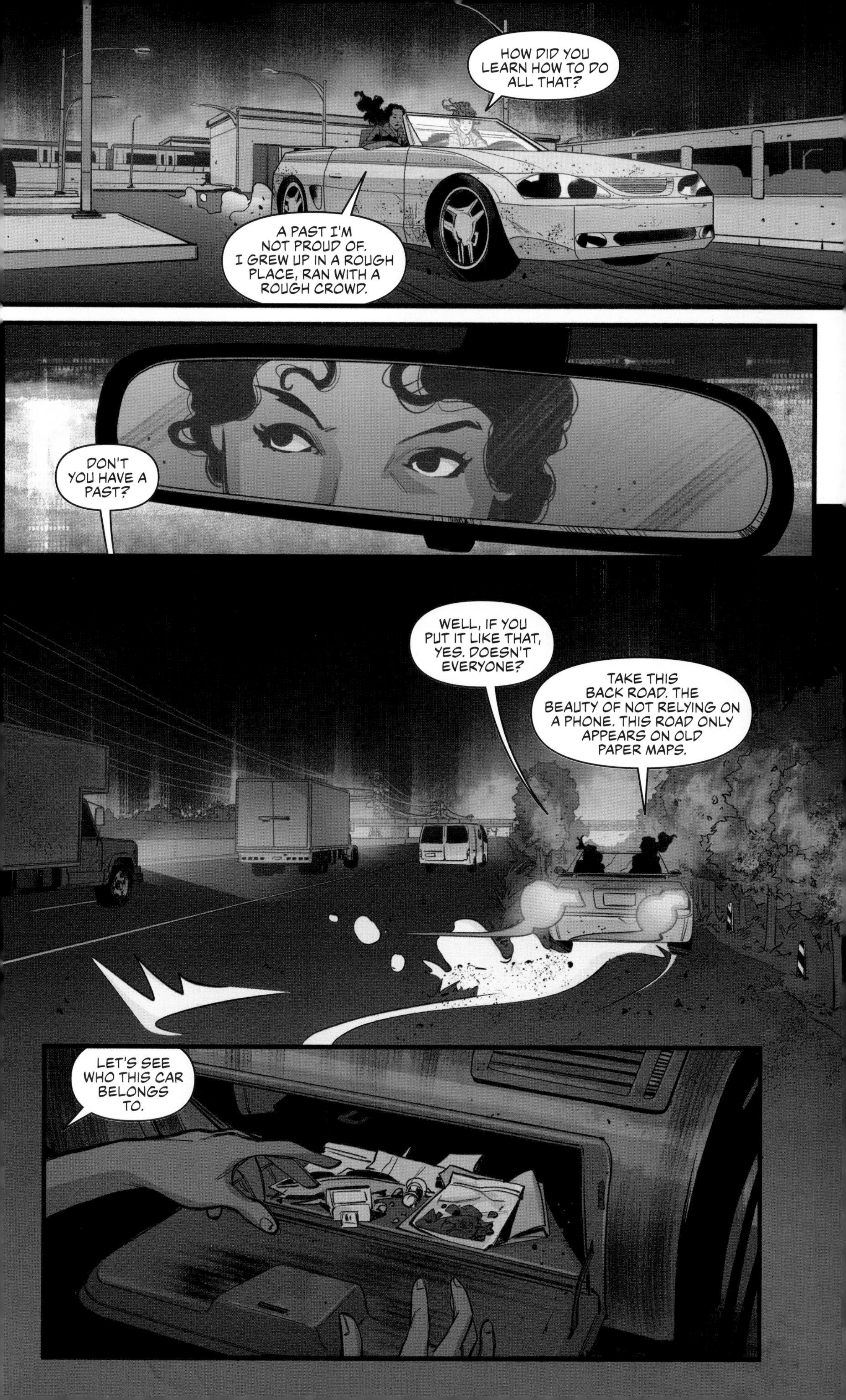
HOW DID YOU LEARN HOW TO DO ALL THAT?
A PAST I'M NOT PROUD OF. I GREW UP IN A ROUGH PLACE, RAN WITH A ROUGH CROWD.
DON'T YOU HAVE A PAST?
WELL, IF YOU PUT IT LIKE THAT, YES. DOESN'T EVERYONE?
TAKE THIS BACK ROAD. THE BEAUTY OF NOT RELYING ON A PHONE. THIS ROAD ONLY APPEARS ON OLD PAPER MAPS.
LET'S SEE WHO THIS CAR BELONGS TO.

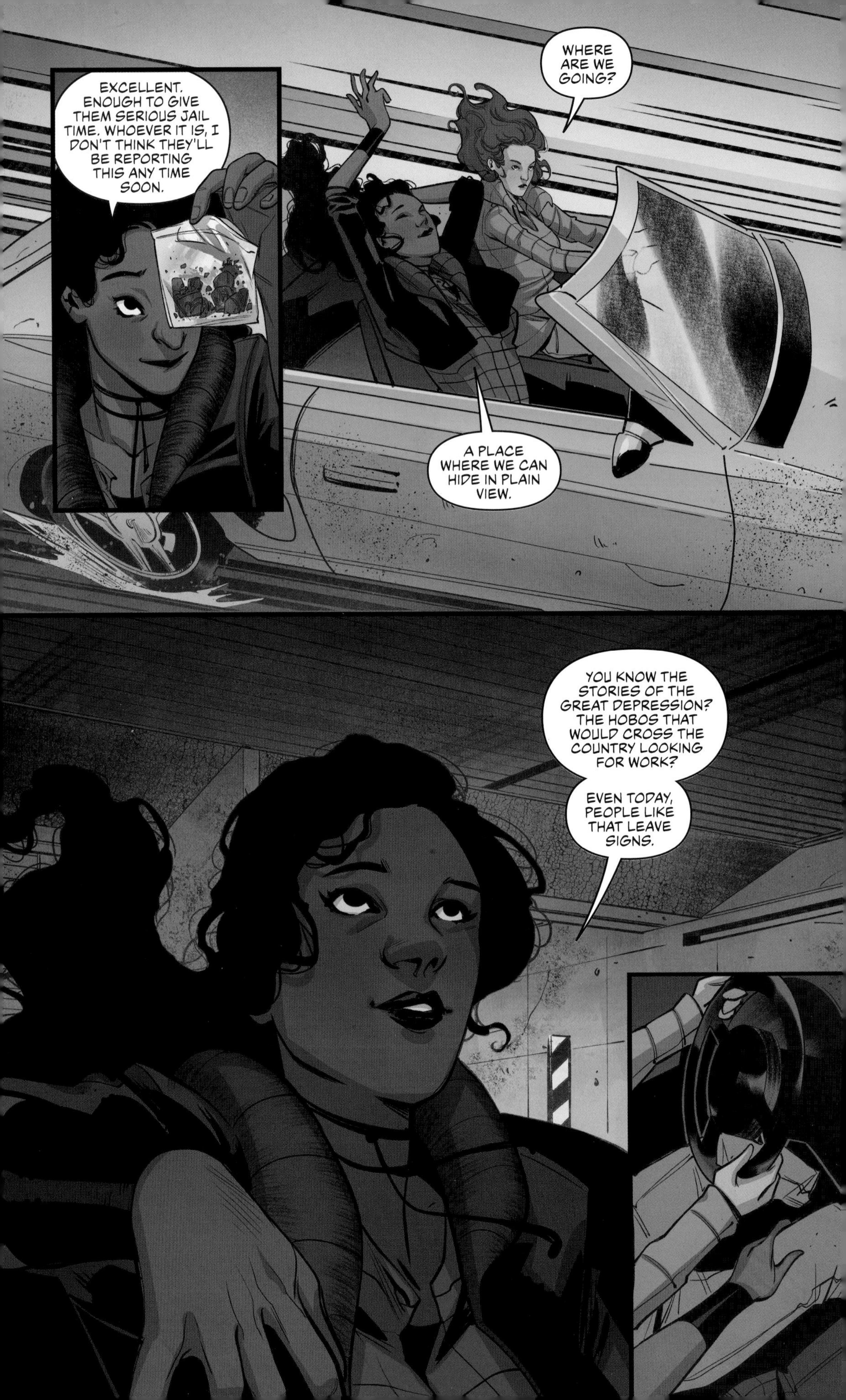
EXCELLENT. ENOUGH TO GIVE THEM SERIOUS JAIL TIME. WHOEVER IT IS, I DON'T THINK THEY'LL BE REPORTING THIS ANY TIME SOON.
WHERE ARE WE GOING?
A PLACE WHERE WE CAN HIDE IN PLAIN VIEW.
YOU KNOW THE STORIES OF THE GREAT DEPRESSION? THE HOBOS THAT WOULD CROSS THE COUNTRY LOOKING FOR WORK?
EVEN TODAY, PEOPLE LIKE THAT LEAVE SIGNS.

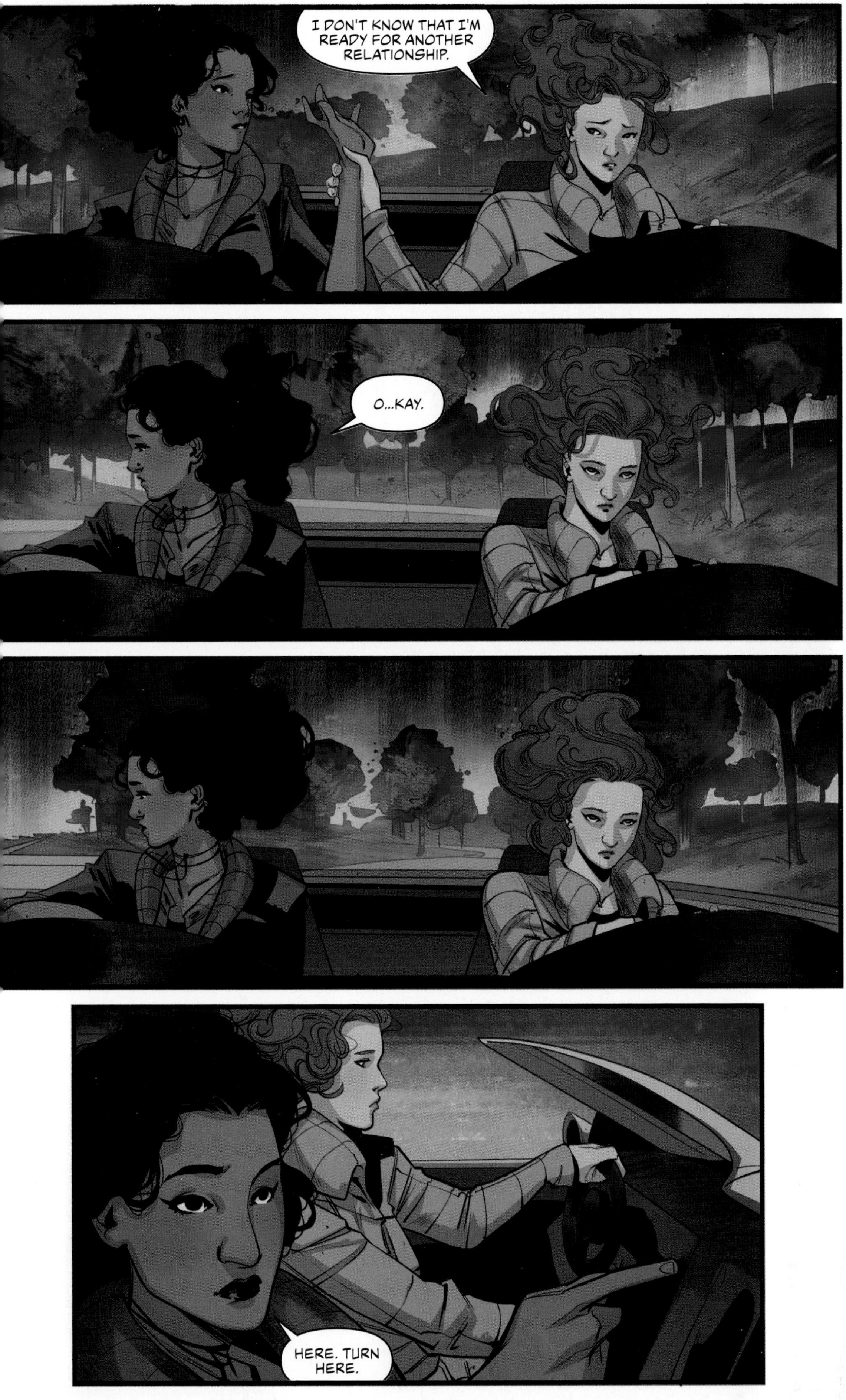
I DON'T KNOW THAT I'M READY FOR ANOTHER RELATIONSHIP.
O...KAY.
HERE. TURN HERE.

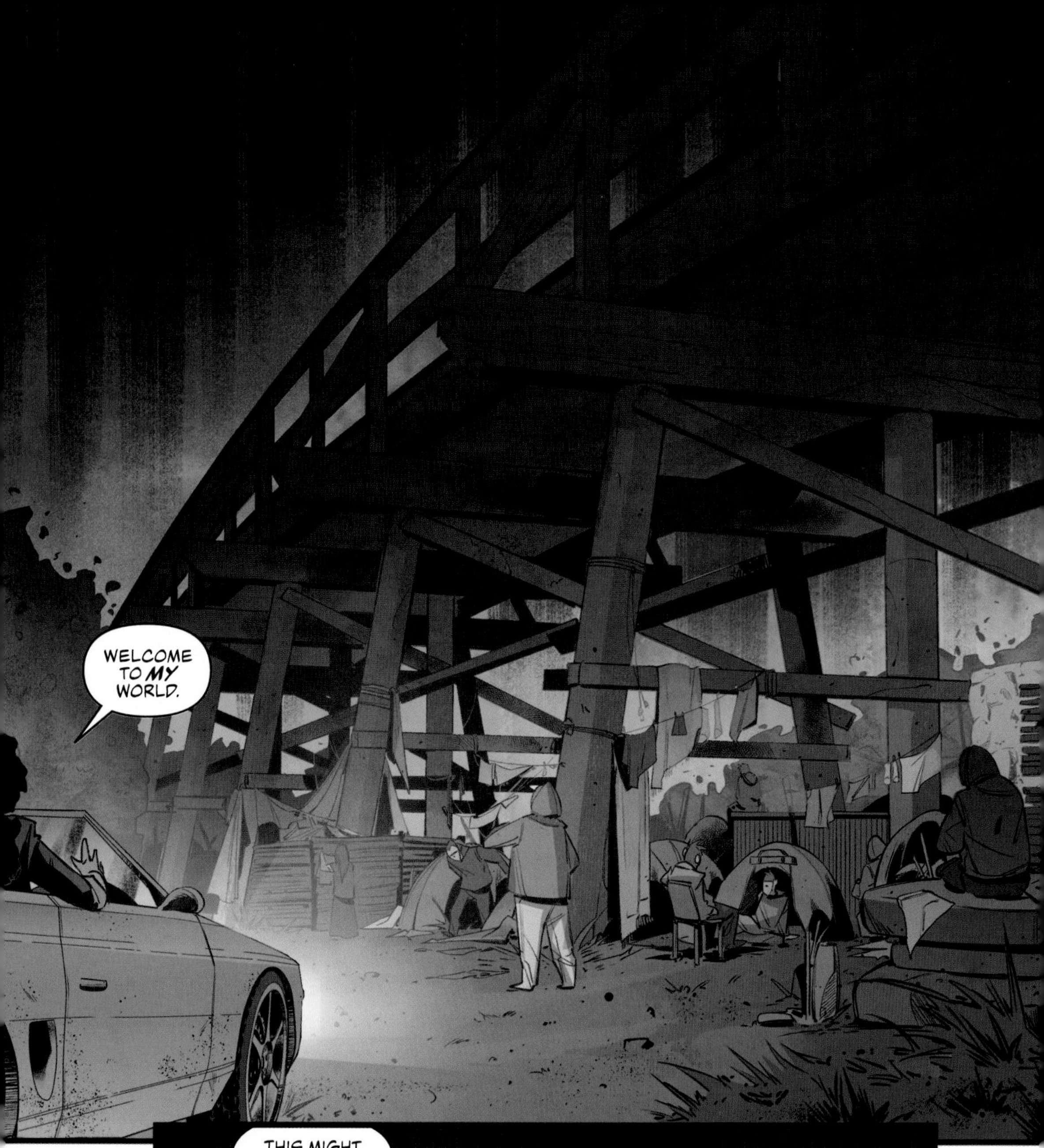
WELCOME TO MY WORLD.

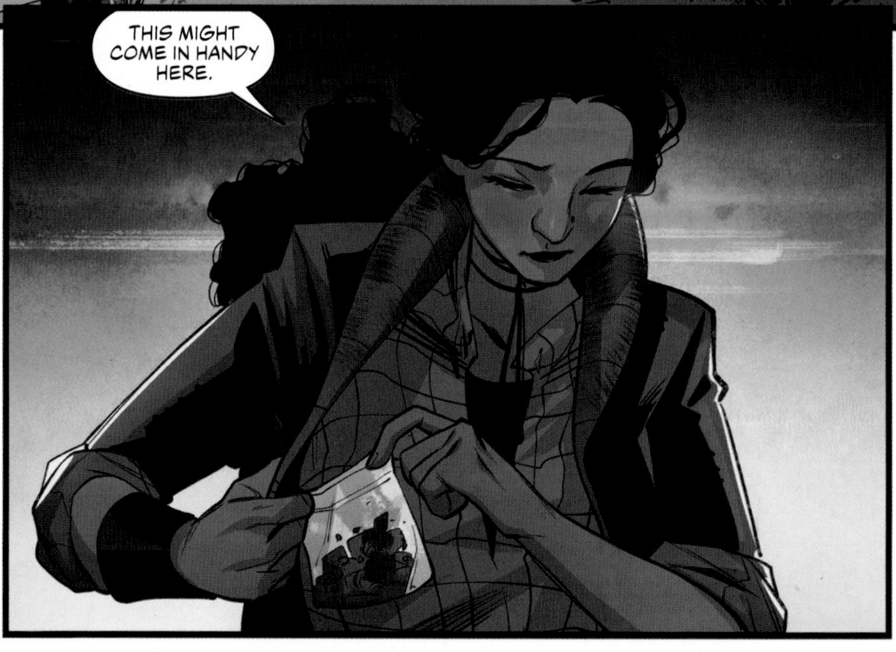
THIS MIGHT COME IN HANDY HERE.

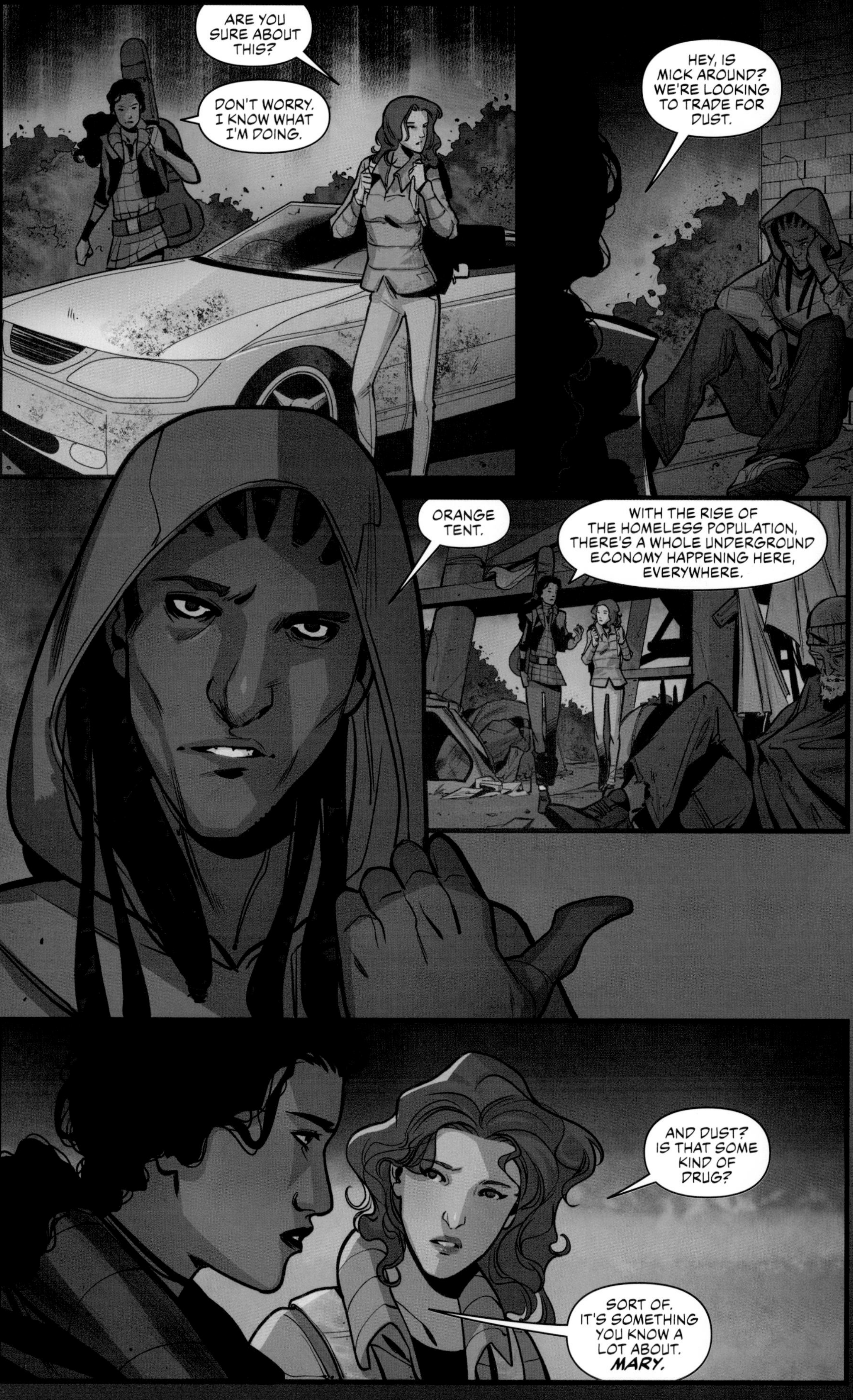
ARE YOU SURE ABOUT THIS?
DON'T WORRY. I KNOW WHAT I'M DOING.
HEY, IS MICK AROUND? WE'RE LOOKING TO TRADE FOR DUST.
ORANGE TENT.
WITH THE RISE OF THE HOMELESS POPULATION, THERE'S A WHOLE UNDERGROUND ECONOMY HAPPENING HERE, EVERYWHERE.
AND DUST? IS THAT SOME KIND OF DRUG?
SORT OF. IT'S SOMETHING YOU KNOW A LOT ABOUT. **MARY.**

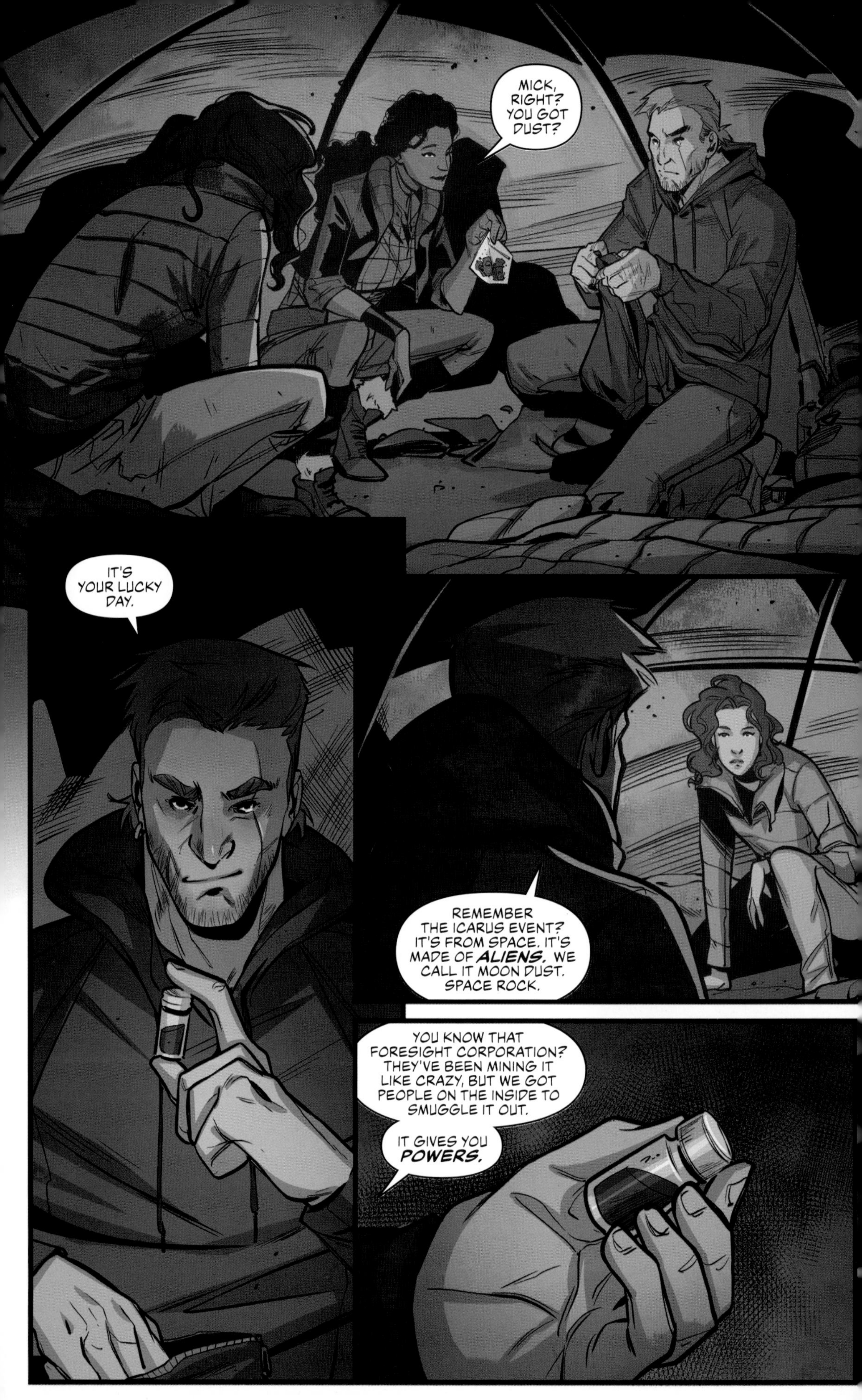
MICK, RIGHT? YOU GOT DUST?
IT'S YOUR LUCKY DAY.
REMEMBER THE ICARUS EVENT? IT'S FROM SPACE. IT'S MADE OF **ALIENS.** WE CALL IT MOON DUST. SPACE ROCK.
YOU KNOW THAT FORESIGHT CORPORATION? THEY'VE BEEN MINING IT LIKE CRAZY, BUT WE GOT PEOPLE ON THE INSIDE TO SMUGGLE IT OUT.
IT GIVES YOU **POWERS.**

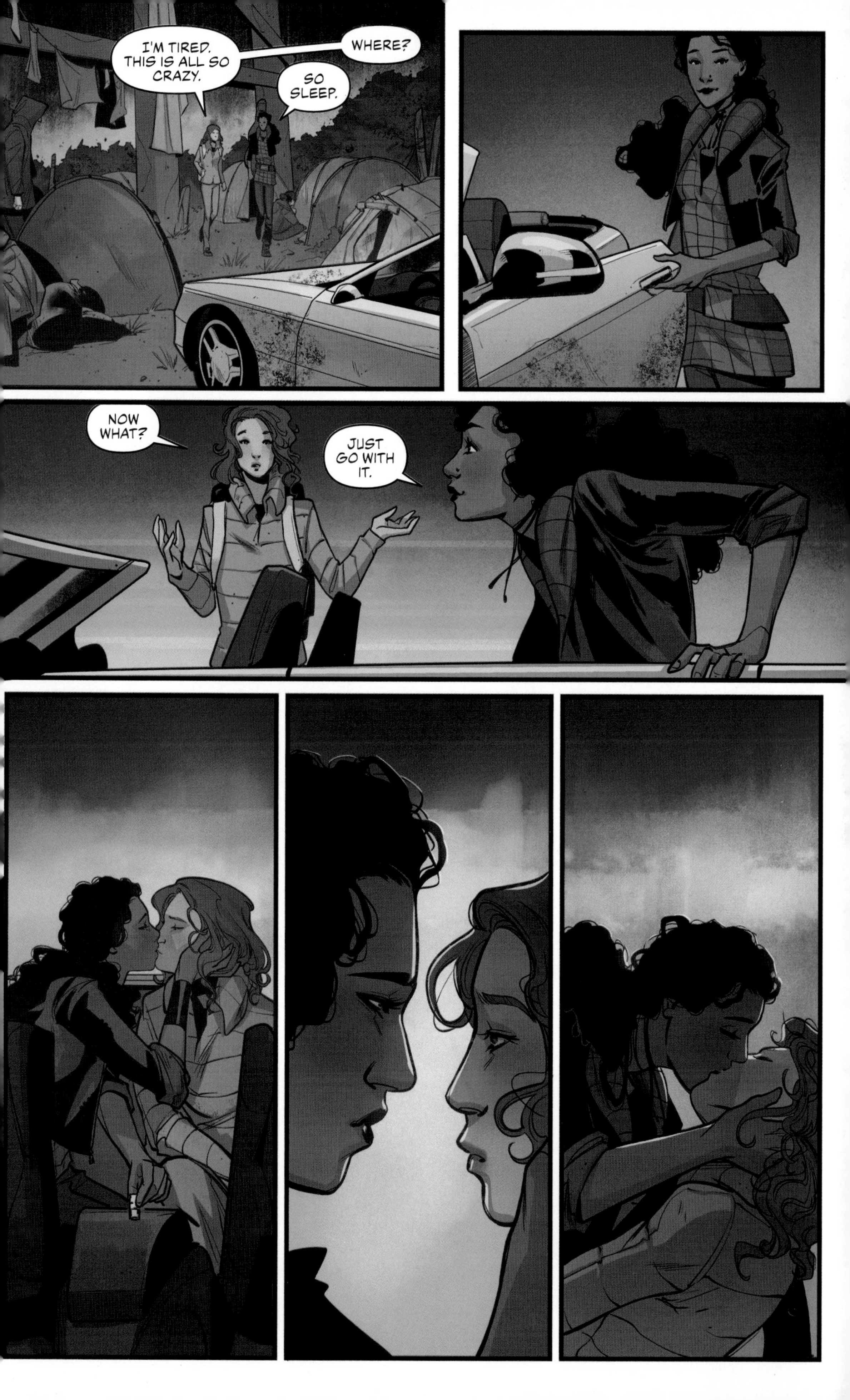
I'M TIRED. THIS IS ALL SO CRAZY.
WHERE?
SO SLEEP.
NOW WHAT?
JUST GO WITH IT.

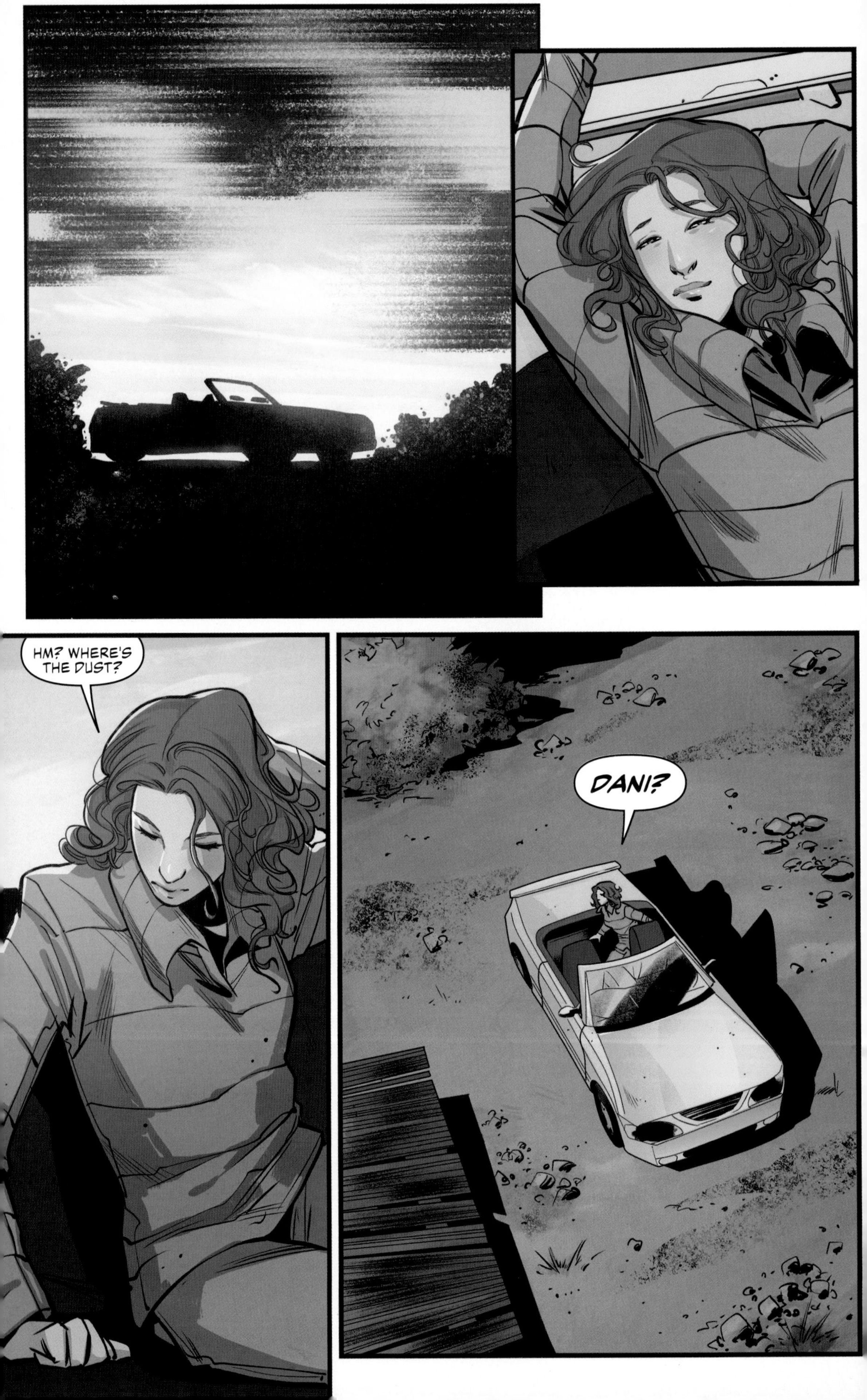
HM? WHERE'S THE DUST?
DANI?

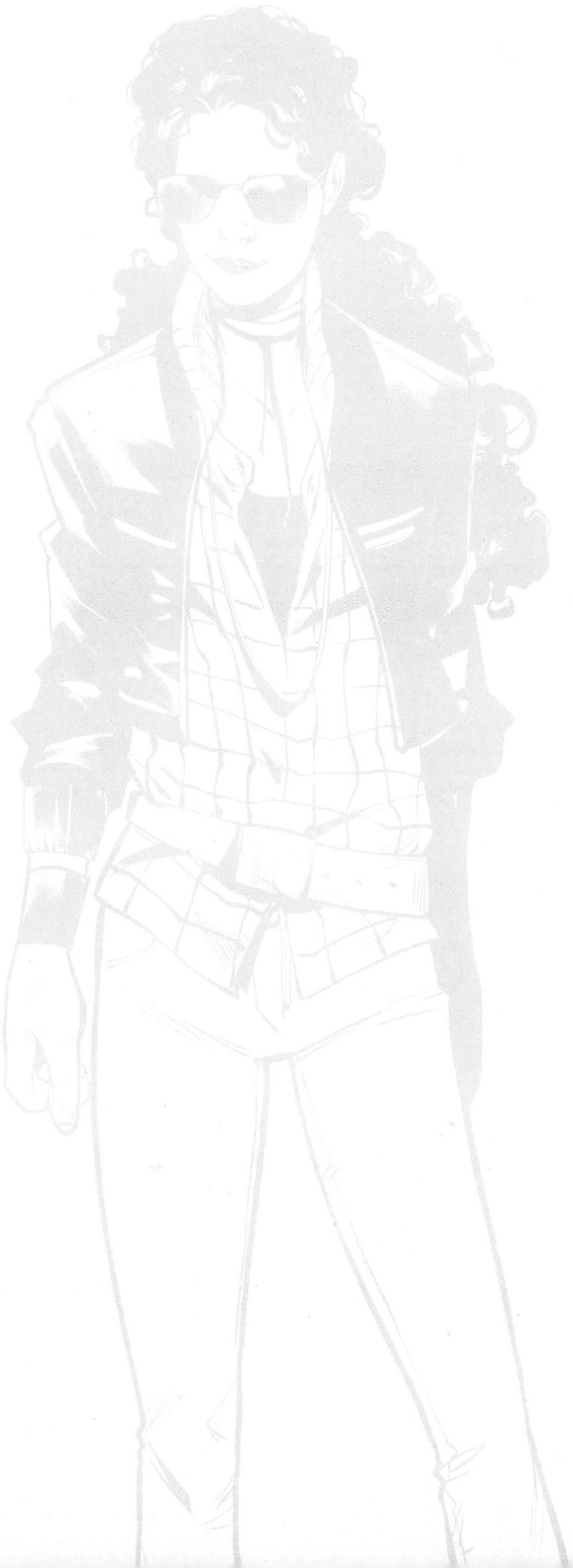

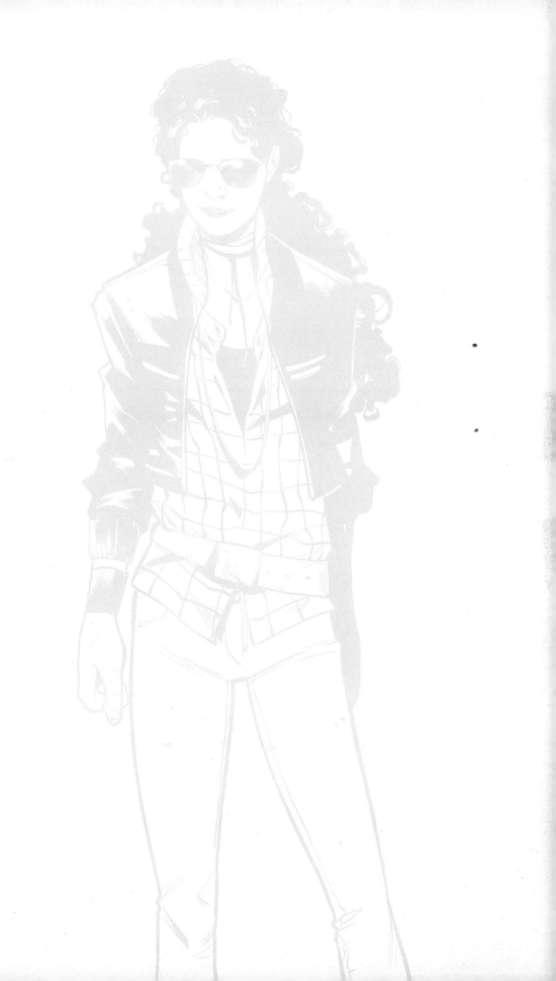

CHAPTER THREE

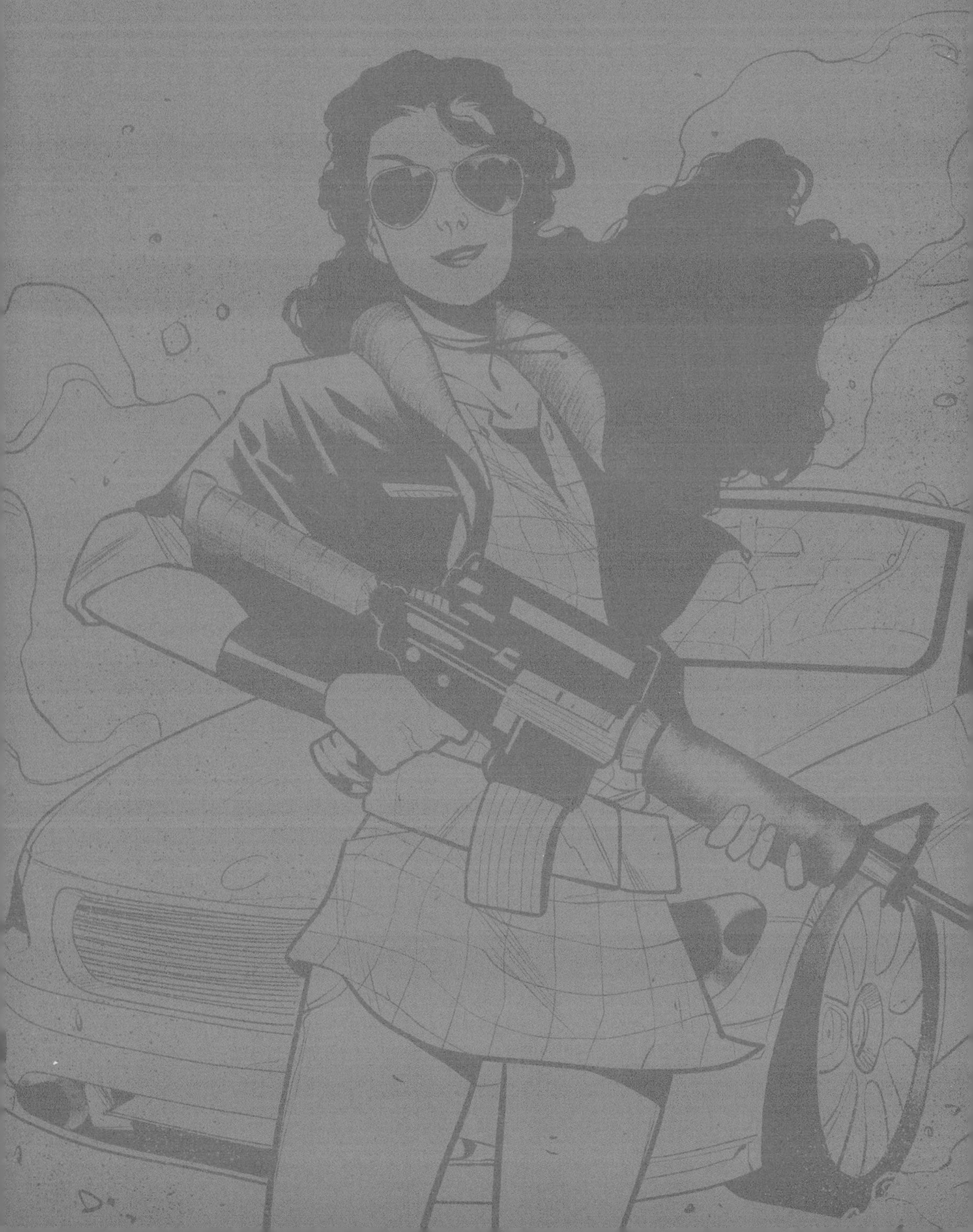

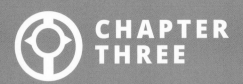

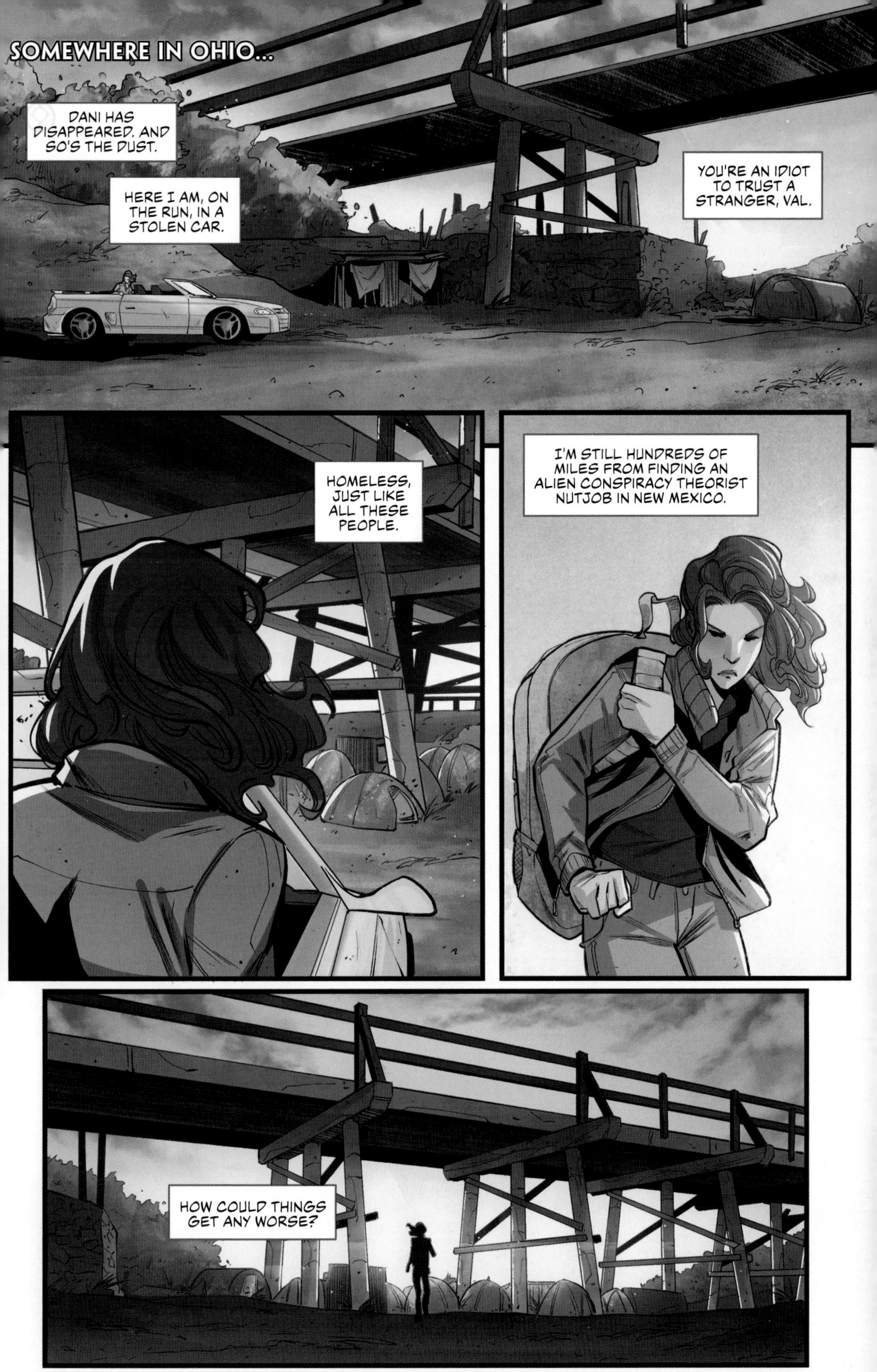
SOMEWHERE IN OHIO...
DANI HAS DISAPPEARED. AND SO'S THE DUST.
HERE I AM, ON THE RUN, IN A STOLEN CAR.
YOU'RE AN IDIOT TO TRUST A STRANGER, VAL.
HOMELESS, JUST LIKE ALL THESE PEOPLE.
I'M STILL HUNDREDS OF MILES FROM FINDING AN ALIEN CONSPIRACY THEORIST NUTJOB IN NEW MEXICO.
HOW COULD THINGS GET ANY WORSE?

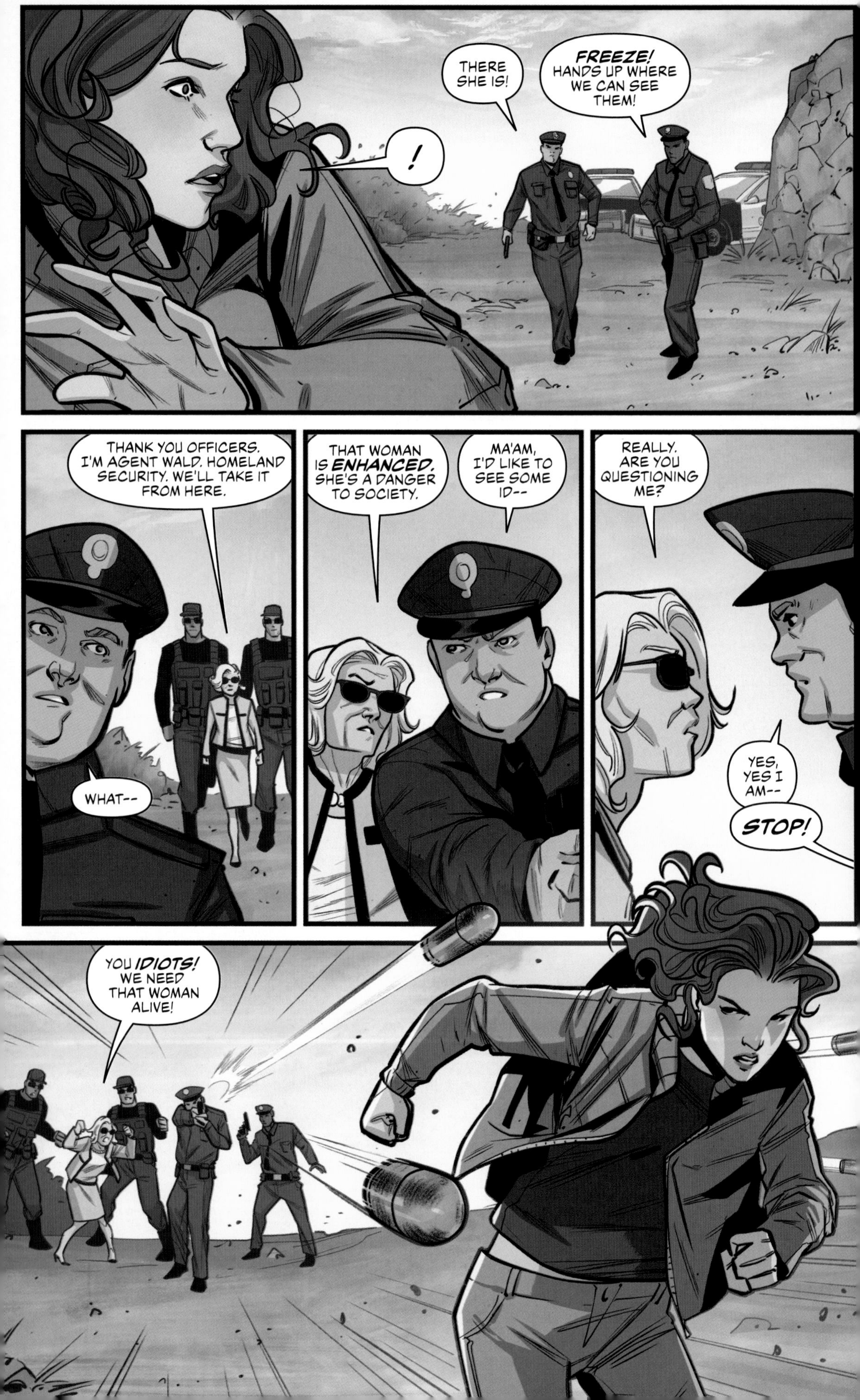
!
THERE SHE IS!
FREEZE! HANDS UP WHERE WE CAN SEE THEM!
THANK YOU OFFICERS. I'M AGENT WALD. HOMELAND SECURITY. WE'LL TAKE IT FROM HERE.
WHAT--
THAT WOMAN IS ENHANCED. SHE'S A DANGER TO SOCIETY.
MA'AM, I'D LIKE TO SEE SOME ID--
REALLY. ARE YOU QUESTIONING ME?
YES, YES I AM--
STOP!
YOU IDIOTS! WE NEED THAT WOMAN ALIVE!

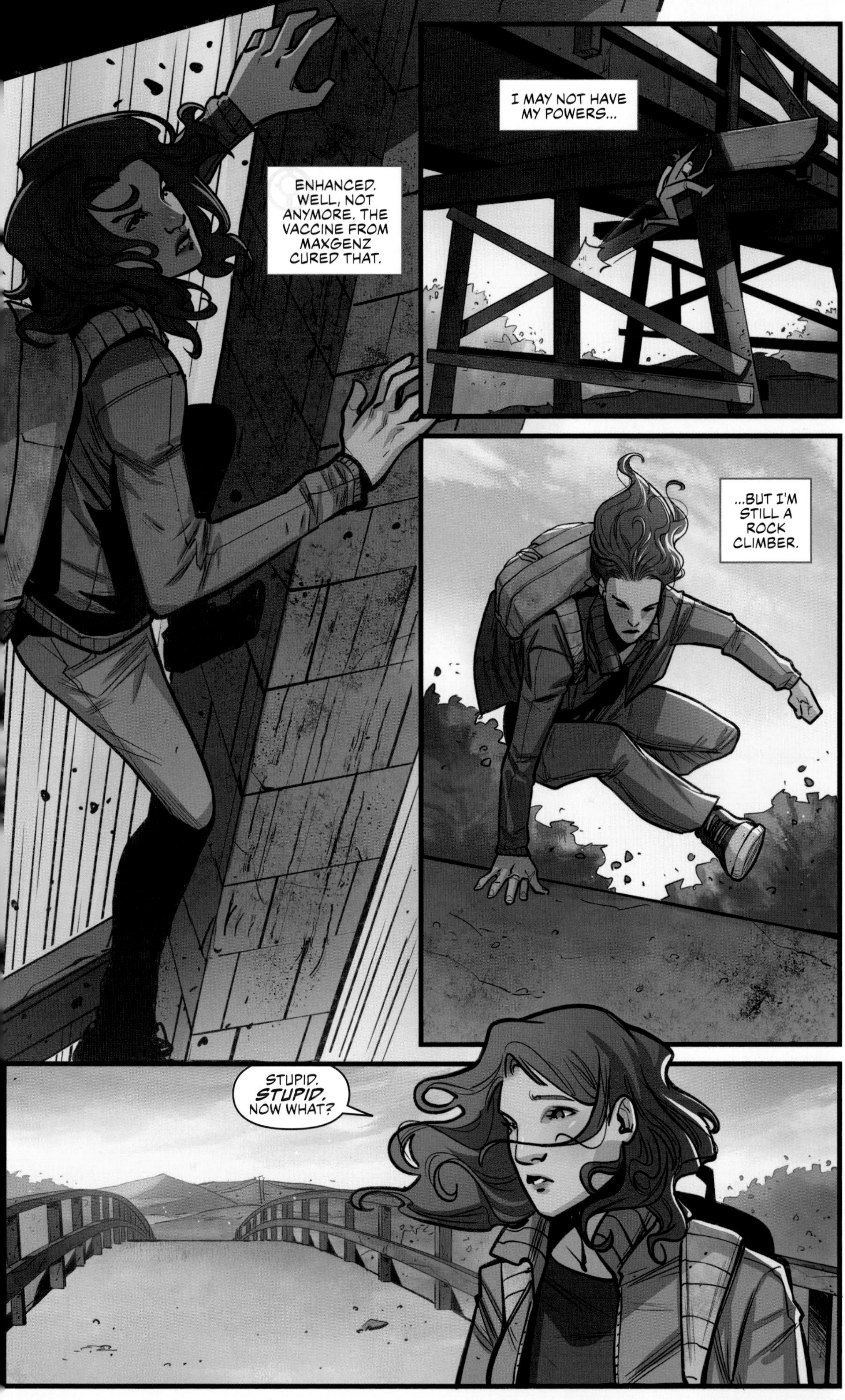
ENHANCED. WELL, NOT ANYMORE. THE VACCINE FROM MAXGENZ CURED THAT.
I MAY NOT HAVE MY POWERS...
...BUT I'M STILL A ROCK CLIMBER.
STUPID. STUPID. NOW WHAT?

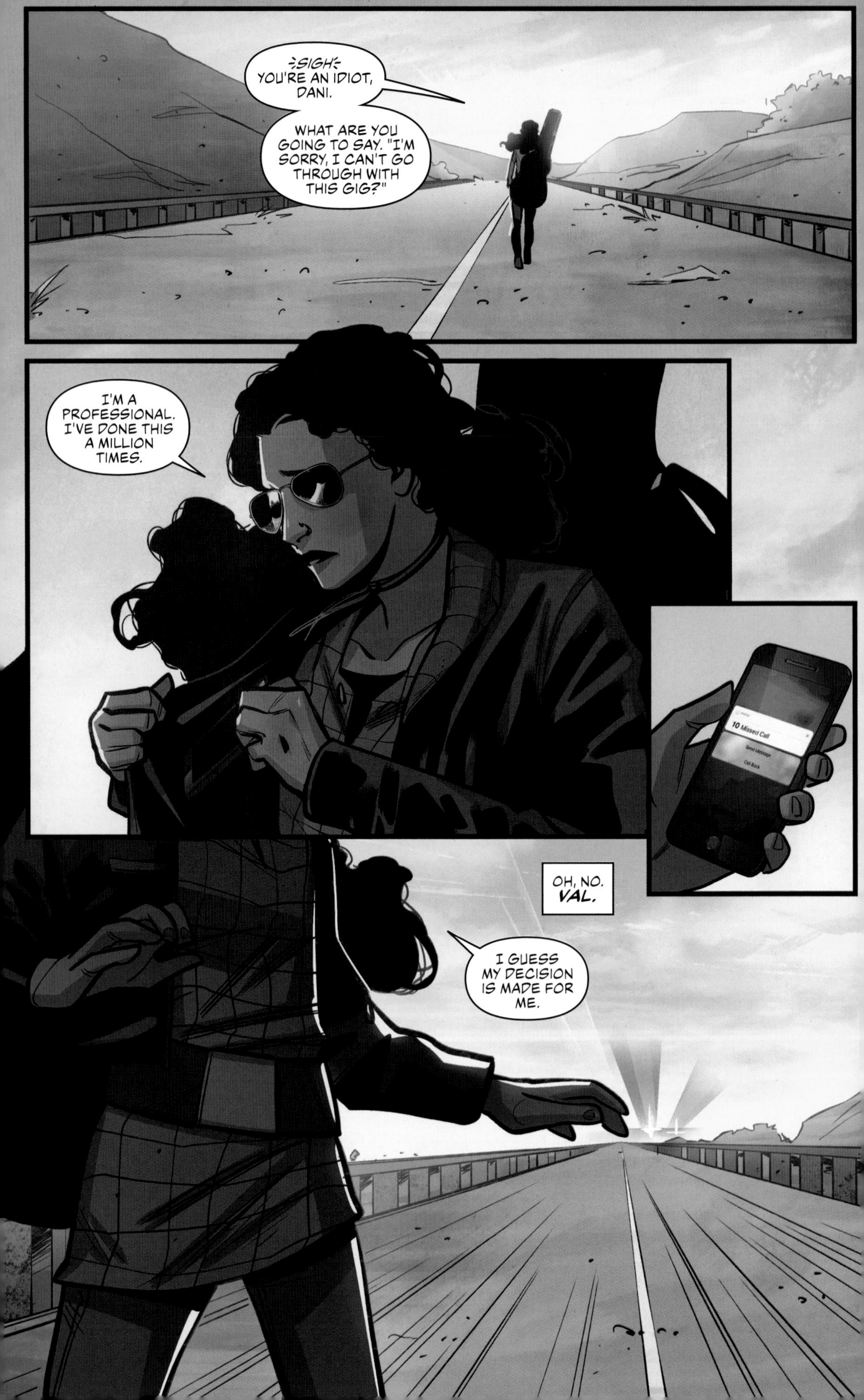
SIGH
YOU'RE AN IDIOT, DANI.
WHAT ARE YOU GOING TO SAY. "I'M SORRY, I CAN'T GO THROUGH WITH THIS GIG?"
I'M A PROFESSIONAL. I'VE DONE THIS A MILLION TIMES.
10 Missed Call
Send Message
Call Back
OH, NO. ***VAL.***
I GUESS MY DECISION IS MADE FOR ME.

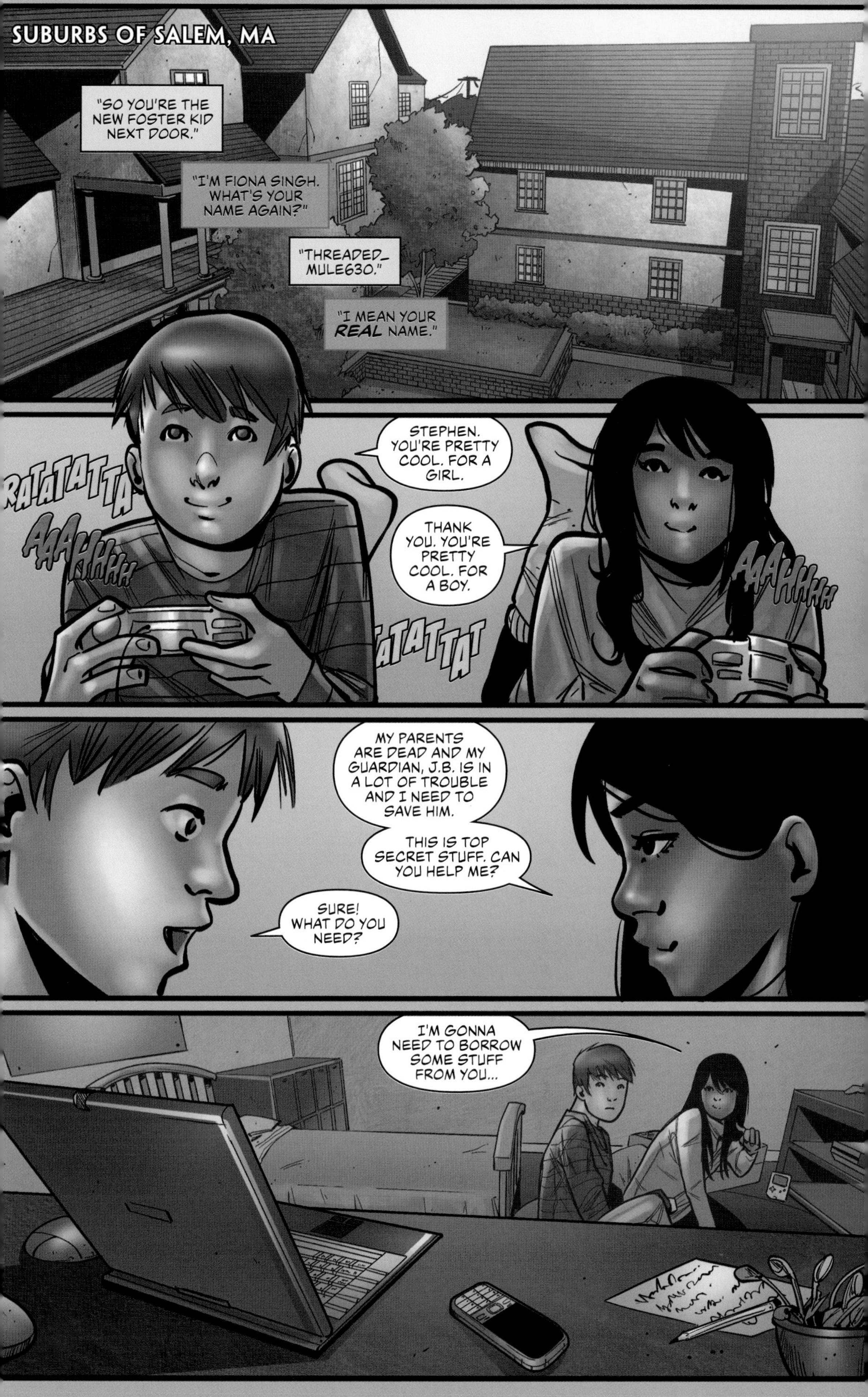
SUBURBS OF SALEM, MA
"SO YOU'RE THE NEW FOSTER KID NEXT DOOR."
"I'M FIONA SINGH. WHAT'S YOUR NAME AGAIN?"
"THREADED_ MULE630."
"I MEAN YOUR *REAL* NAME."
STEPHEN. YOU'RE PRETTY COOL. FOR A GIRL.
RATATATTA
AAAHHHH
THANK YOU. YOU'RE PRETTY COOL. FOR A BOY.
TATATTAT
AAAHHHH
MY PARENTS ARE DEAD AND MY GUARDIAN, J.B. IS IN A LOT OF TROUBLE AND I NEED TO SAVE HIM.
THIS IS TOP SECRET STUFF. CAN YOU HELP ME?
SURE! WHAT DO YOU NEED?
I'M GONNA NEED TO BORROW SOME STUFF FROM YOU...

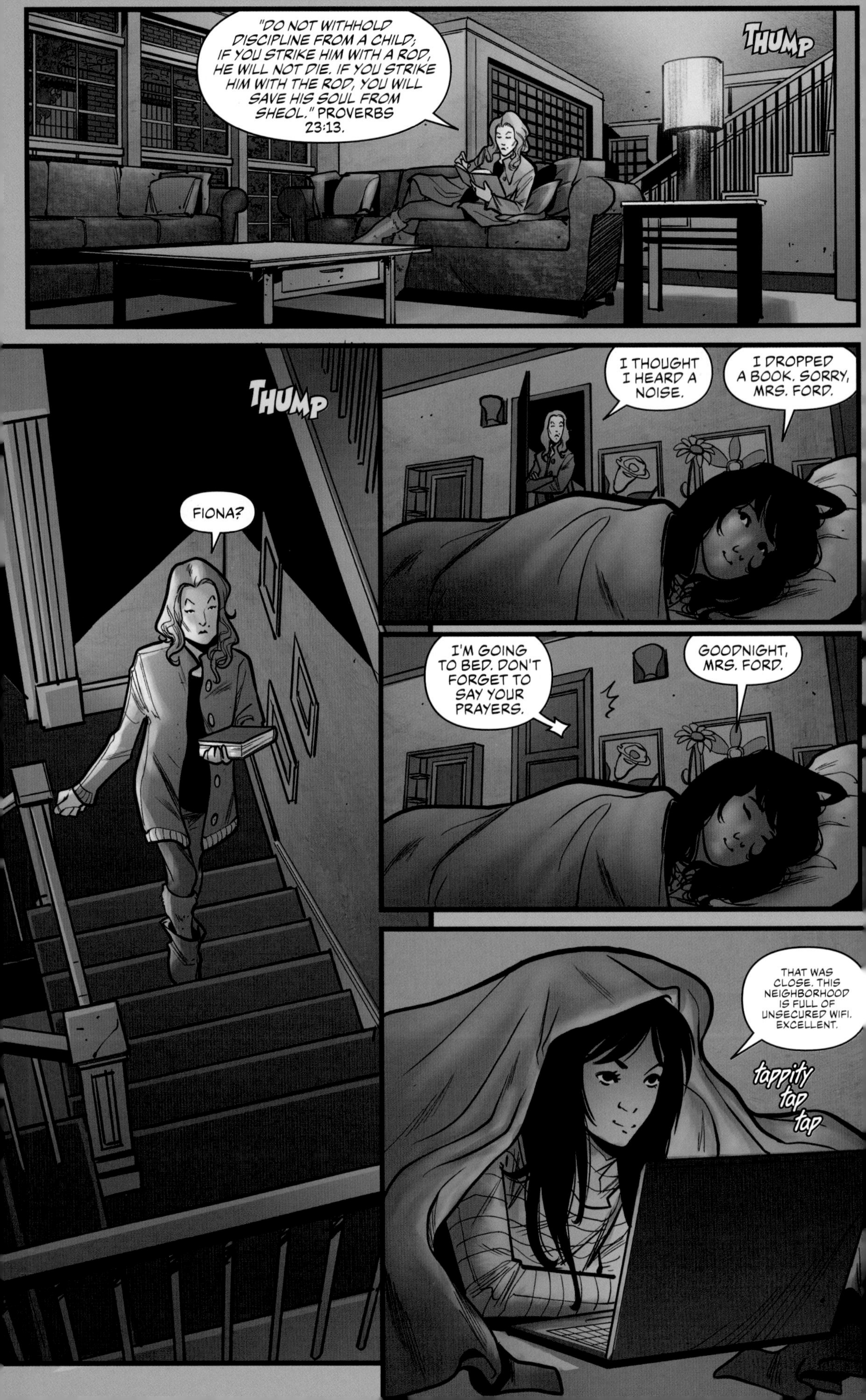
"DO NOT WITHHOLD DISCIPLINE FROM A CHILD; IF YOU STRIKE HIM WITH A ROD, HE WILL NOT DIE. IF YOU STRIKE HIM WITH THE ROD, YOU WILL SAVE HIS SOUL FROM SHEOL." PROVERBS 23:13.
THUMP
THUMP
FIONA?
I THOUGHT I HEARD A NOISE.
I DROPPED A BOOK. SORRY, MRS. FORD.
I'M GOING TO BED. DON'T FORGET TO SAY YOUR PRAYERS.
GOODNIGHT, MRS. FORD.
THAT WAS CLOSE. THIS NEIGHBORHOOD IS FULL OF UNSECURED WIFI. EXCELLENT.
tappity tap tap

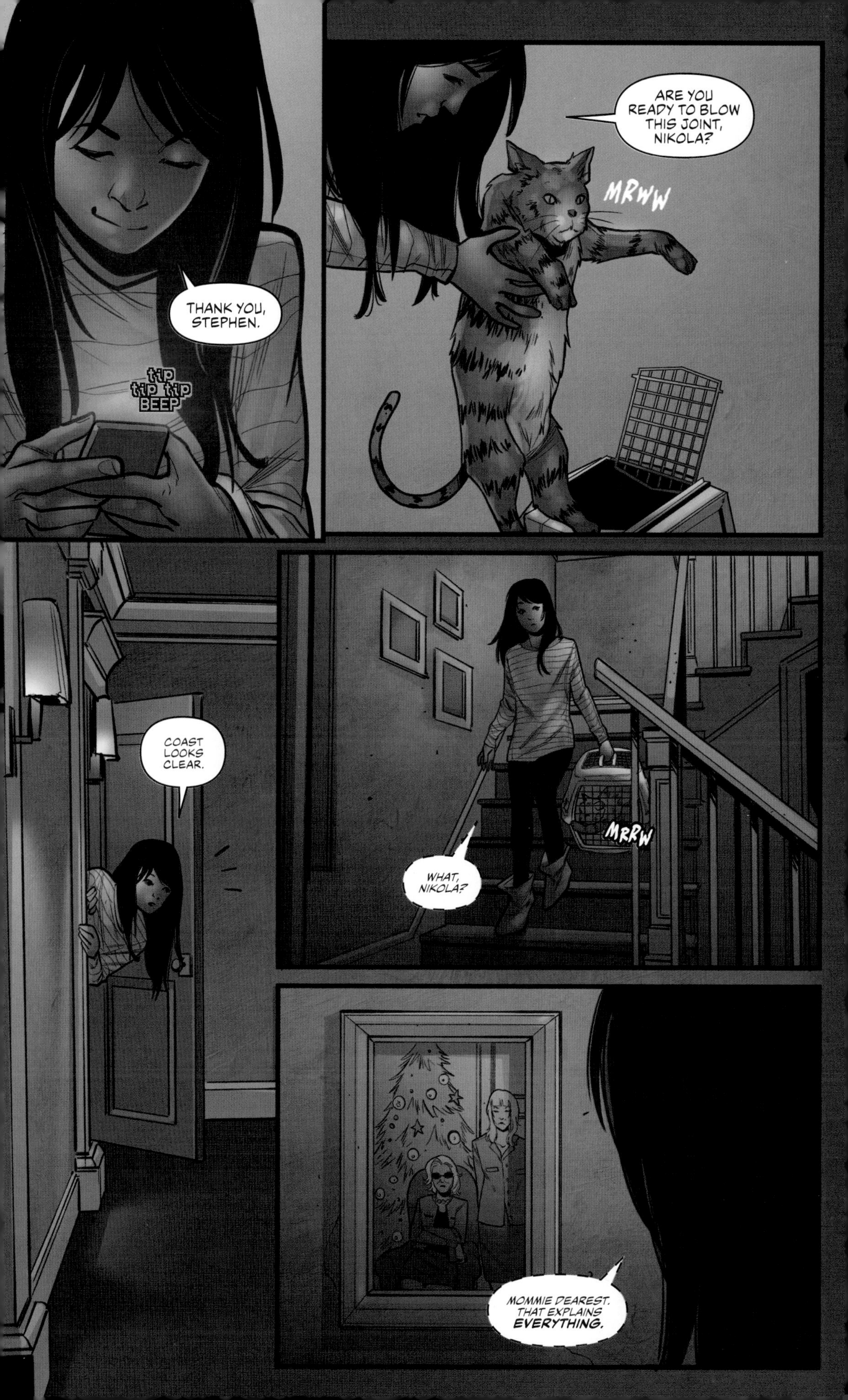
THANK YOU, STEPHEN.
tip tip tip BEEP
ARE YOU READY TO BLOW THIS JOINT, NIKOLA?
MRWW
COAST LOOKS CLEAR.
MRRW
WHAT, NIKOLA?
MOMMIE DEAREST. THAT EXPLAINS **EVERYTHING.**

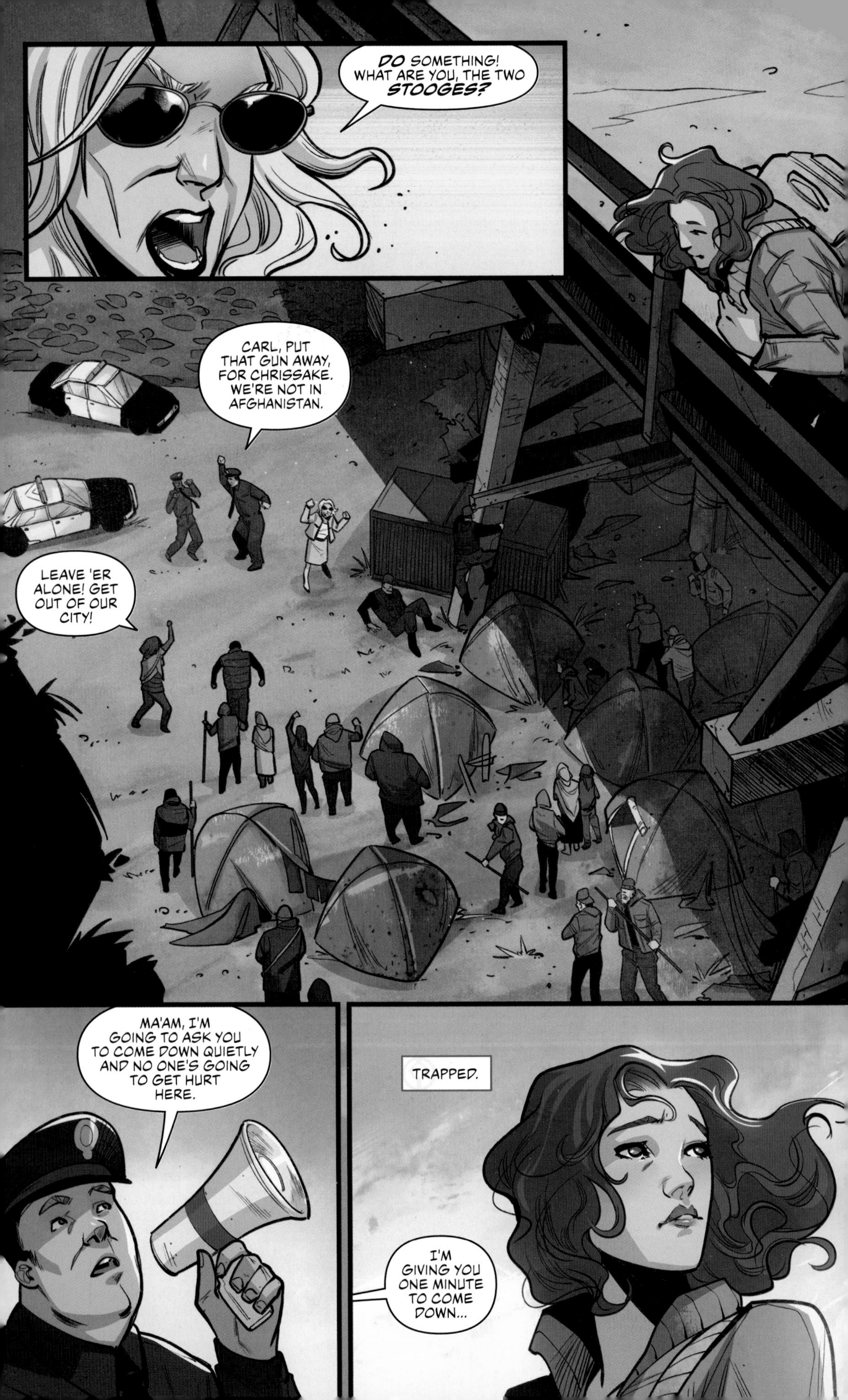
DO SOMETHING! WHAT ARE YOU, THE TWO STOOGES?
CARL, PUT THAT GUN AWAY, FOR CHRISSAKE. WE'RE NOT IN AFGHANISTAN.
LEAVE 'ER ALONE! GET OUT OF OUR CITY!
MA'AM, I'M GOING TO ASK YOU TO COME DOWN QUIETLY AND NO ONE'S GOING TO GET HURT HERE.
TRAPPED.
I'M GIVING YOU ONE MINUTE TO COME DOWN...

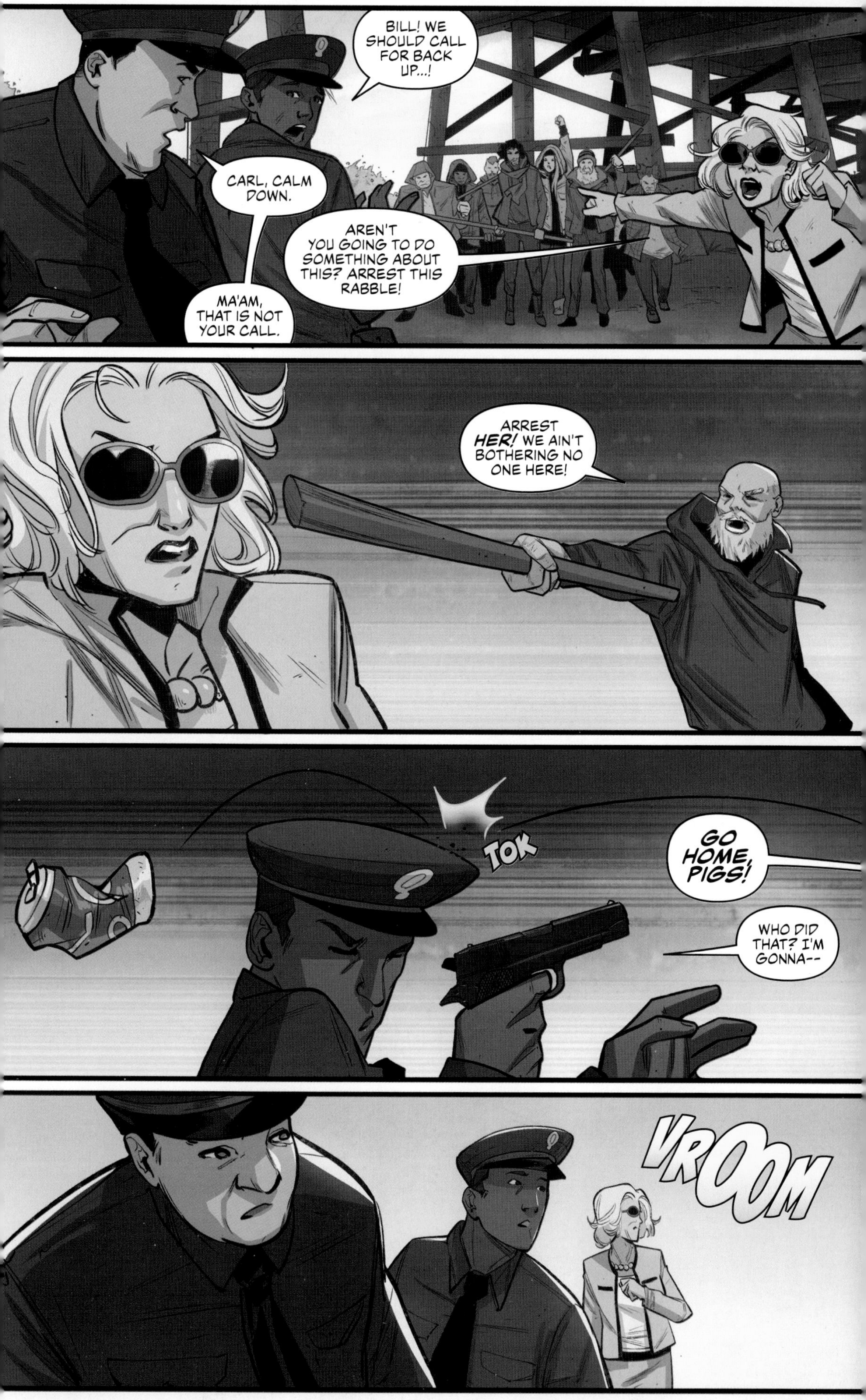
BILL! WE SHOULD CALL FOR BACK UP...!
CARL, CALM DOWN.
AREN'T YOU GOING TO DO SOMETHING ABOUT THIS? ARREST THIS RABBLE!
MA'AM, THAT IS NOT YOUR CALL.
ARREST HER! WE AIN'T BOTHERING NO ONE HERE!
TOK
GO HOME, PIGS!
WHO DID THAT? I'M GONNA--
VROOOM

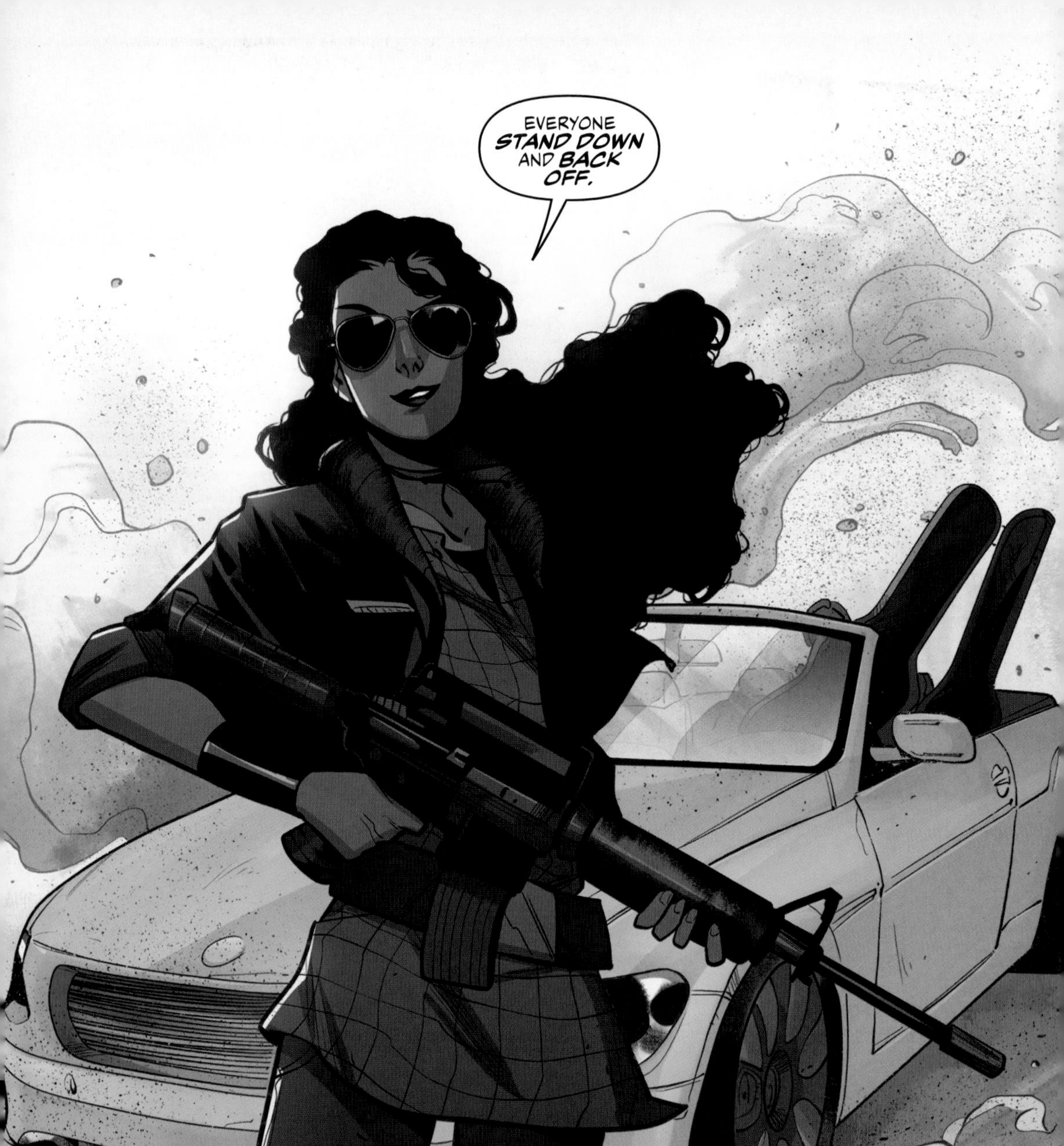
EVERYONE STAND DOWN AND BACK OFF.

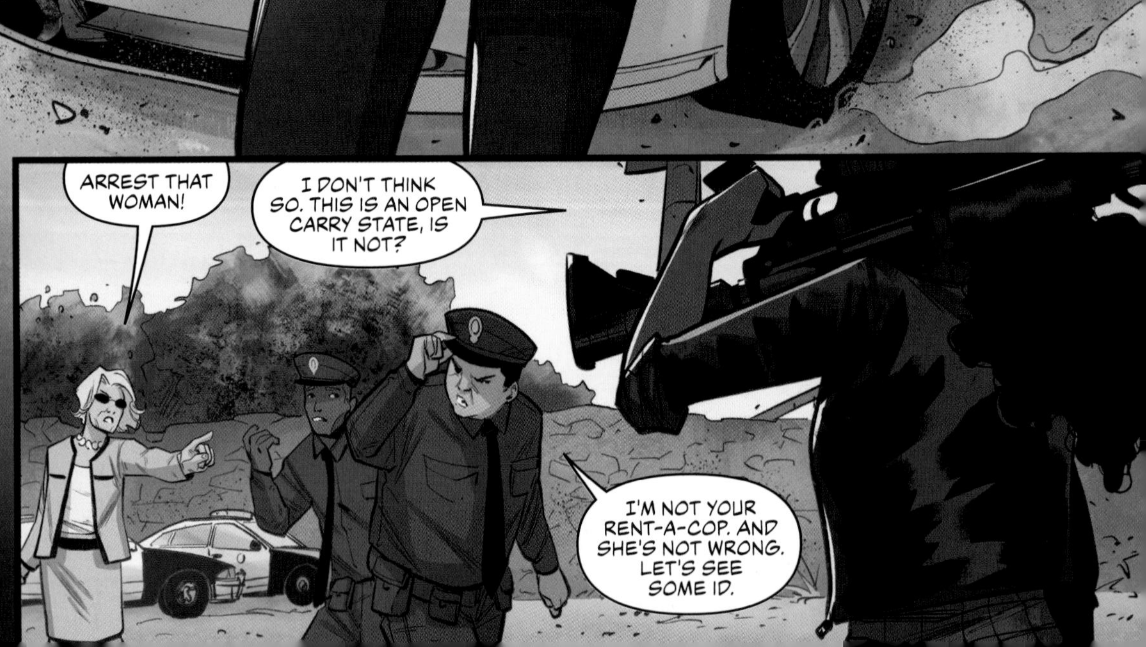
ARREST THAT WOMAN!
I DON'T THINK SO. THIS IS AN OPEN CARRY STATE, IS IT NOT?
I'M NOT YOUR RENT-A-COP. AND SHE'S NOT WRONG. LET'S SEE SOME ID.

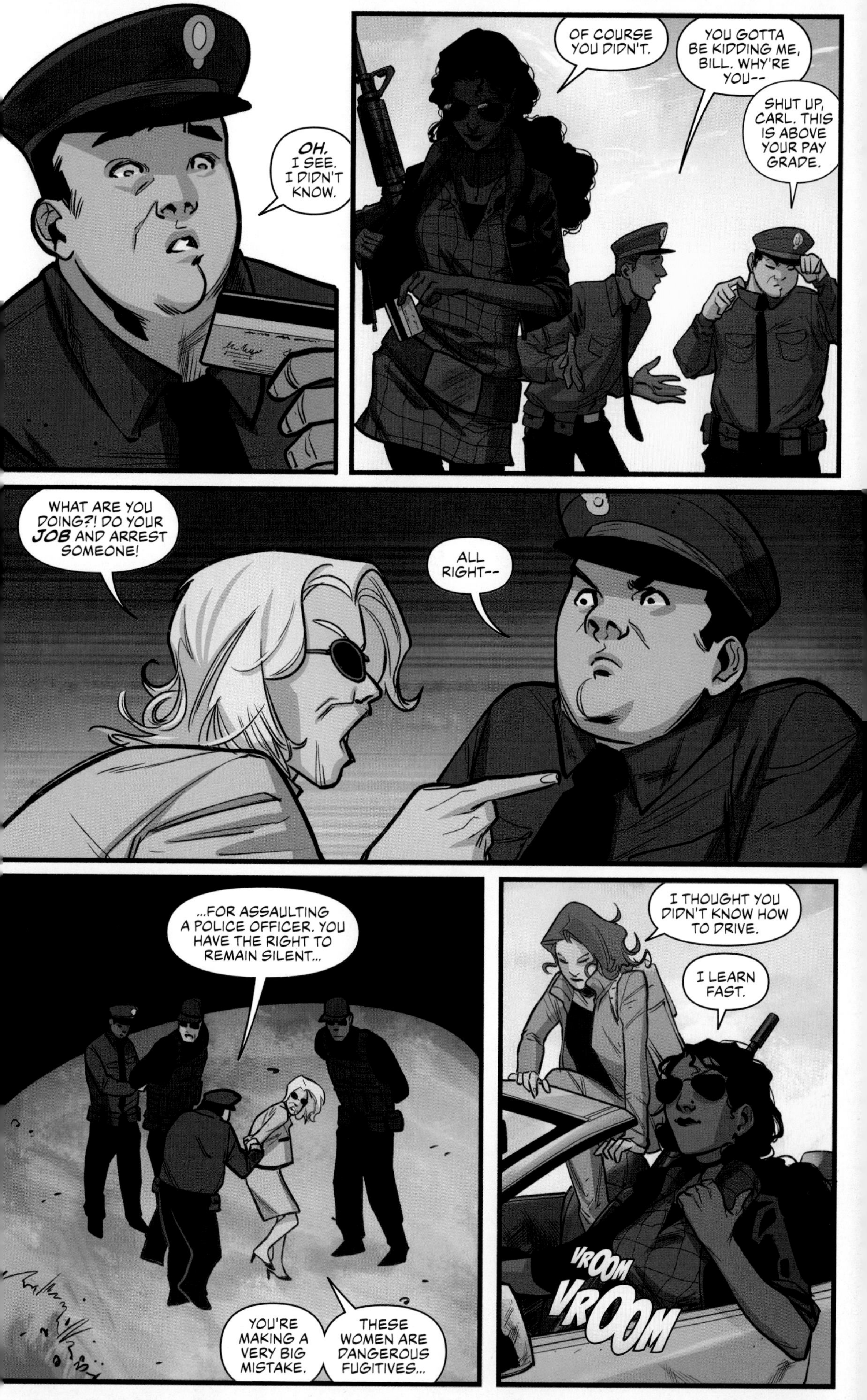
OH. I SEE. I DIDN'T KNOW.
OF COURSE YOU DIDN'T.
YOU GOTTA BE KIDDING ME, BILL. WHY'RE YOU--
SHUT UP, CARL. THIS IS ABOVE YOUR PAY GRADE.
WHAT ARE YOU DOING?! DO YOUR JOB AND ARREST SOMEONE!
ALL RIGHT--
...FOR ASSAULTING A POLICE OFFICER. YOU HAVE THE RIGHT TO REMAIN SILENT...
YOU'RE MAKING A VERY BIG MISTAKE.
THESE WOMEN ARE DANGEROUS FUGITIVES...
I THOUGHT YOU DIDN'T KNOW HOW TO DRIVE.
I LEARN FAST.
VROOM
VROOM

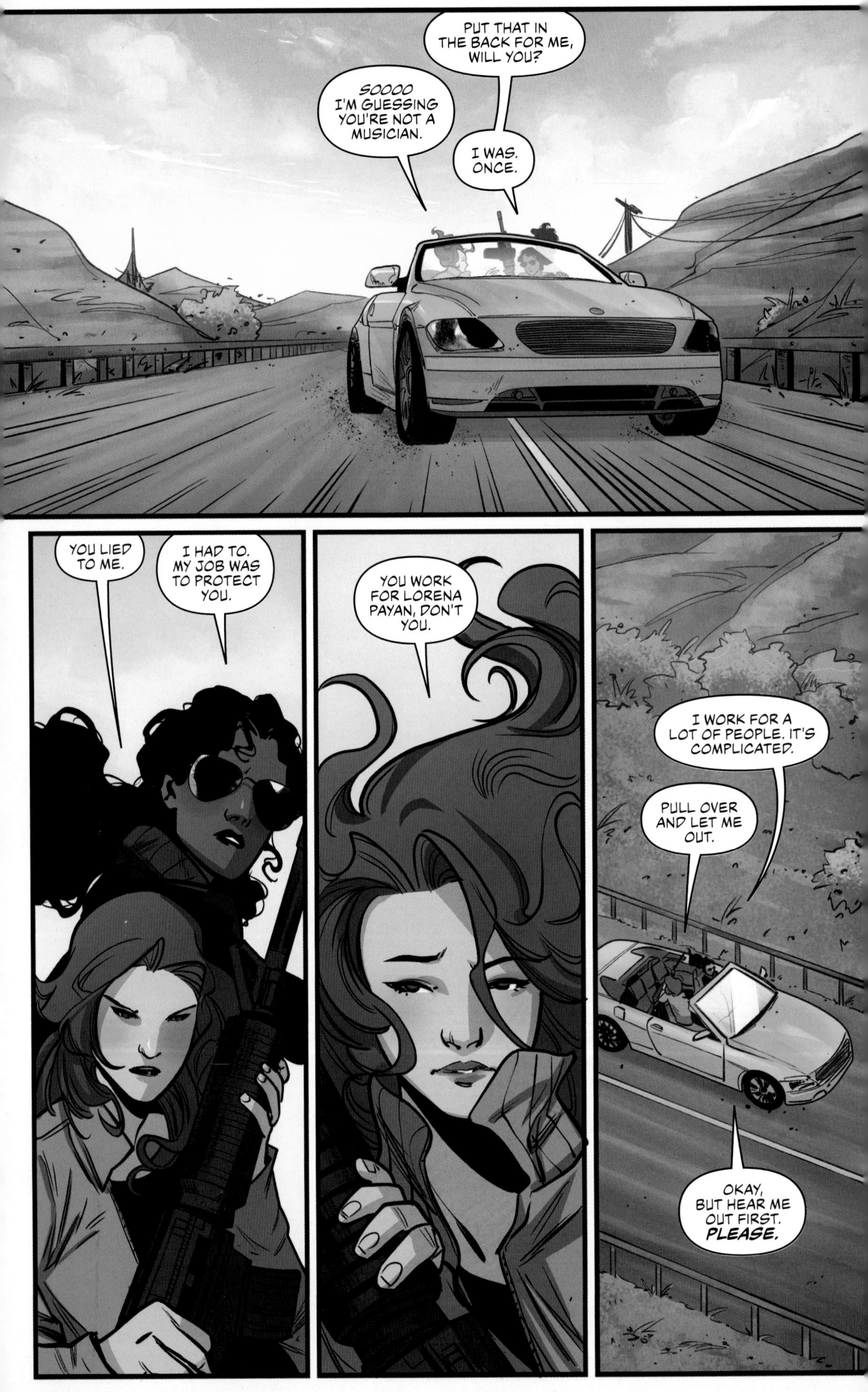
PUT THAT IN THE BACK FOR ME, WILL YOU?
SOOOO I'M GUESSING YOU'RE NOT A MUSICIAN.
I WAS. ONCE.
YOU LIED TO ME.
I HAD TO. MY JOB WAS TO PROTECT YOU.
YOU WORK FOR LORENA PAYAN, DON'T YOU.
I WORK FOR A LOT OF PEOPLE. IT'S COMPLICATED.
PULL OVER AND LET ME OUT.
OKAY, BUT HEAR ME OUT FIRST. *PLEASE.*

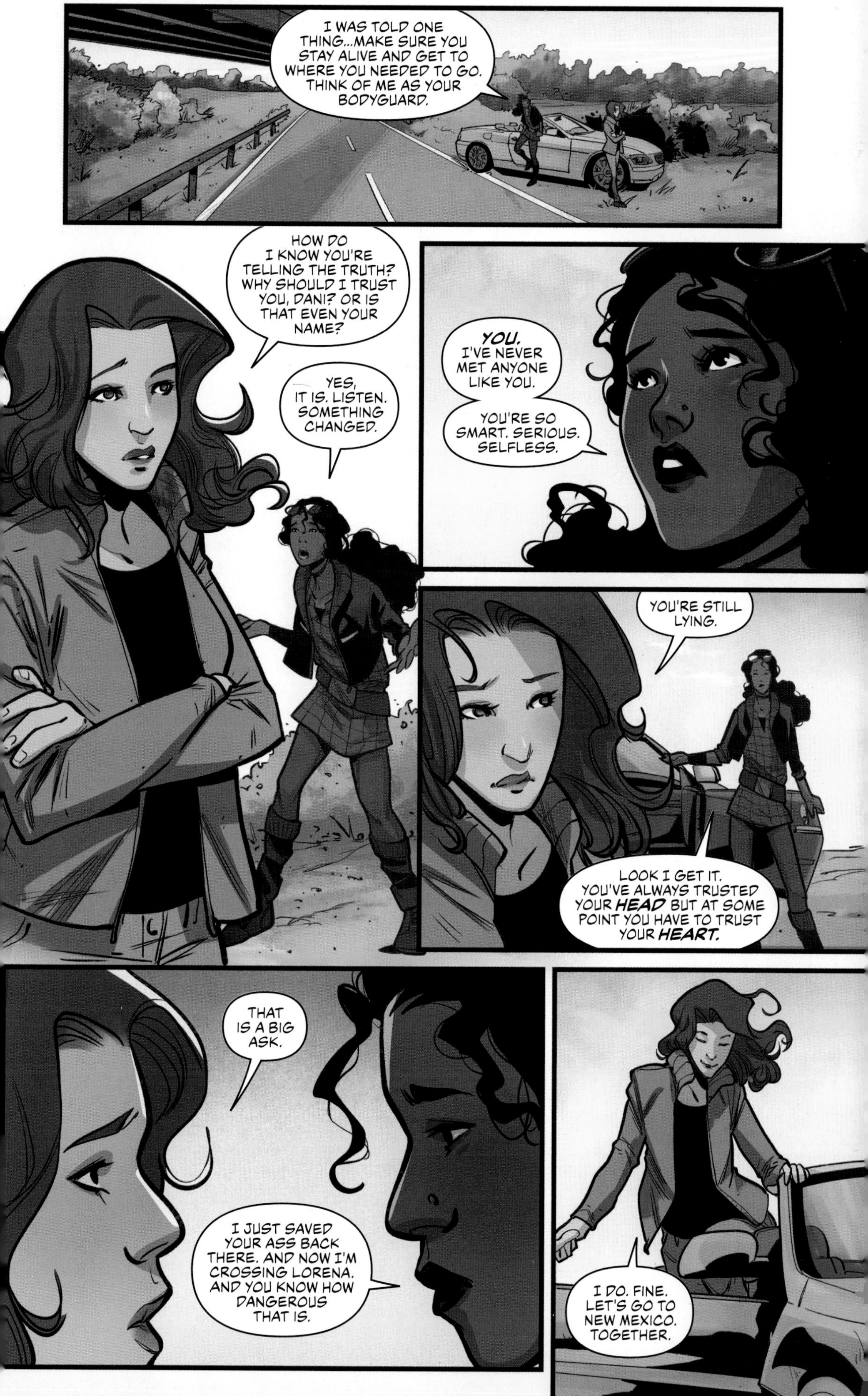
I WAS TOLD ONE THING...MAKE SURE YOU STAY ALIVE AND GET TO WHERE YOU NEEDED TO GO. THINK OF ME AS YOUR BODYGUARD.
HOW DO I KNOW YOU'RE TELLING THE TRUTH? WHY SHOULD I TRUST YOU, DANI? OR IS THAT EVEN YOUR NAME?
YES, IT IS. LISTEN. SOMETHING CHANGED.
YOU. I'VE NEVER MET ANYONE LIKE YOU.
YOU'RE SO SMART. SERIOUS. SELFLESS.
YOU'RE STILL LYING.
LOOK I GET IT. YOU'VE ALWAYS TRUSTED YOUR HEAD BUT AT SOME POINT YOU HAVE TO TRUST YOUR HEART.
THAT IS A BIG ASK.
I JUST SAVED YOUR ASS BACK THERE. AND NOW I'M CROSSING LORENA. AND YOU KNOW HOW DANGEROUS THAT IS.
I DO. FINE. LET'S GO TO NEW MEXICO. TOGETHER.

MISSOURI.

OKLAHOMA.

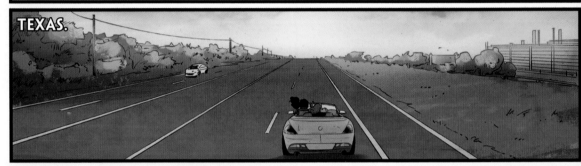

TEXAS.

WELCOME TO HOPE,
NEW MEXICO
POPULATION 105

WAKE UP, VAL. WE'RE HERE. WE MADE IT.

DANI--

AHEM!

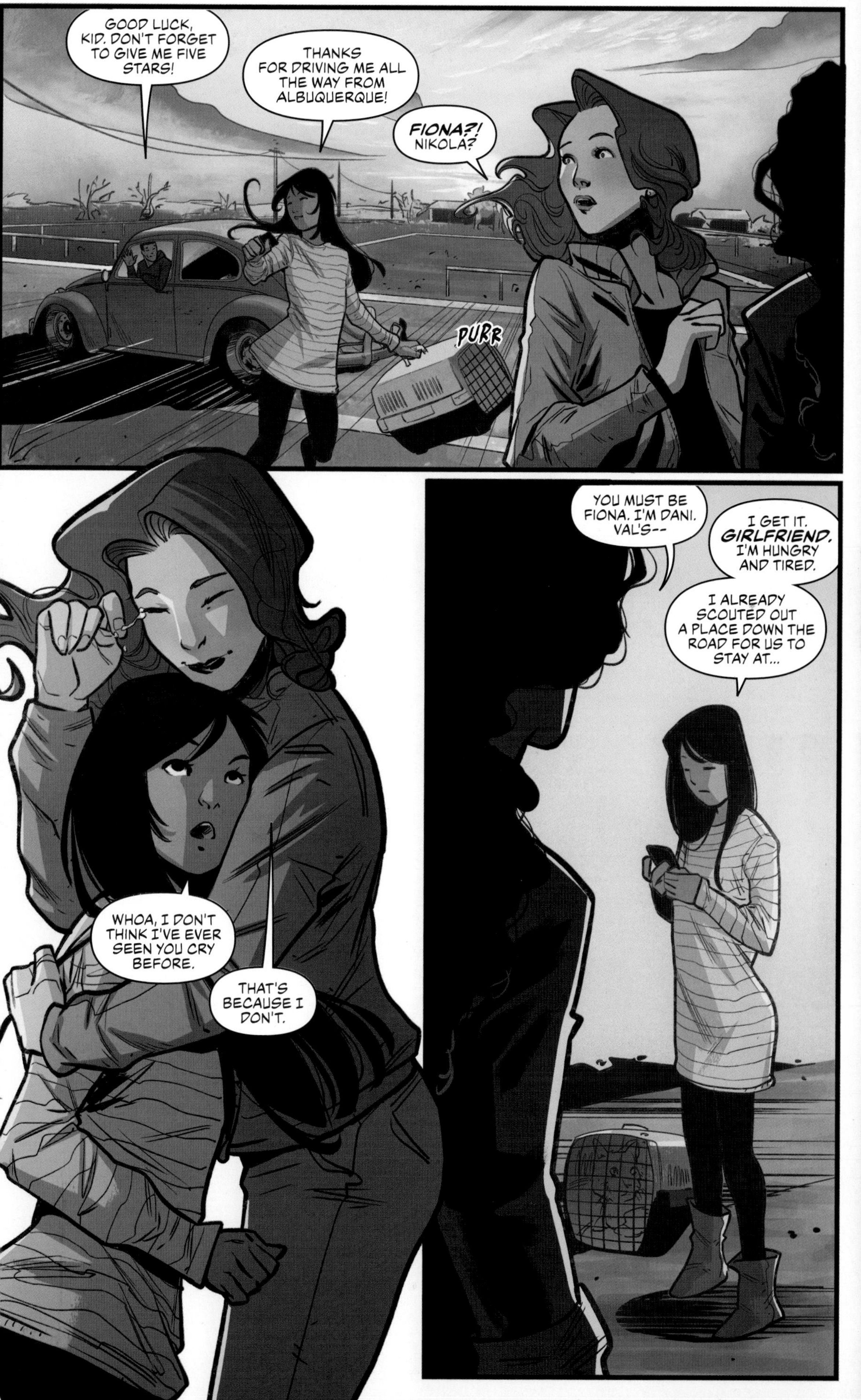
GOOD LUCK, KID. DON'T FORGET TO GIVE ME FIVE STARS!
THANKS FOR DRIVING ME ALL THE WAY FROM ALBUQUERQUE!
FIONA?! NIKOLA?
PURR
WHOA, I DON'T THINK I'VE EVER SEEN YOU CRY BEFORE.
THAT'S BECAUSE I DON'T.
YOU MUST BE FIONA. I'M DANI. VAL'S--
I GET IT. GIRLFRIEND. I'M HUNGRY AND TIRED.
I ALREADY SCOUTED OUT A PLACE DOWN THE ROAD FOR US TO STAY AT...

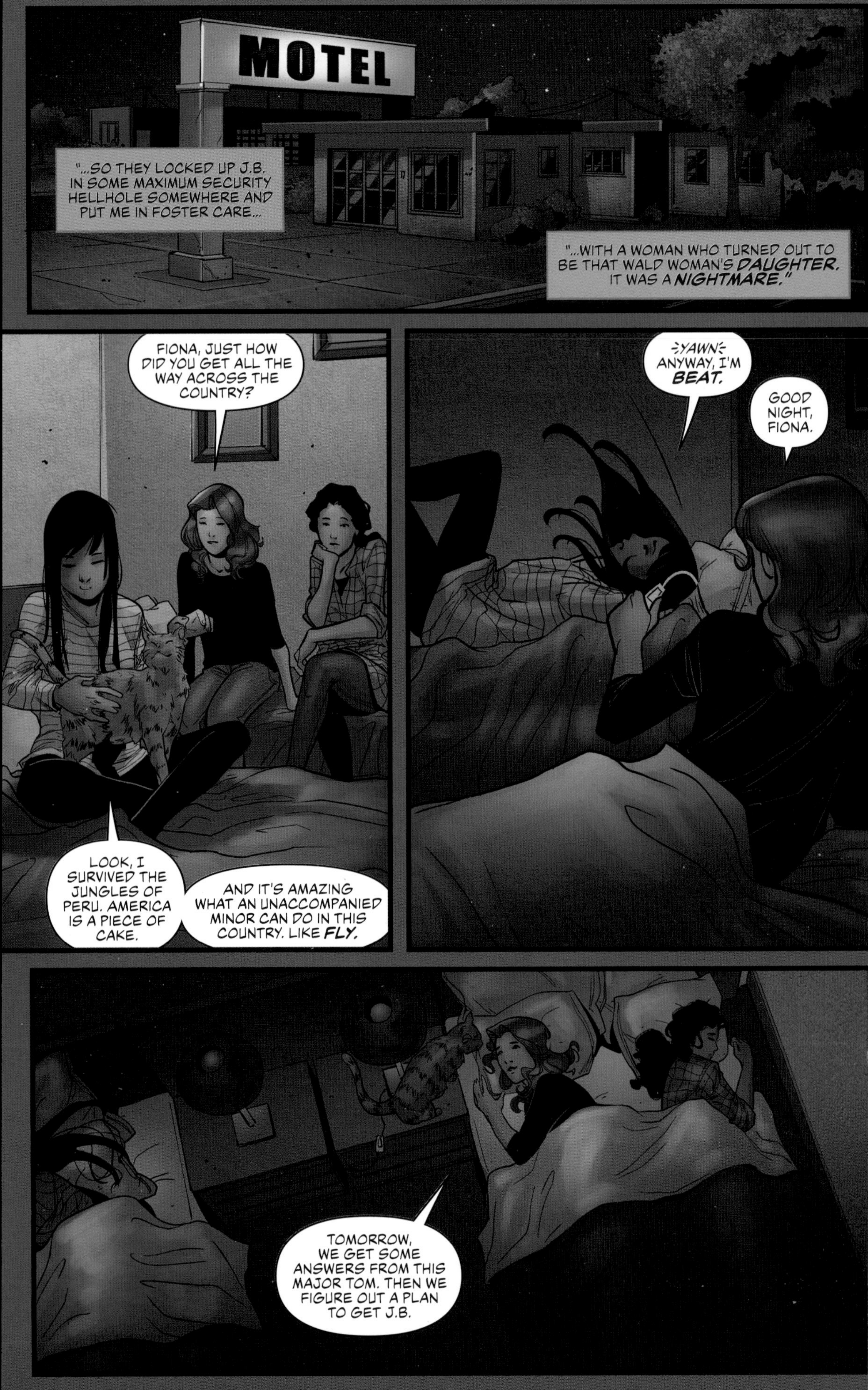
MOTEL
"...SO THEY LOCKED UP J.B. IN SOME MAXIMUM SECURITY HELLHOLE SOMEWHERE AND PUT ME IN FOSTER CARE...
"...WITH A WOMAN WHO TURNED OUT TO BE THAT WALD WOMAN'S DAUGHTER. IT WAS A NIGHTMARE."
FIONA, JUST HOW DID YOU GET ALL THE WAY ACROSS THE COUNTRY?
LOOK, I SURVIVED THE JUNGLES OF PERU. AMERICA IS A PIECE OF CAKE.
AND IT'S AMAZING WHAT AN UNACCOMPANIED MINOR CAN DO IN THIS COUNTRY. LIKE FLY.
YAWN ANYWAY, I'M BEAT.
GOOD NIGHT, FIONA.
TOMORROW, WE GET SOME ANSWERS FROM THIS MAJOR TOM. THEN WE FIGURE OUT A PLAN TO GET J.B.

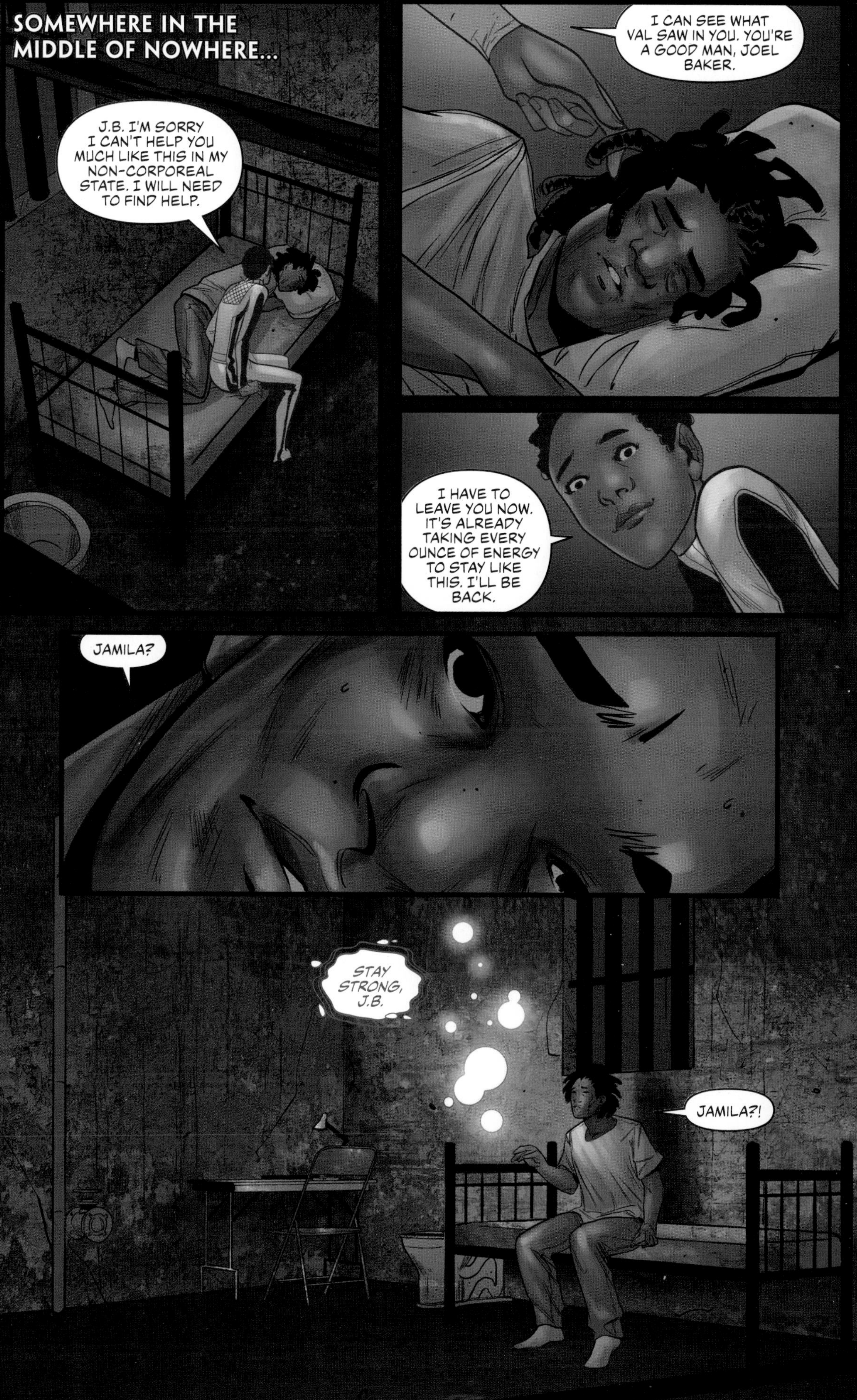
SOMEWHERE IN THE MIDDLE OF NOWHERE...
J.B. I'M SORRY I CAN'T HELP YOU MUCH LIKE THIS IN MY NON-CORPOREAL STATE. I WILL NEED TO FIND HELP.
I CAN SEE WHAT VAL SAW IN YOU. YOU'RE A GOOD MAN, JOEL BAKER.
I HAVE TO LEAVE YOU NOW. IT'S ALREADY TAKING EVERY OUNCE OF ENERGY TO STAY LIKE THIS. I'LL BE BACK.
JAMILA?
STAY STRONG, J.B.
JAMILA?!

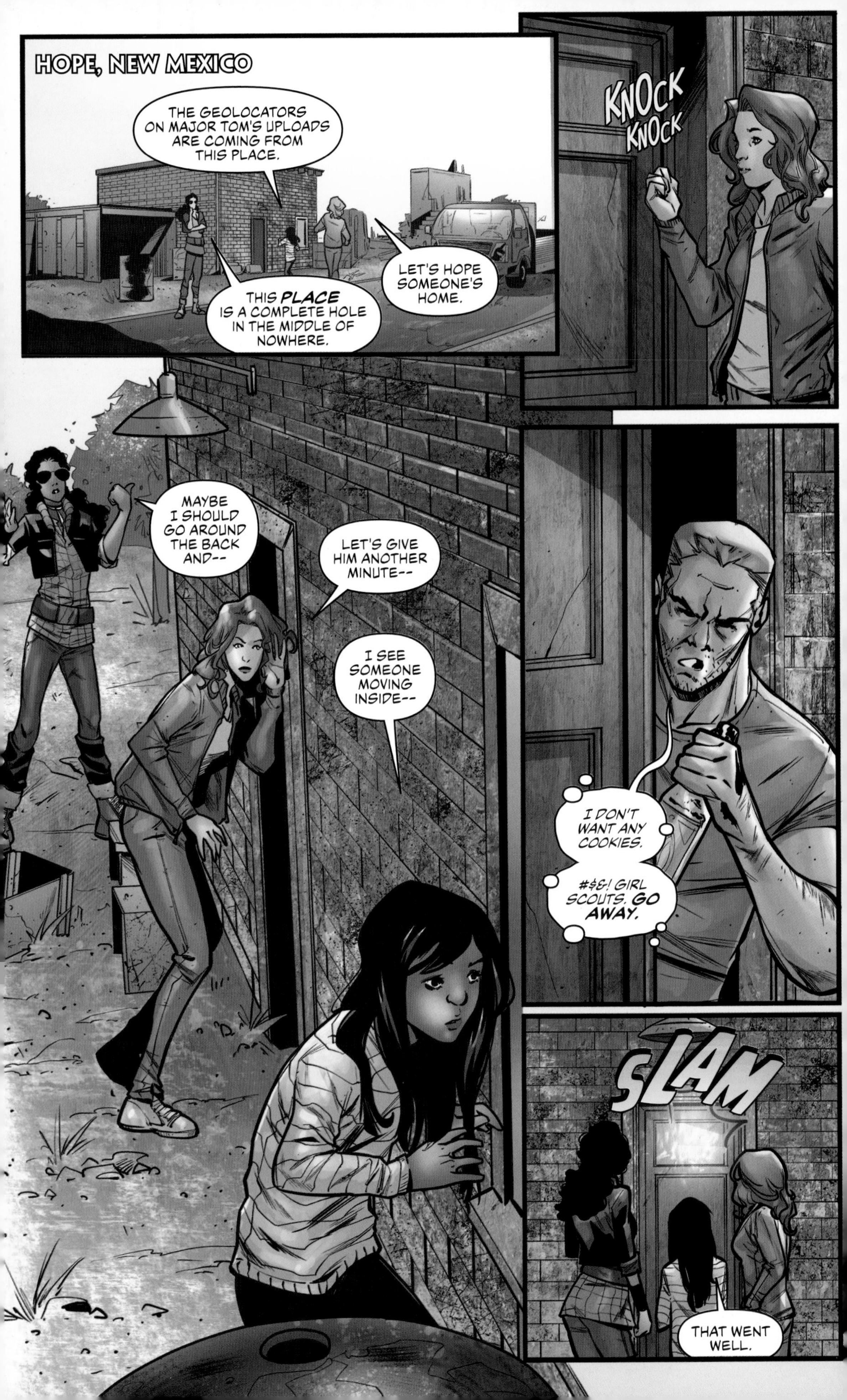
HOPE, NEW MEXICO
THE GEOLOCATORS ON MAJOR TOM'S UPLOADS ARE COMING FROM THIS PLACE.
THIS *PLACE* IS A COMPLETE HOLE IN THE MIDDLE OF NOWHERE.
LET'S HOPE SOMEONE'S HOME.
KNOCK KNOCK
MAYBE I SHOULD GO AROUND THE BACK AND--
LET'S GIVE HIM ANOTHER MINUTE--
I SEE SOMEONE MOVING INSIDE--
I DON'T WANT ANY COOKIES.
#$&! GIRL SCOUTS. **GO AWAY.**
SLAM
THAT WENT WELL.

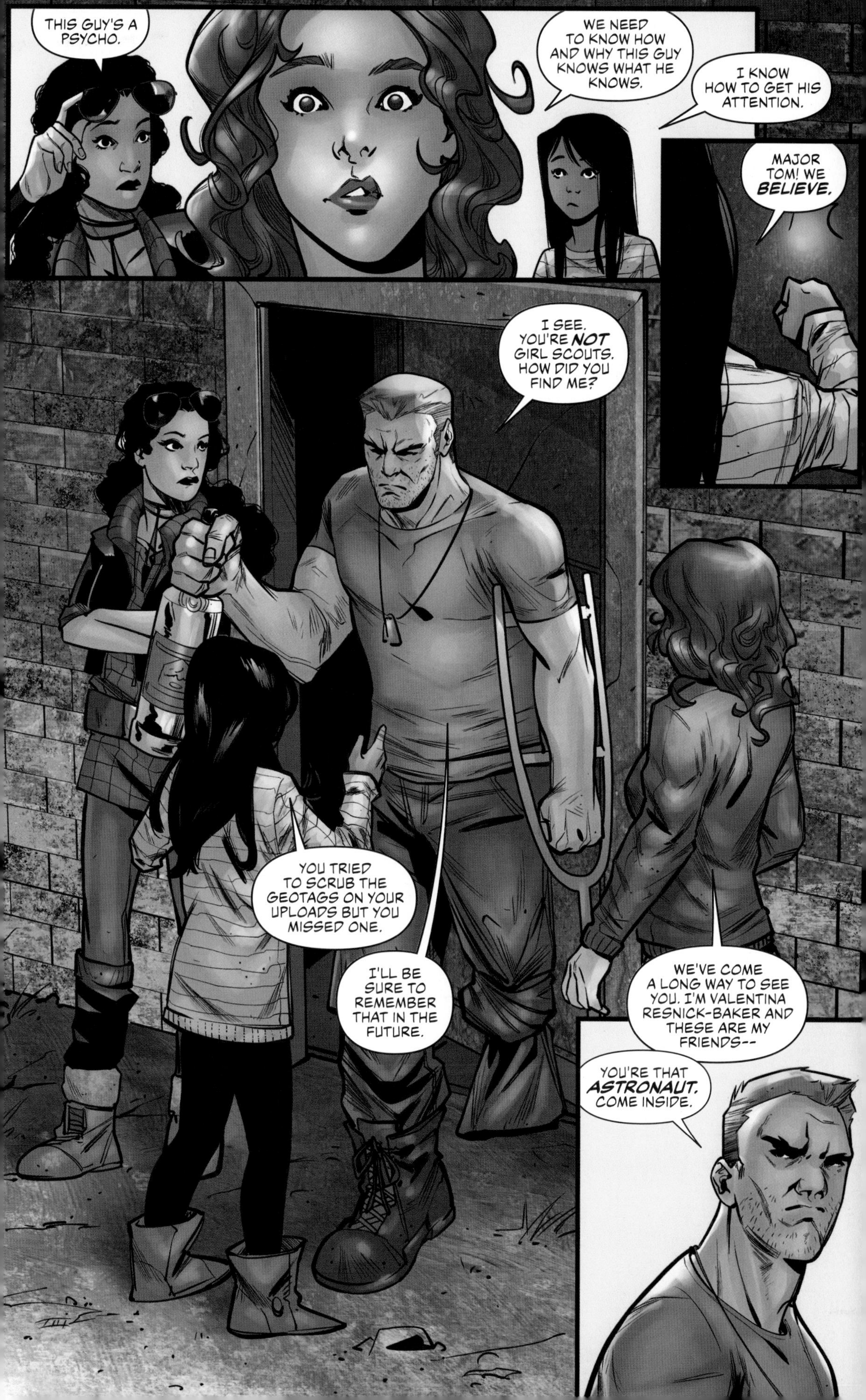
THIS GUY'S A PSYCHO.
WE NEED TO KNOW HOW AND WHY THIS GUY KNOWS WHAT HE KNOWS.
I KNOW HOW TO GET HIS ATTENTION.
MAJOR TOM! WE **BELIEVE.**
I SEE. YOU'RE **NOT** GIRL SCOUTS. HOW DID YOU FIND ME?
YOU TRIED TO SCRUB THE GEOTAGS ON YOUR UPLOADS BUT YOU MISSED ONE.
I'LL BE SURE TO REMEMBER THAT IN THE FUTURE.
WE'VE COME A LONG WAY TO SEE YOU. I'M VALENTINA RESNICK-BAKER AND THESE ARE MY FRIENDS--
YOU'RE THAT **ASTRONAUT.** COME INSIDE.

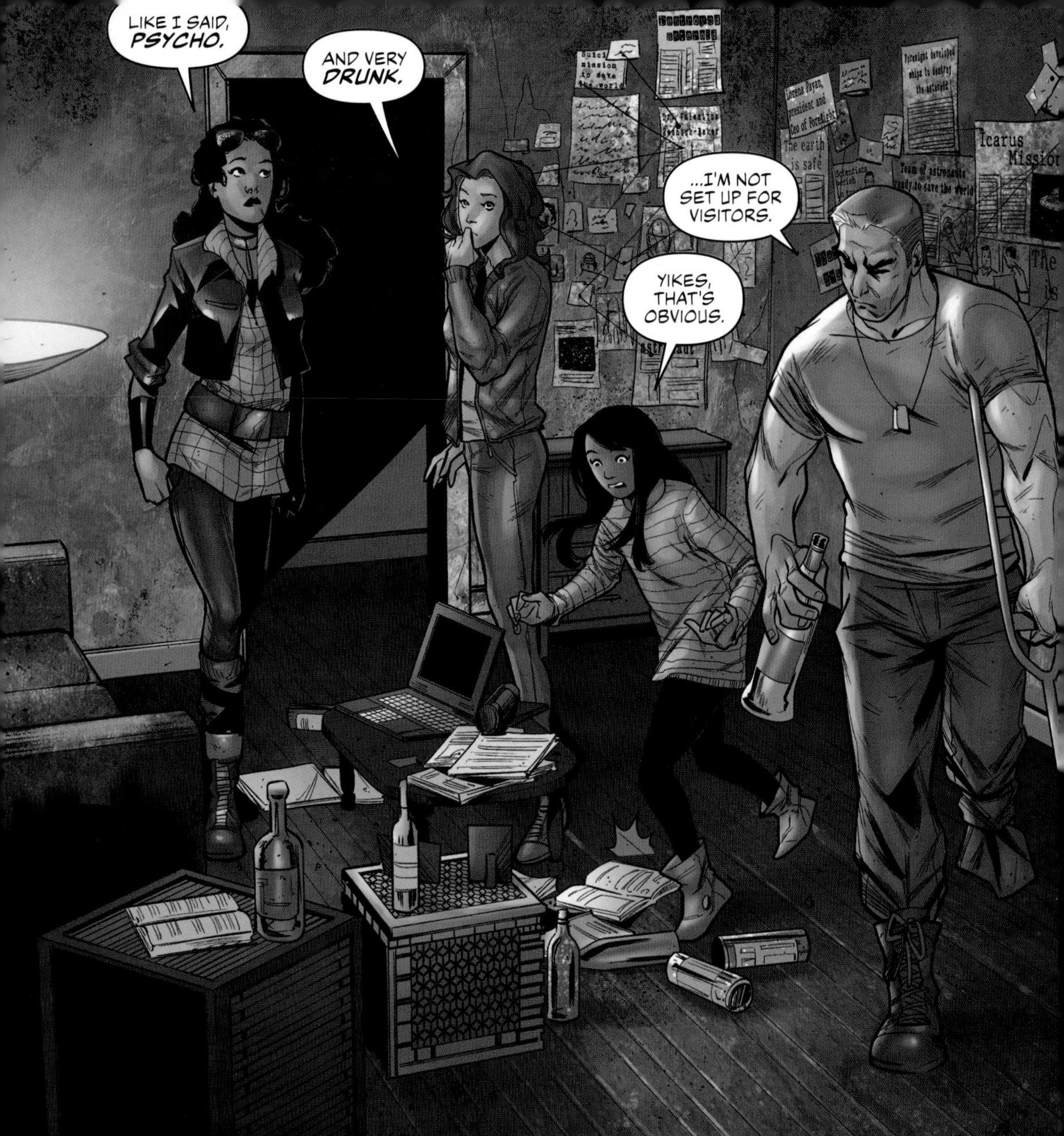
LIKE I SAID, PSYCHO.
AND VERY DRUNK.
...I'M NOT SET UP FOR VISITORS.
YIKES, THAT'S OBVIOUS.

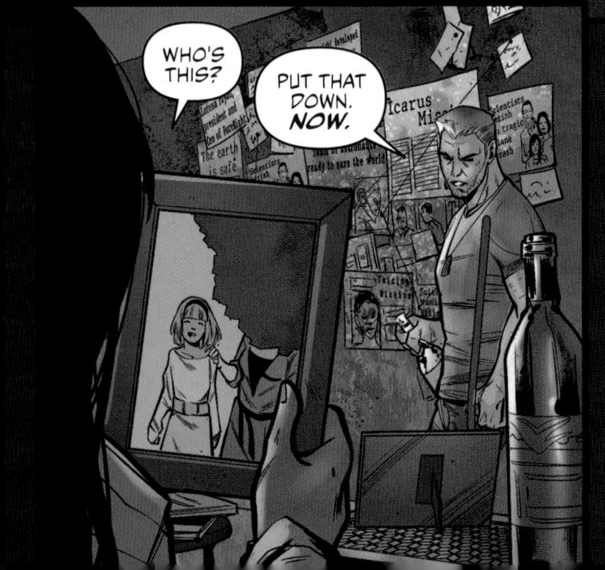
WHO'S THIS?
PUT THAT DOWN. NOW.

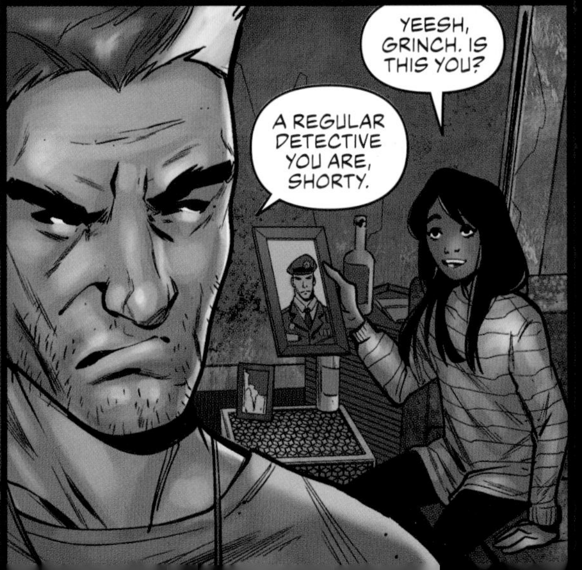
YEESH, GRINCH. IS THIS YOU?
A REGULAR DETECTIVE YOU ARE, SHORTY.

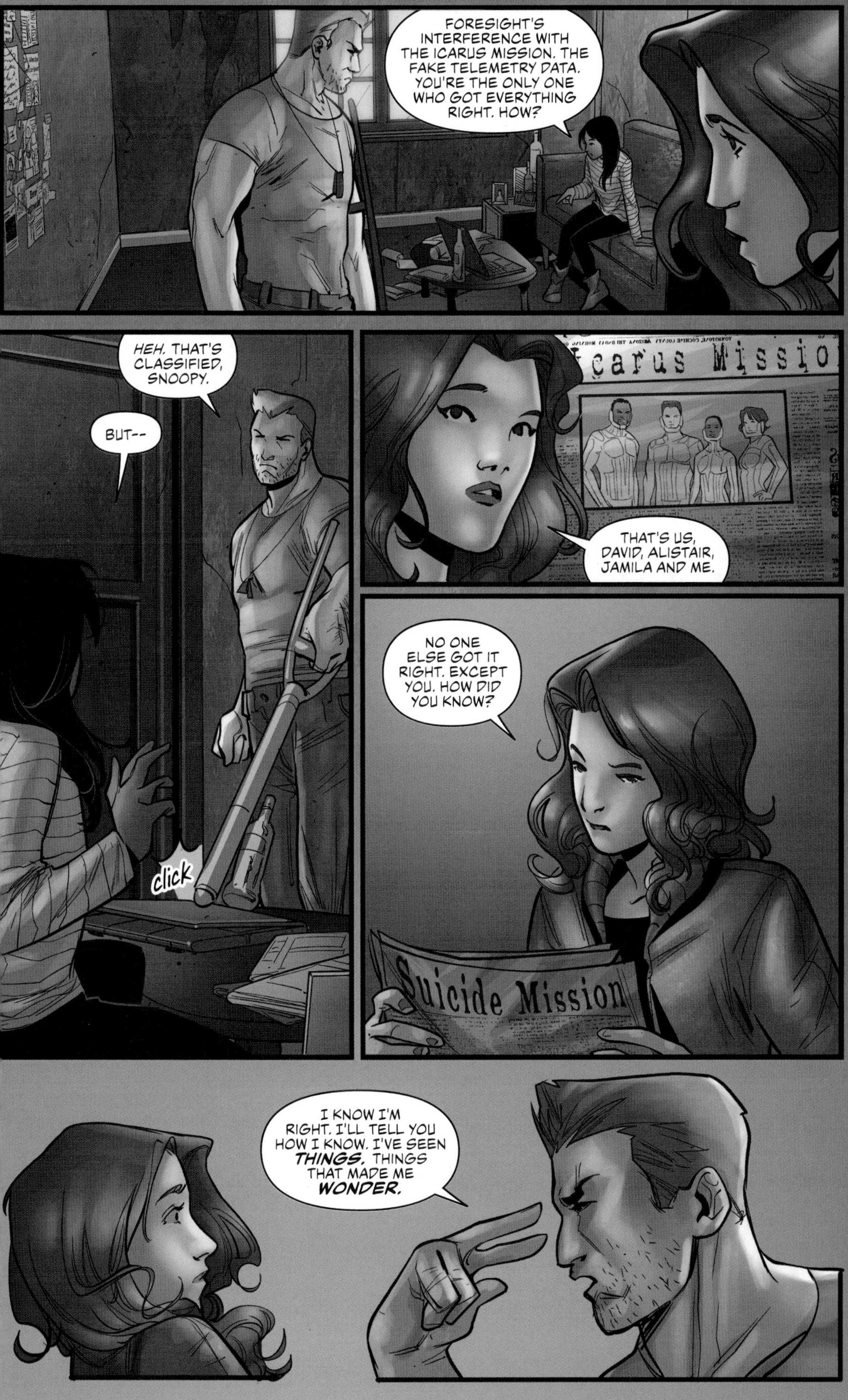
FORESIGHT'S INTERFERENCE WITH THE ICARUS MISSION. THE FAKE TELEMETRY DATA. YOU'RE THE ONLY ONE WHO GOT EVERYTHING RIGHT. HOW?
HEH. THAT'S CLASSIFIED, SNOOPY.
BUT--
click
Icarus Missio
THAT'S US, DAVID, ALISTAIR, JAMILA AND ME.
NO ONE ELSE GOT IT RIGHT. EXCEPT YOU. HOW DID YOU KNOW?
Suicide Mission
I KNOW I'M RIGHT. I'LL TELL YOU HOW I KNOW. I'VE SEEN THINGS. THINGS THAT MADE ME WONDER.

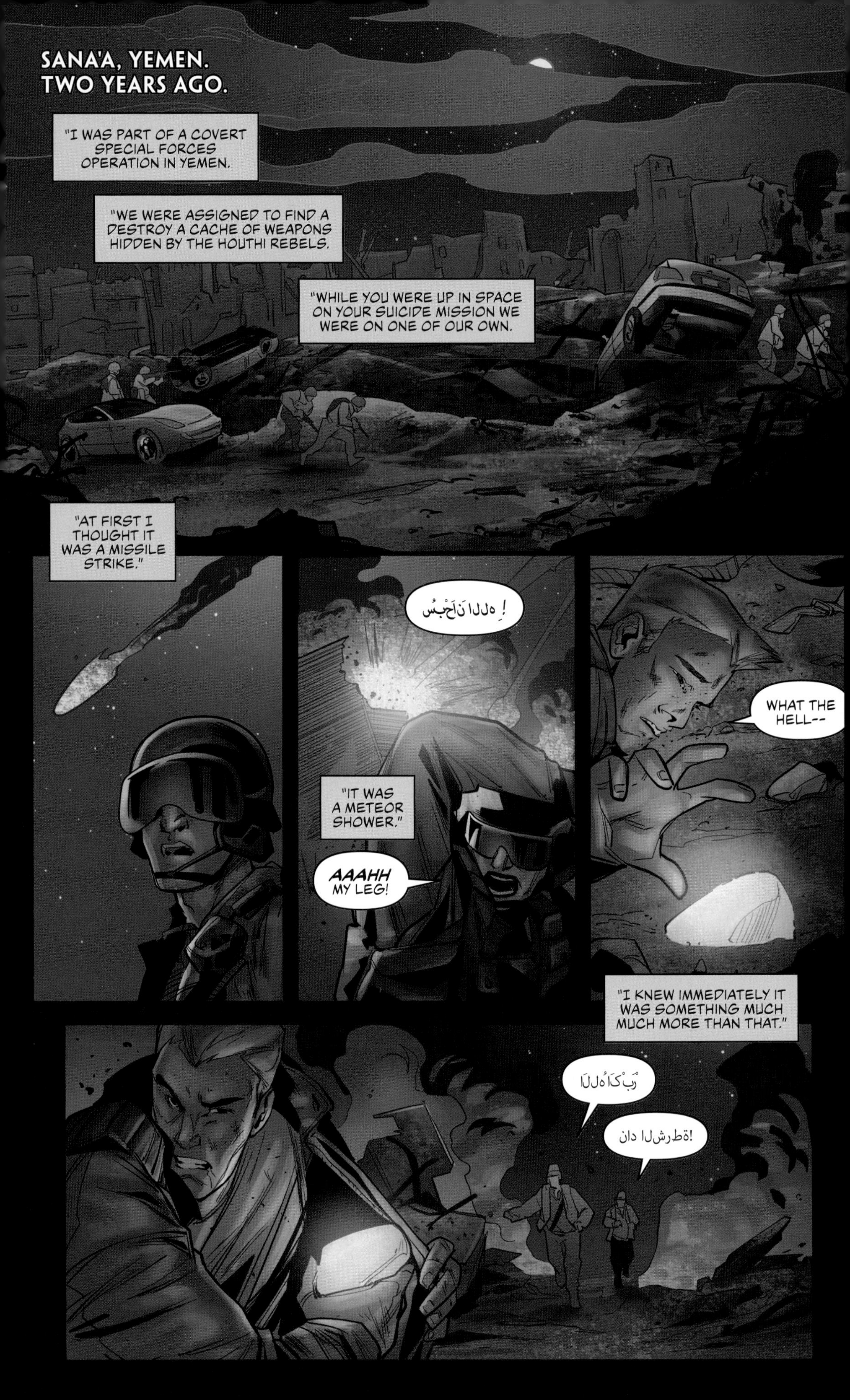
SANA'A, YEMEN.
TWO YEARS AGO.
"I WAS PART OF A COVERT SPECIAL FORCES OPERATION IN YEMEN.
"WE WERE ASSIGNED TO FIND A DESTROY A CACHE OF WEAPONS HIDDEN BY THE HOUTHI REBELS.
"WHILE YOU WERE UP IN SPACE ON YOUR SUICIDE MISSION WE WERE ON ONE OF OUR OWN.
"AT FIRST I THOUGHT IT WAS A MISSILE STRIKE."
!ِهللا نَاحْبُس
"IT WAS A METEOR SHOWER."
AAAHH MY LEG!
WHAT THE HELL--
"I KNEW IMMEDIATELY IT WAS SOMETHING MUCH MUCH MORE THAN THAT."
رُبْكَاهُللَا
!ةطرشلا دان

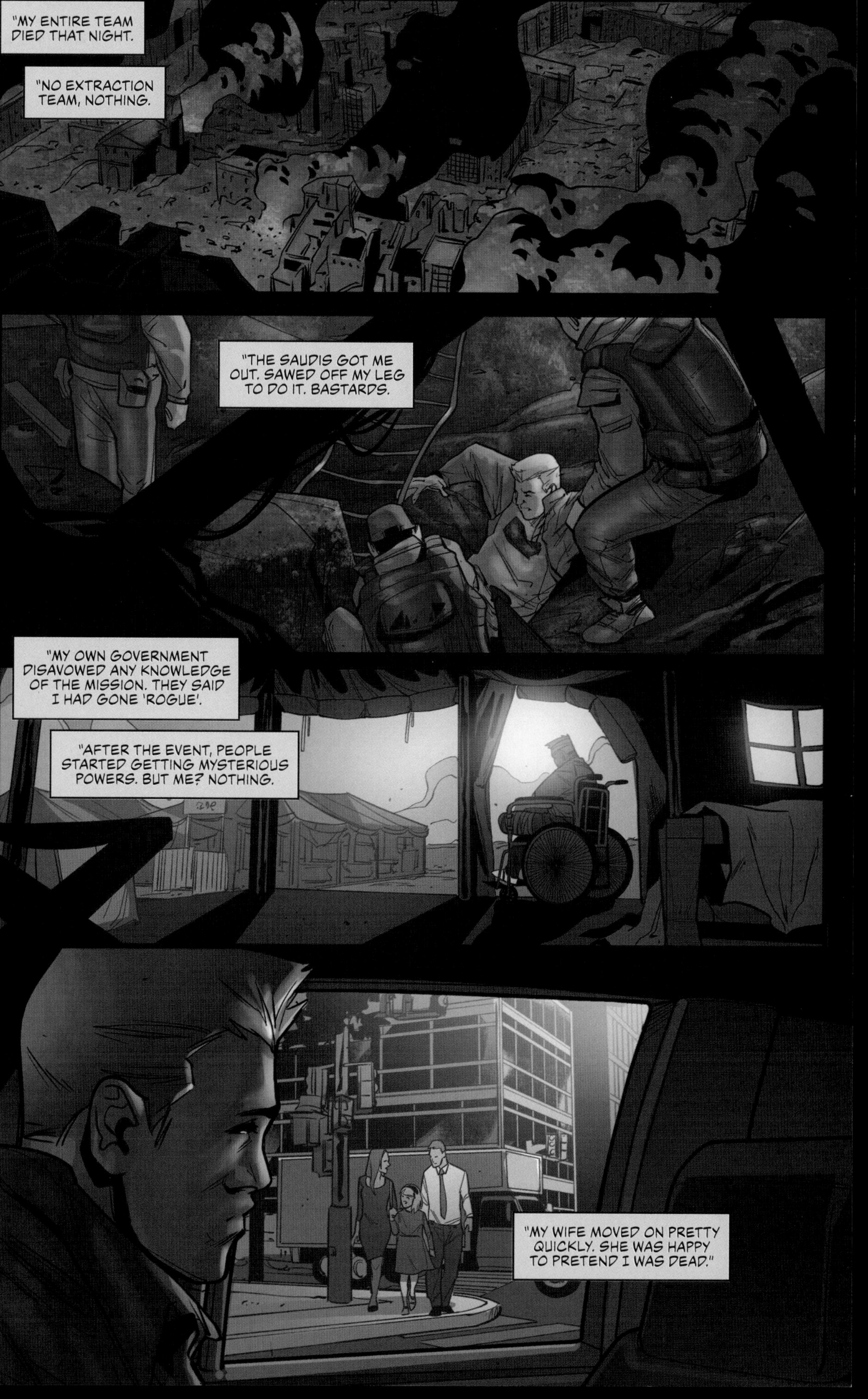
"MY ENTIRE TEAM DIED THAT NIGHT.
"NO EXTRACTION TEAM, NOTHING.
"THE SAUDIS GOT ME OUT. SAWED OFF MY LEG TO DO IT. BASTARDS.
"MY OWN GOVERNMENT DISAVOWED ANY KNOWLEDGE OF THE MISSION. THEY SAID I HAD GONE 'ROGUE'.
"AFTER THE EVENT, PEOPLE STARTED GETTING MYSTERIOUS POWERS. BUT ME? NOTHING.
"MY WIFE MOVED ON PRETTY QUICKLY. SHE WAS HAPPY TO PRETEND I WAS DEAD."

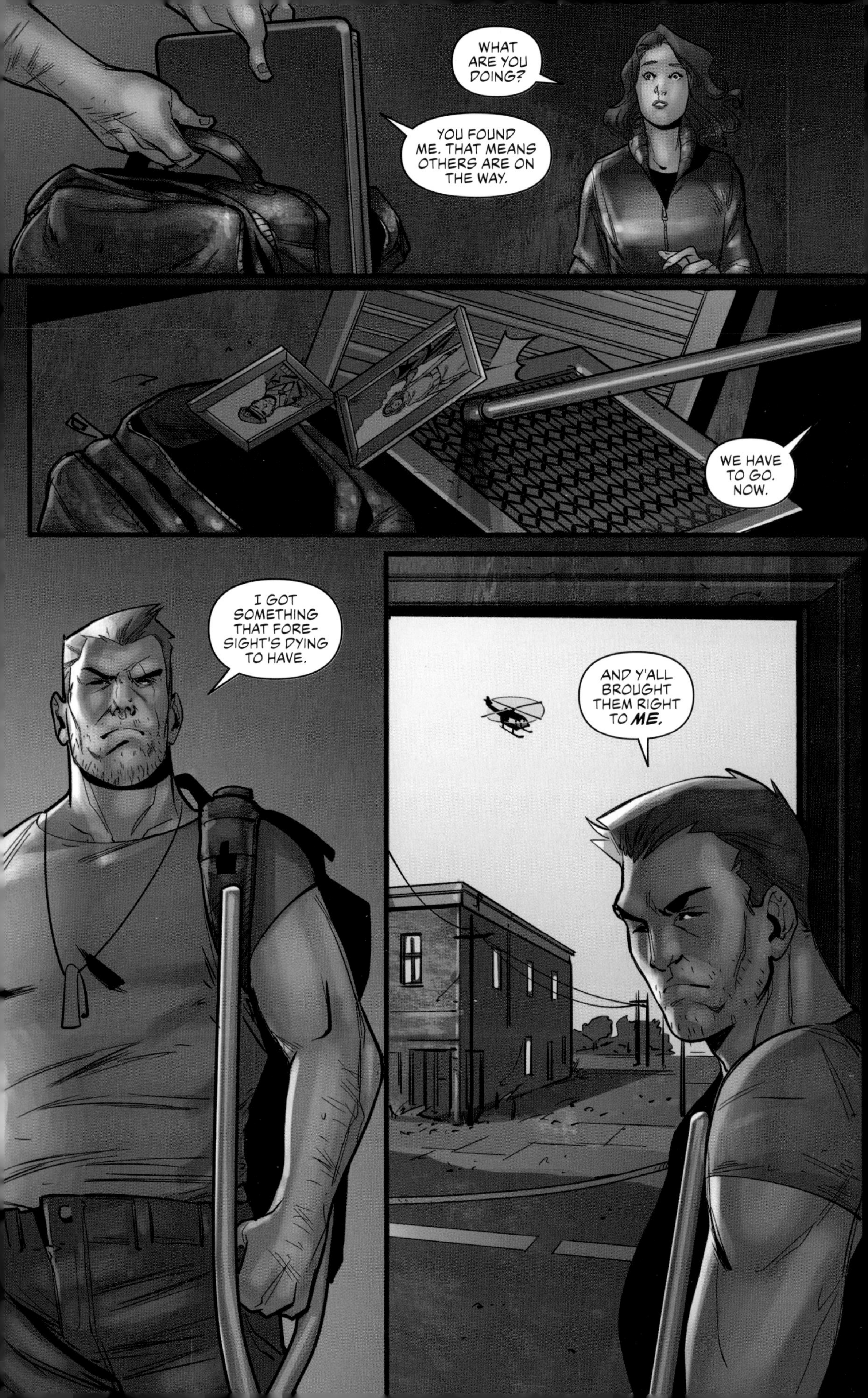
WHAT ARE YOU DOING?
YOU FOUND ME. THAT MEANS OTHERS ARE ON THE WAY.
WE HAVE TO GO. NOW.
I GOT SOMETHING THAT FORE-SIGHT'S DYING TO HAVE.
AND Y'ALL BROUGHT THEM RIGHT TO ***ME.***

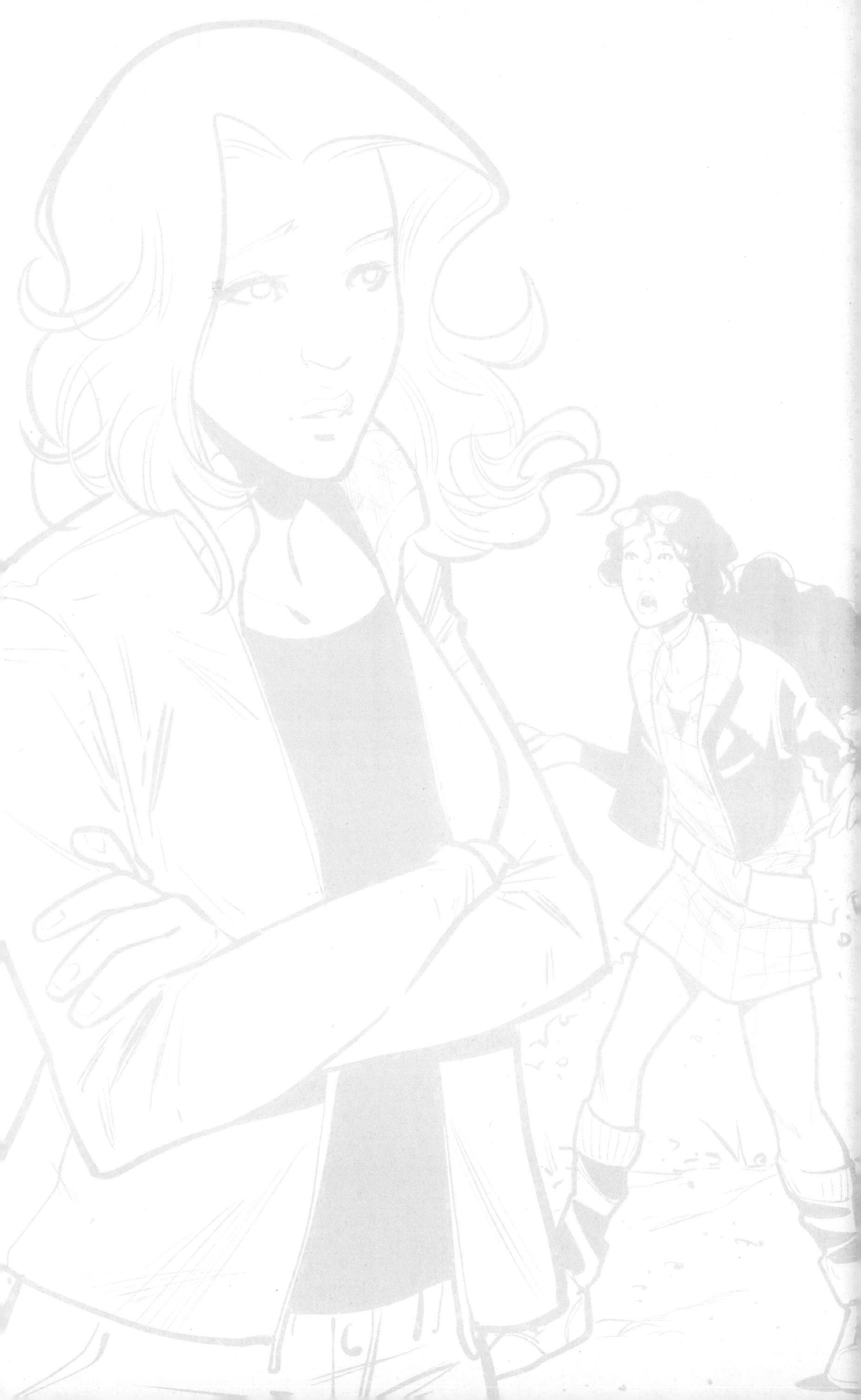

CHAPTER FOUR

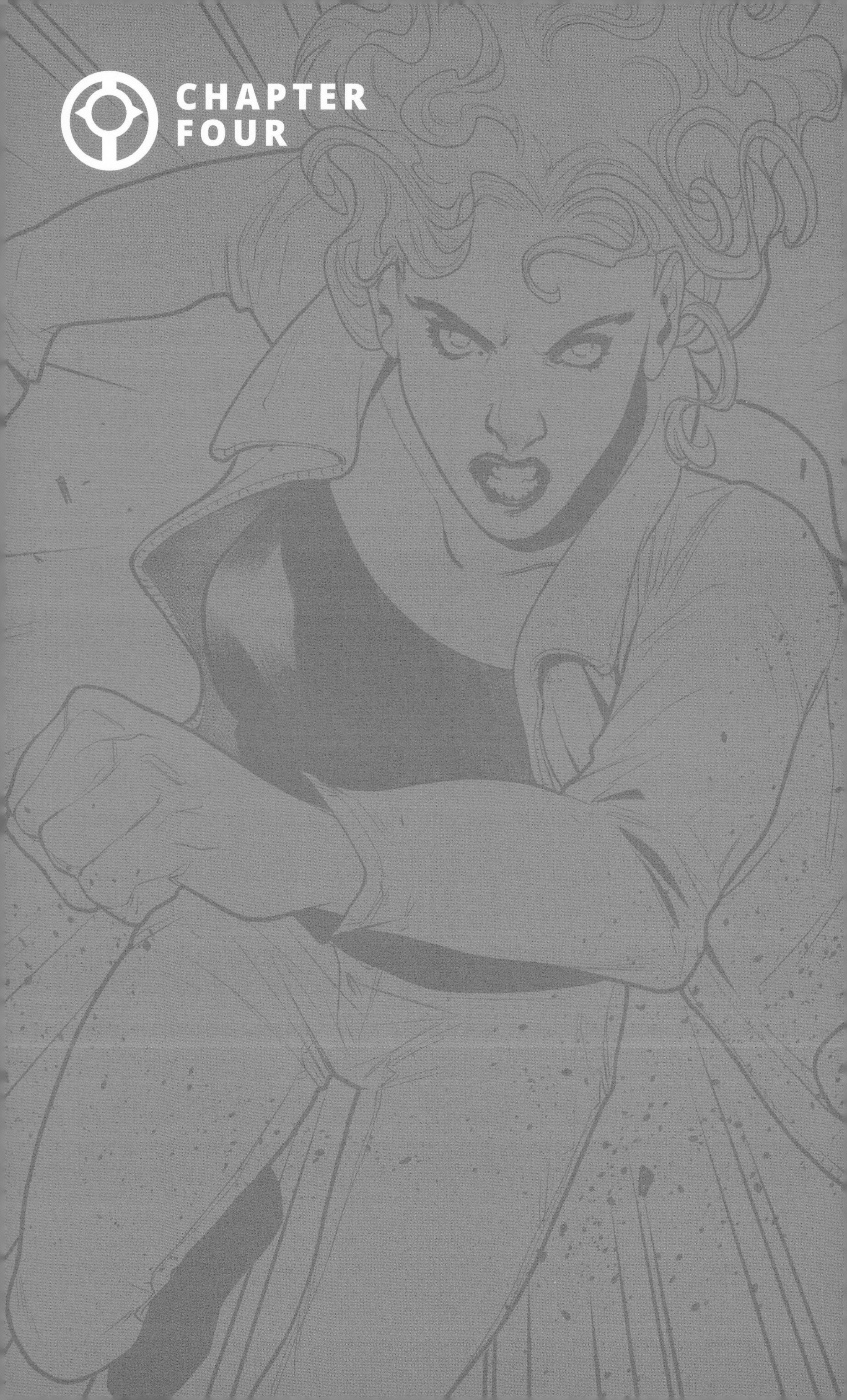

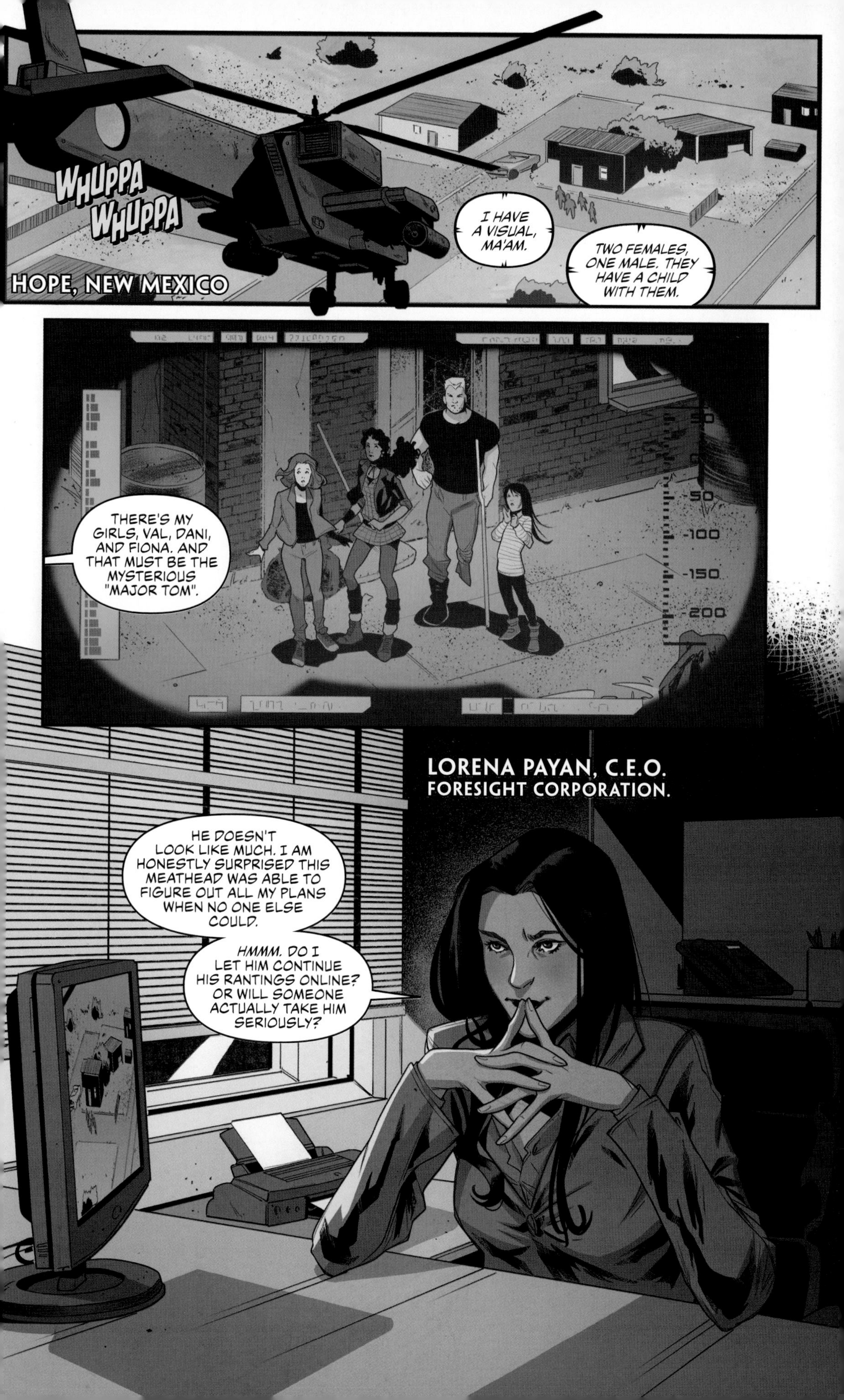
WHUPPA WHUPPA
HOPE, NEW MEXICO
I HAVE A VISUAL, MA'AM.
TWO FEMALES, ONE MALE. THEY HAVE A CHILD WITH THEM.
THERE'S MY GIRLS, VAL, DANI, AND FIONA. AND THAT MUST BE THE MYSTERIOUS "MAJOR TOM".
LORENA PAYAN, C.E.O. FORESIGHT CORPORATION.
HE DOESN'T LOOK LIKE MUCH. I AM HONESTLY SURPRISED THIS MEATHEAD WAS ABLE TO FIGURE OUT ALL MY PLANS WHEN NO ONE ELSE COULD.
HMMM. DO I LET HIM CONTINUE HIS RANTINGS ONLINE? OR WILL SOMEONE ACTUALLY TAKE HIM SERIOUSLY?

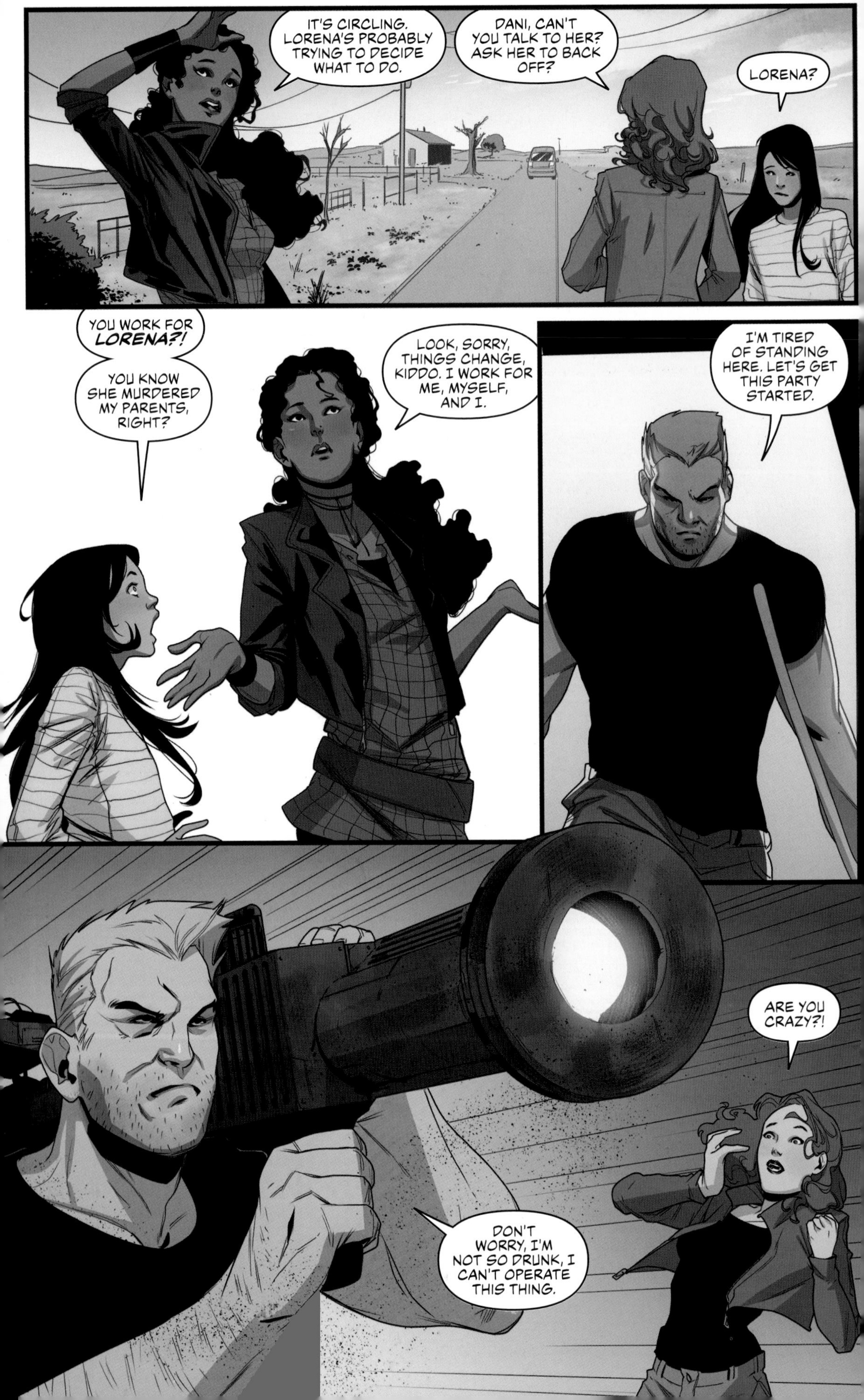
IT'S CIRCLING. LORENA'S PROBABLY TRYING TO DECIDE WHAT TO DO.
DANI, CAN'T YOU TALK TO HER? ASK HER TO BACK OFF?
LORENA?
YOU WORK FOR LORENA?!
YOU KNOW SHE MURDERED MY PARENTS, RIGHT?
LOOK, SORRY, THINGS CHANGE, KIDDO. I WORK FOR ME, MYSELF, AND I.
I'M TIRED OF STANDING HERE. LET'S GET THIS PARTY STARTED.
ARE YOU CRAZY?!
DON'T WORRY, I'M NOT SO DRUNK, I CAN'T OPERATE THIS THING.

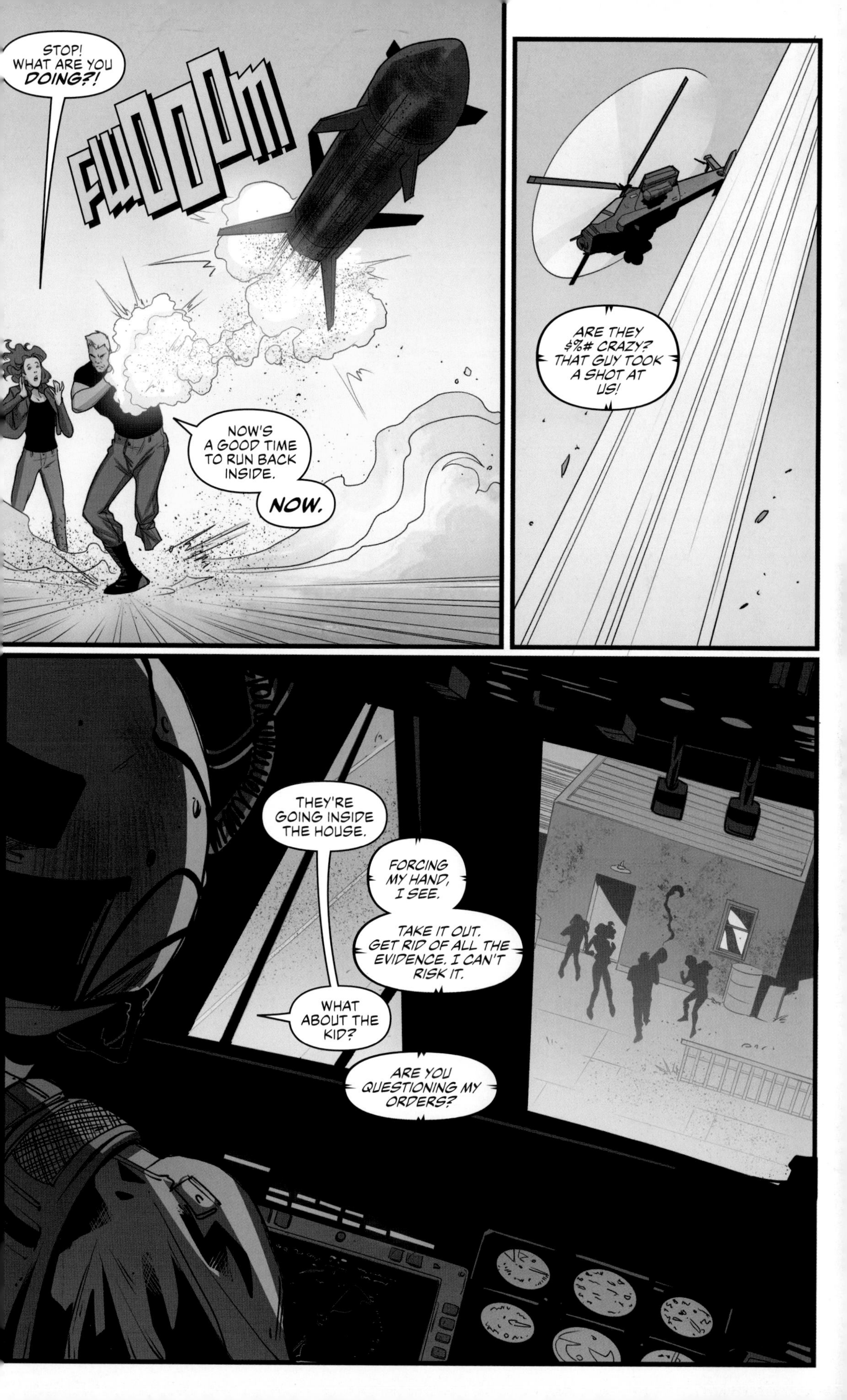
STOP! WHAT ARE YOU DOING?!
FWOOOM
NOW'S A GOOD TIME TO RUN BACK INSIDE.
NOW.
ARE THEY $%# CRAZY? THAT GUY TOOK A SHOT AT US!
THEY'RE GOING INSIDE THE HOUSE.
FORCING MY HAND, I SEE.
TAKE IT OUT. GET RID OF ALL THE EVIDENCE. I CAN'T RISK IT.
WHAT ABOUT THE KID?
ARE YOU QUESTIONING MY ORDERS?

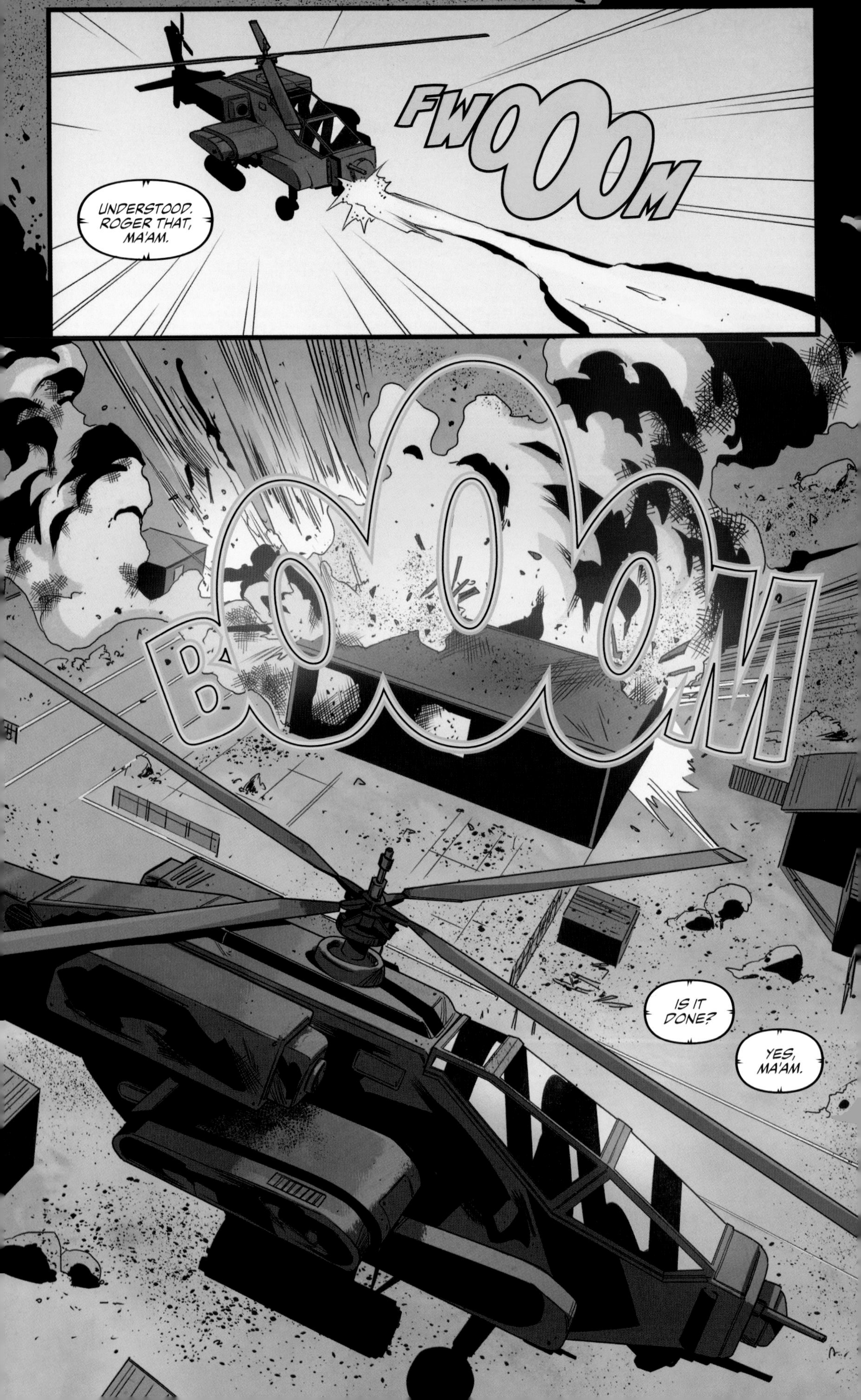
UNDERSTOOD. ROGER THAT, MA'AM.
FWOOOOM
BOOOOM
IS IT DONE?
YES, MA'AM.

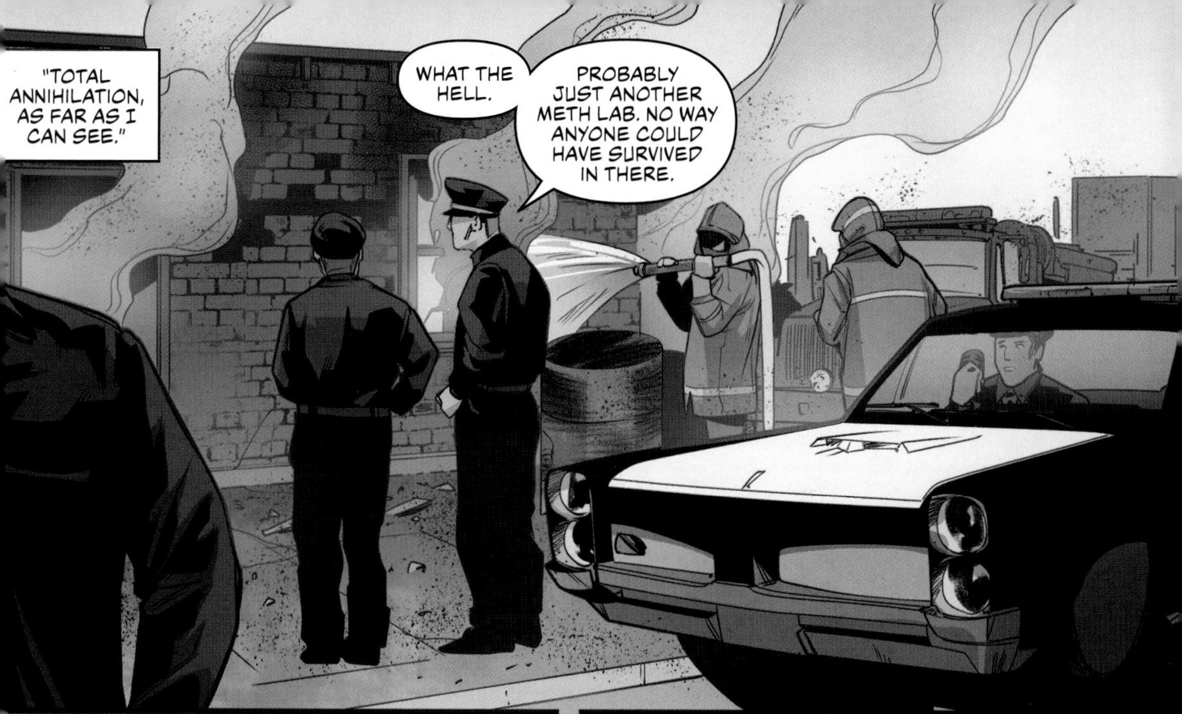
"TOTAL ANNIHILATION, AS FAR AS I CAN SEE."
WHAT THE HELL.
PROBABLY JUST ANOTHER METH LAB. NO WAY ANYONE COULD HAVE SURVIVED IN THERE.

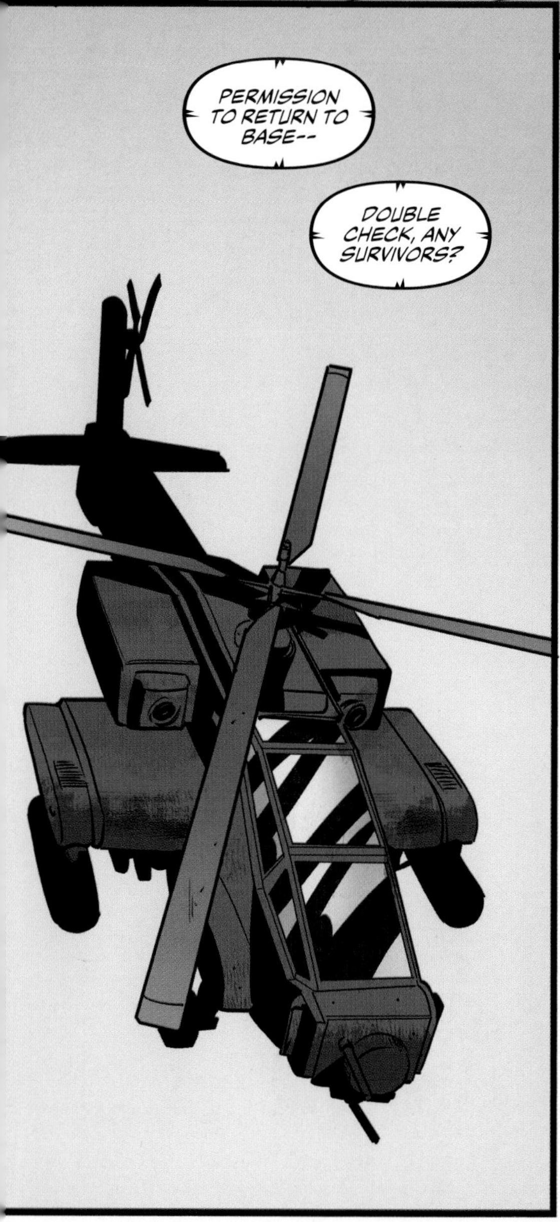
PERMISSION TO RETURN TO BASE--
DOUBLE CHECK, ANY SURVIVORS?

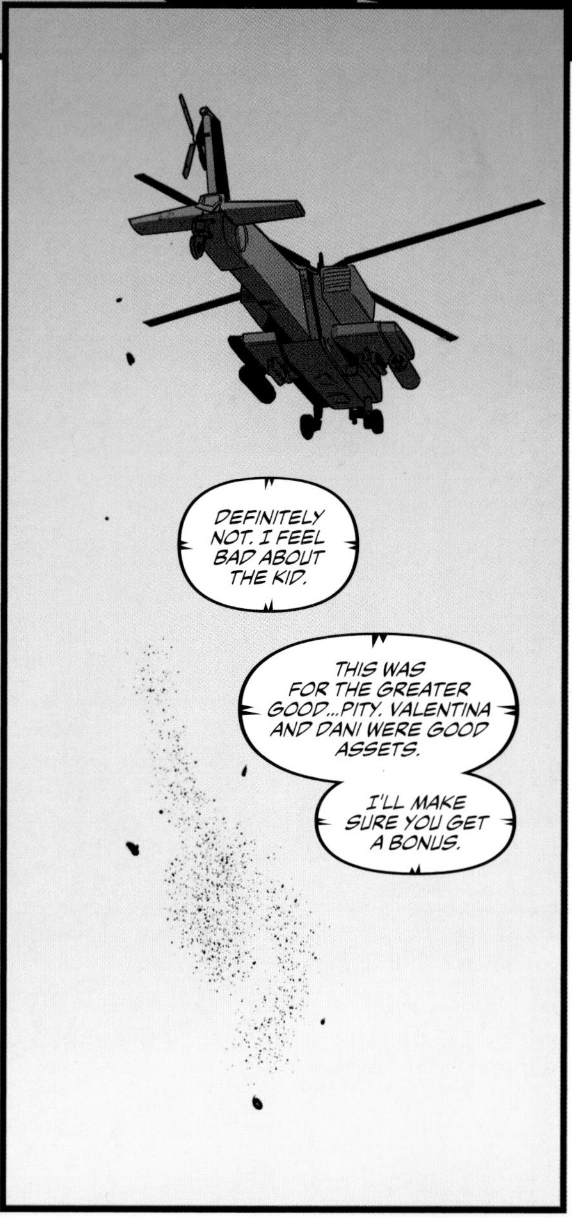
DEFINITELY NOT. I FEEL BAD ABOUT THE KID.
THIS WAS FOR THE GREATER GOOD...PITY. VALENTINA AND DANI WERE GOOD ASSETS.
I'LL MAKE SURE YOU GET A BONUS.

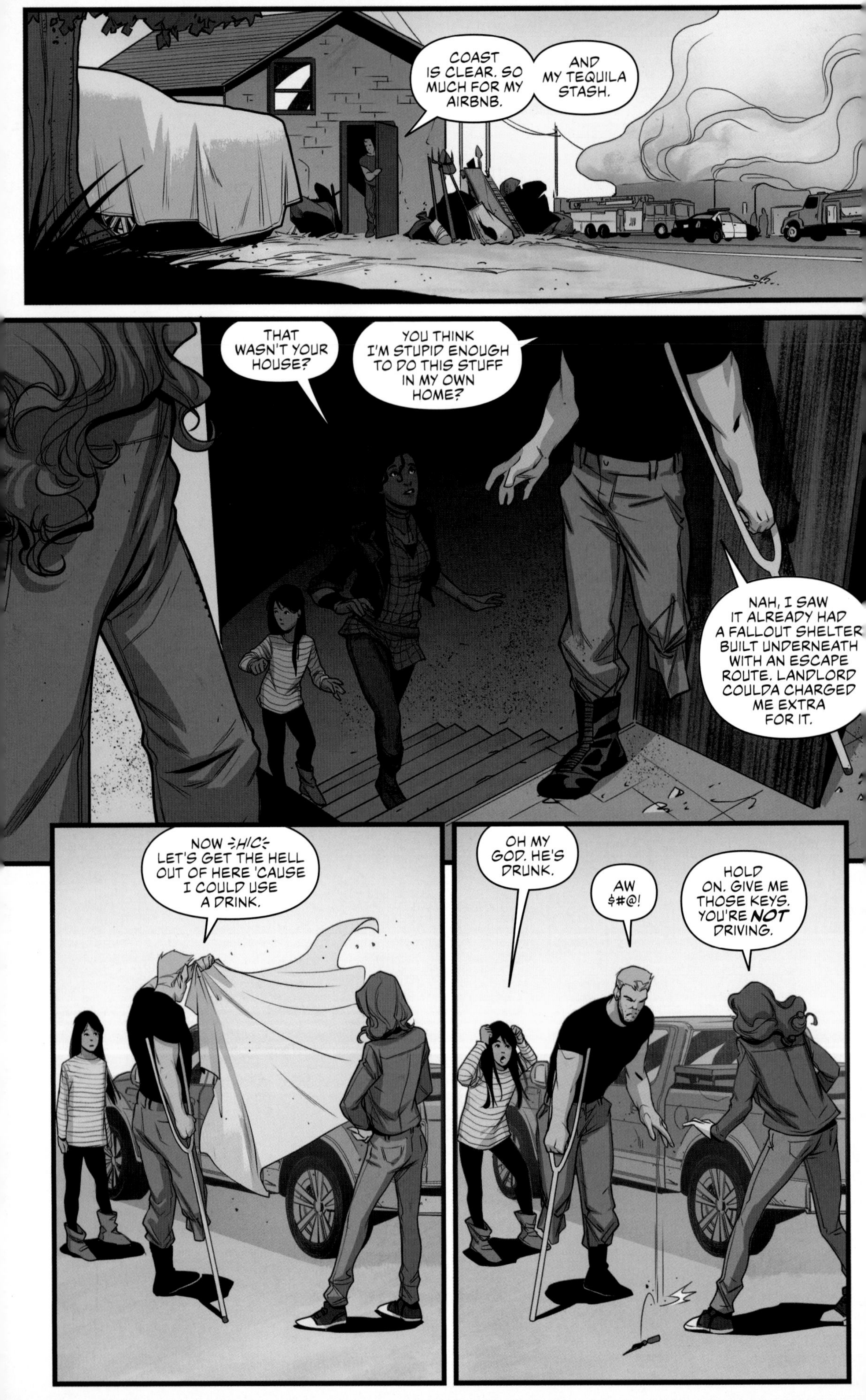
COAST IS CLEAR. SO MUCH FOR MY AIRBNB.
AND MY TEQUILA STASH.
THAT WASN'T YOUR HOUSE?
YOU THINK I'M STUPID ENOUGH TO DO THIS STUFF IN MY OWN HOME?
NAH, I SAW IT ALREADY HAD A FALLOUT SHELTER BUILT UNDERNEATH WITH AN ESCAPE ROUTE. LANDLORD COULDA CHARGED ME EXTRA FOR IT.
NOW *HIC* LET'S GET THE HELL OUT OF HERE 'CAUSE I COULD USE A DRINK.
OH MY GOD. HE'S DRUNK.
AW $#@!
HOLD ON. GIVE ME THOSE KEYS. YOU'RE ***NOT*** DRIVING.

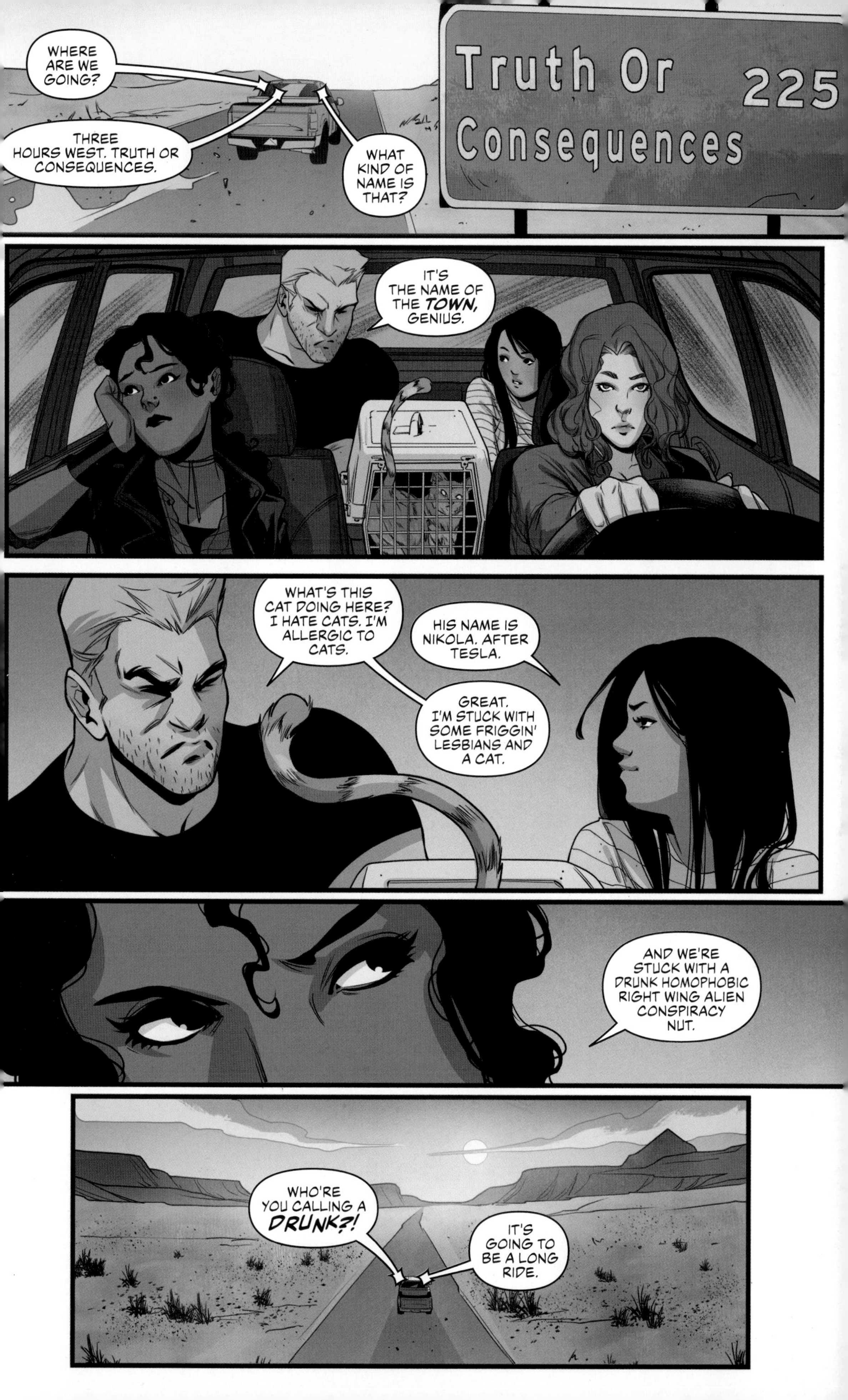
WHERE ARE WE GOING?
THREE HOURS WEST. TRUTH OR CONSEQUENCES.
WHAT KIND OF NAME IS THAT?
Truth Or Consequences 225
IT'S THE NAME OF THE TOWN, GENIUS.
WHAT'S THIS CAT DOING HERE? I HATE CATS. I'M ALLERGIC TO CATS.
HIS NAME IS NIKOLA. AFTER TESLA.
GREAT. I'M STUCK WITH SOME FRIGGIN' LESBIANS AND A CAT.
AND WE'RE STUCK WITH A DRUNK HOMOPHOBIC RIGHT WING ALIEN CONSPIRACY NUT.
WHO'RE YOU CALLING A DRUNK?!
IT'S GOING TO BE A LONG RIDE.

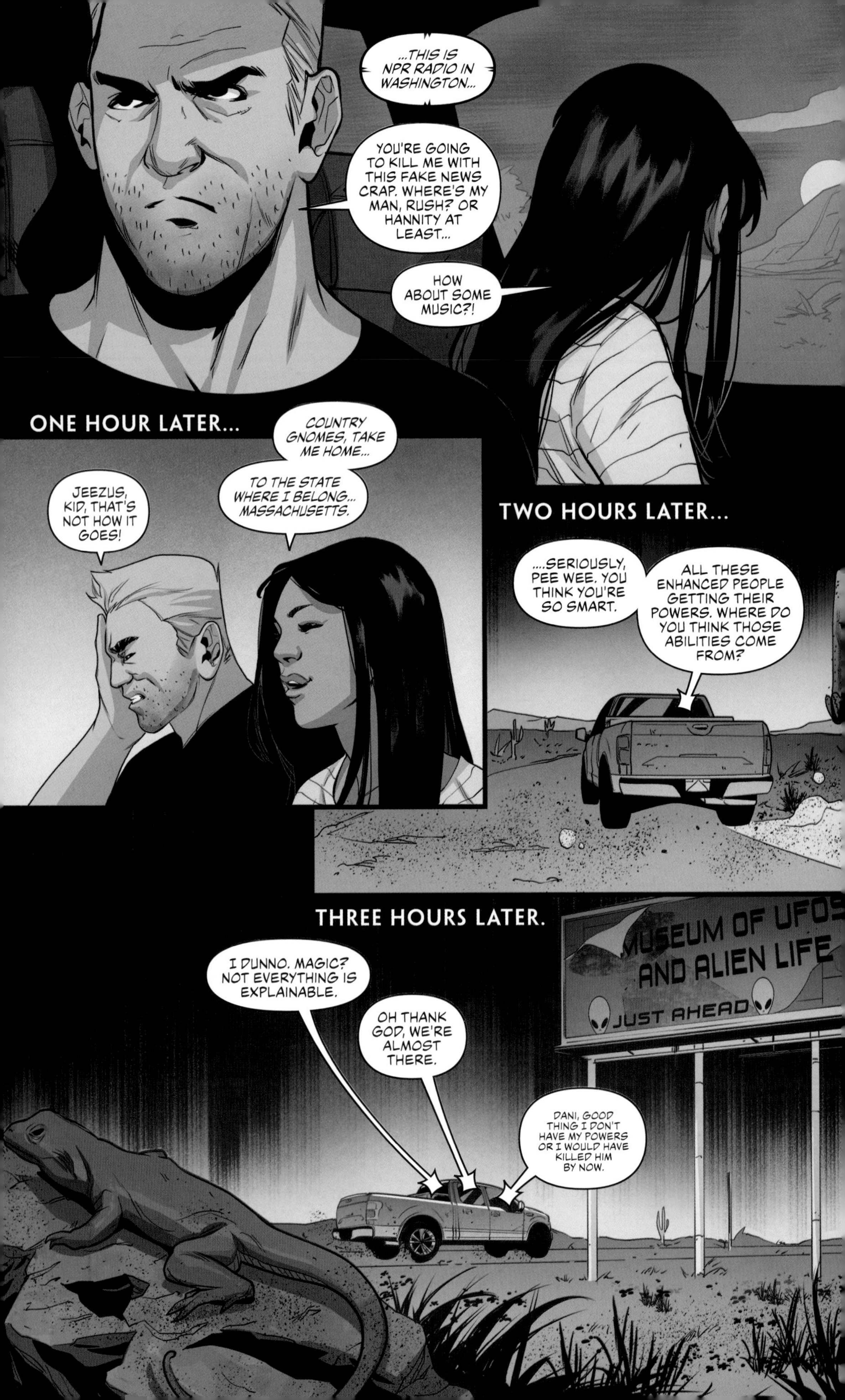
...THIS IS NPR RADIO IN WASHINGTON...
YOU'RE GOING TO KILL ME WITH THIS FAKE NEWS CRAP. WHERE'S MY MAN, RUSH? OR HANNITY AT LEAST...
HOW ABOUT SOME MUSIC?!
ONE HOUR LATER...
COUNTRY GNOMES, TAKE ME HOME...
TO THE STATE WHERE I BELONG... MASSACHUSETTS.
JEEZUS, KID, THAT'S NOT HOW IT GOES!
TWO HOURS LATER...
....SERIOUSLY, PEE WEE. YOU THINK YOU'RE SO SMART.
ALL THESE ENHANCED PEOPLE GETTING THEIR POWERS. WHERE DO YOU THINK THOSE ABILITIES COME FROM?
THREE HOURS LATER.
MUSEUM OF UFOS AND ALIEN LIFE
JUST AHEAD
I DUNNO. MAGIC? NOT EVERYTHING IS EXPLAINABLE.
OH THANK GOD, WE'RE ALMOST THERE.
DANI, GOOD THING I DON'T HAVE MY POWERS OR I WOULD HAVE KILLED HIM BY NOW.

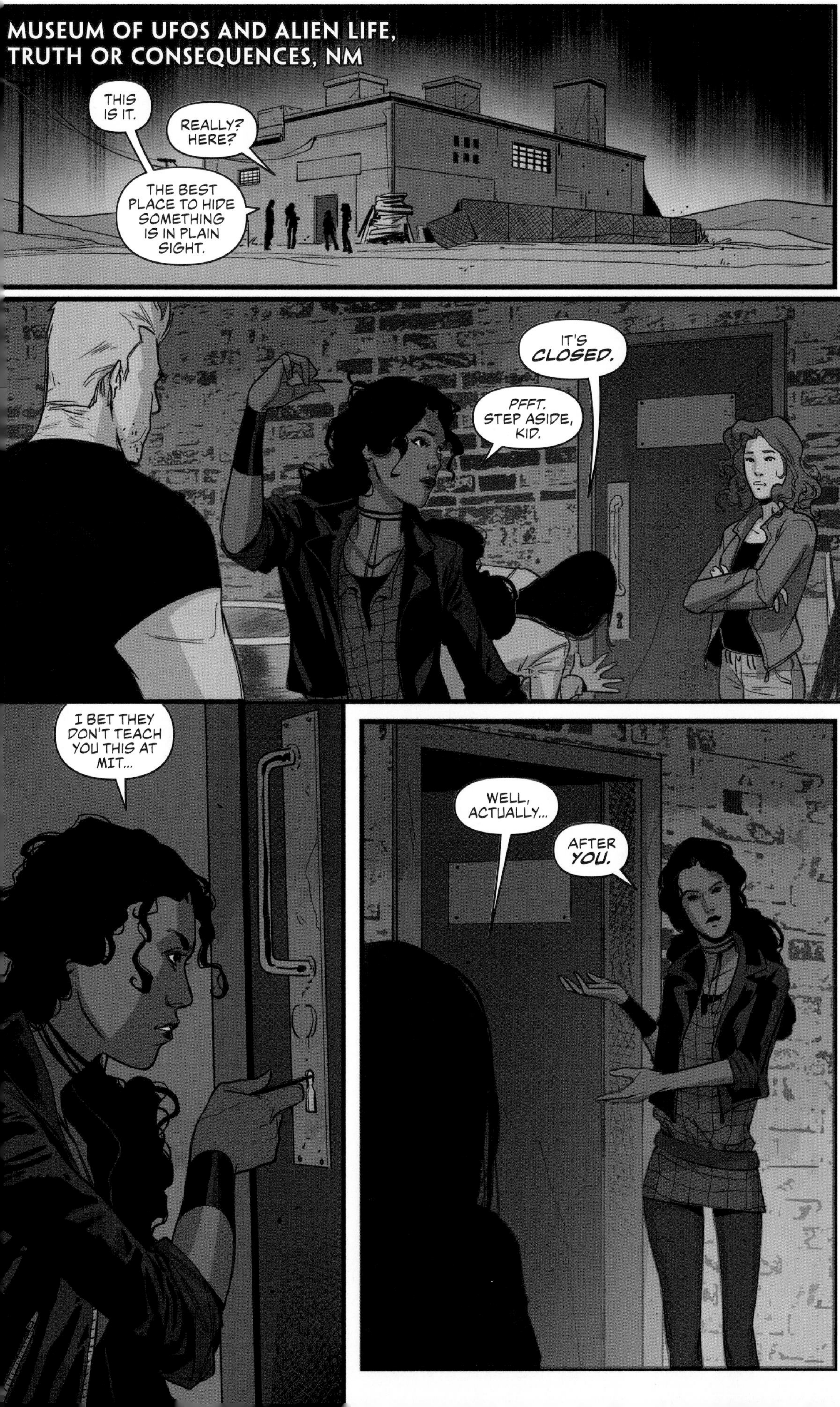
MUSEUM OF UFOS AND ALIEN LIFE, TRUTH OR CONSEQUENCES, NM
THIS IS IT.
REALLY? HERE?
THE BEST PLACE TO HIDE SOMETHING IS IN PLAIN SIGHT.
IT'S CLOSED.
PFFT. STEP ASIDE, KID.
I BET THEY DON'T TEACH YOU THIS AT MIT...
WELL, ACTUALLY...
AFTER YOU.

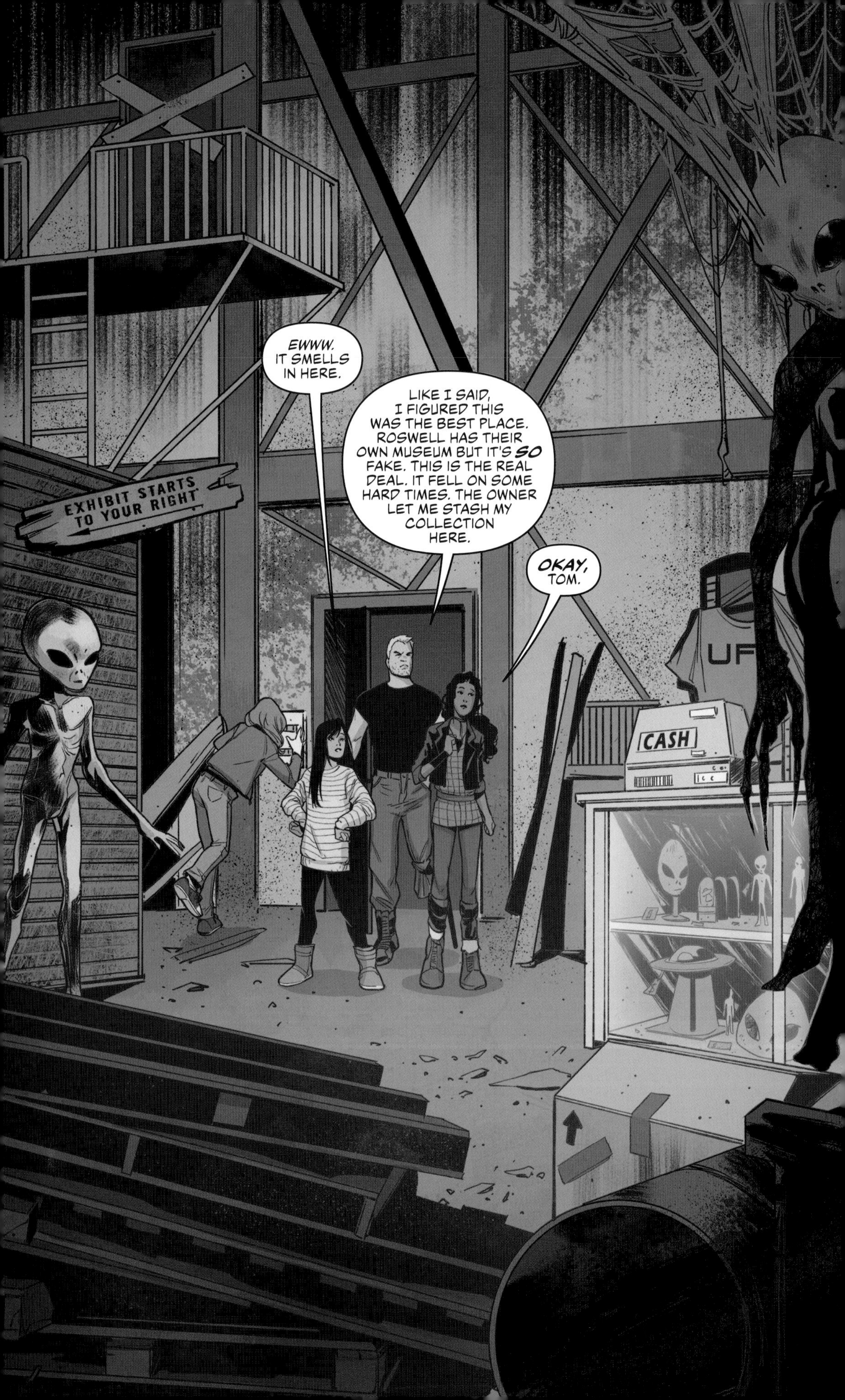
EXHIBIT STARTS TO YOUR RIGHT
EWWW. IT SMELLS IN HERE.
LIKE I SAID, I FIGURED THIS WAS THE BEST PLACE. ROSWELL HAS THEIR OWN MUSEUM BUT IT'S SO FAKE. THIS IS THE REAL DEAL. IT FELL ON SOME HARD TIMES. THE OWNER LET ME STASH MY COLLECTION HERE.
OKAY, TOM.
CASH
UF

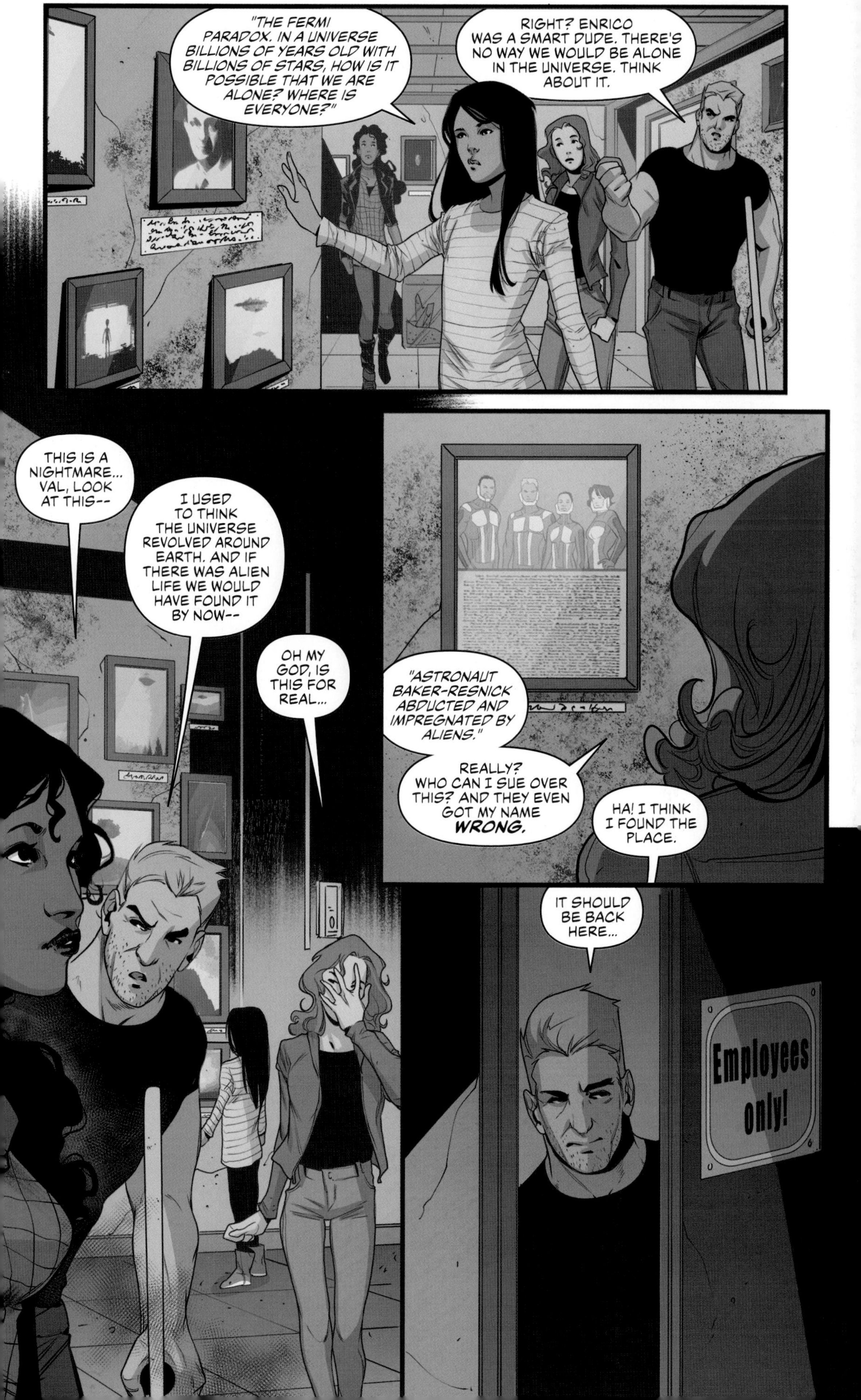
"THE FERMI PARADOX. IN A UNIVERSE BILLIONS OF YEARS OLD WITH BILLIONS OF STARS, HOW IS IT POSSIBLE THAT WE ARE ALONE? WHERE IS EVERYONE?"
RIGHT? ENRICO WAS A SMART DUDE. THERE'S NO WAY WE WOULD BE ALONE IN THE UNIVERSE. THINK ABOUT IT.
THIS IS A NIGHTMARE... VAL, LOOK AT THIS--
I USED TO THINK THE UNIVERSE REVOLVED AROUND EARTH. AND IF THERE WAS ALIEN LIFE WE WOULD HAVE FOUND IT BY NOW--
OH MY GOD, IS THIS FOR REAL...
"ASTRONAUT BAKER-RESNICK ABDUCTED AND IMPREGNATED BY ALIENS."
REALLY? WHO CAN I SUE OVER THIS? AND THEY EVEN GOT MY NAME **WRONG.**
HA! I THINK I FOUND THE PLACE.
IT SHOULD BE BACK HERE...
Employees only!

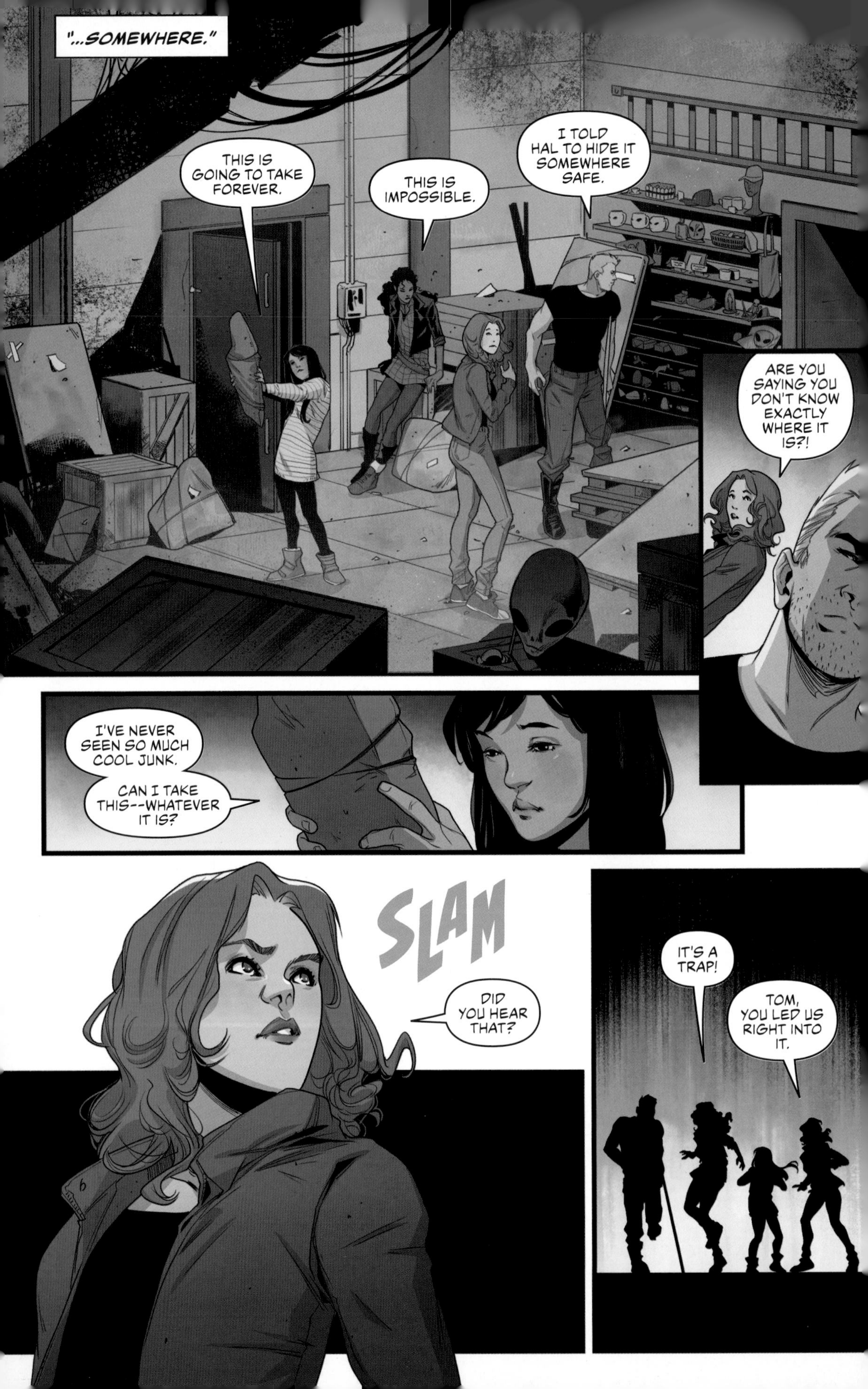
"...SOMEWHERE."
THIS IS GOING TO TAKE FOREVER.
THIS IS IMPOSSIBLE.
I TOLD HAL TO HIDE IT SOMEWHERE SAFE.
ARE YOU SAYING YOU DON'T KNOW EXACTLY WHERE IT IS?!
I'VE NEVER SEEN SO MUCH COOL JUNK.
CAN I TAKE THIS--WHATEVER IT IS?
SLAM
DID YOU HEAR THAT?
IT'S A TRAP!
TOM, YOU LED US RIGHT INTO IT.

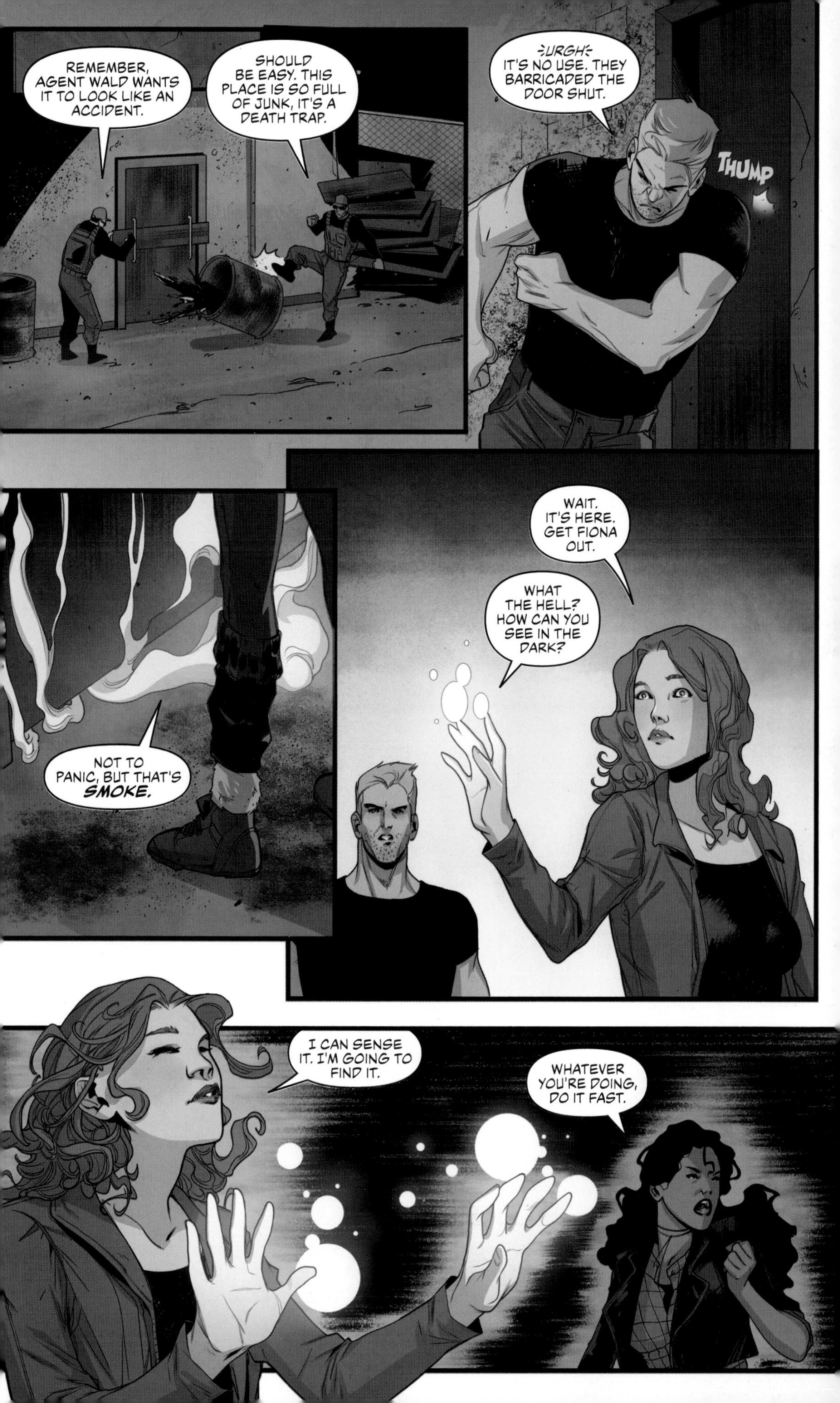

REMEMBER, AGENT WALD WANTS IT TO LOOK LIKE AN ACCIDENT.
SHOULD BE EASY. THIS PLACE IS SO FULL OF JUNK, IT'S A DEATH TRAP.
URGH
IT'S NO USE. THEY BARRICADED THE DOOR SHUT.
THUMP
NOT TO PANIC, BUT THAT'S SMOKE.
WAIT. IT'S HERE. GET FIONA OUT.
WHAT THE HELL? HOW CAN YOU SEE IN THE DARK?
I CAN SENSE IT. I'M GOING TO FIND IT.
WHATEVER YOU'RE DOING, DO IT FAST.

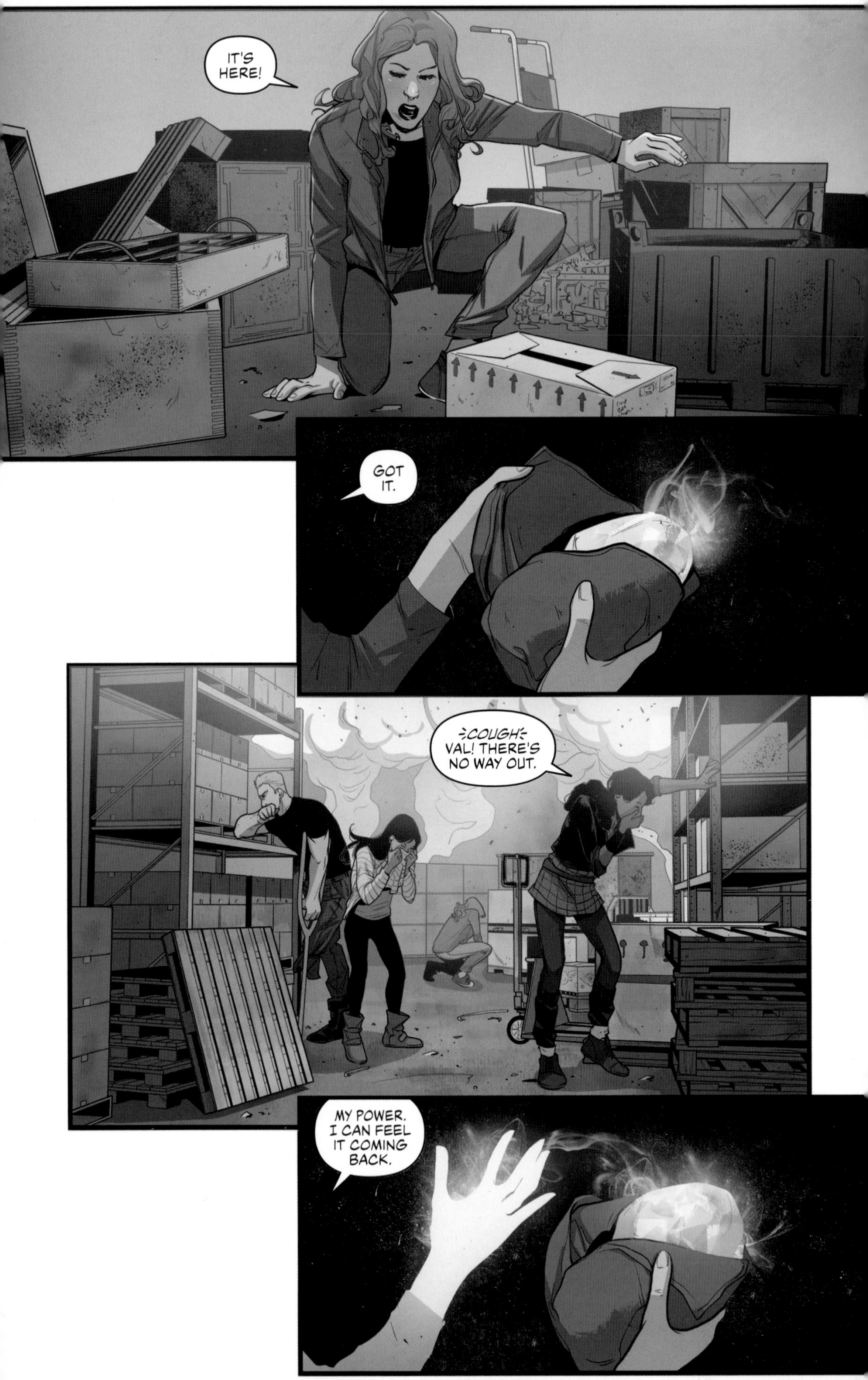
IT'S HERE!
GOT IT.
COUGH VAL! THERE'S NO WAY OUT.
MY POWER. I CAN FEEL IT COMING BACK.

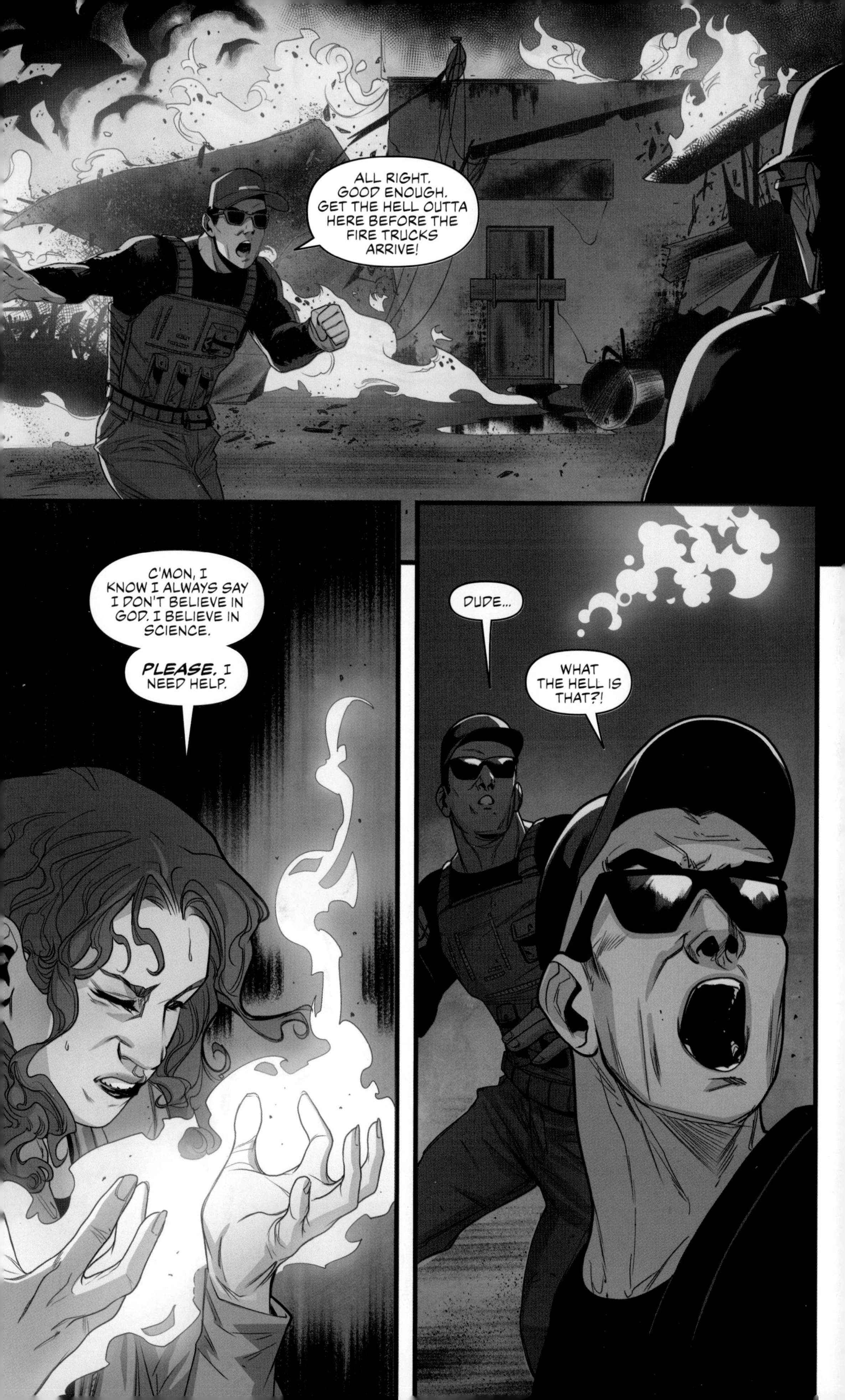
ALL RIGHT. GOOD ENOUGH. GET THE HELL OUTTA HERE BEFORE THE FIRE TRUCKS ARRIVE!
C'MON, I KNOW I ALWAYS SAY I DON'T BELIEVE IN GOD. I BELIEVE IN SCIENCE.
PLEASE. I NEED HELP.
DUDE...
WHAT THE HELL IS THAT?!

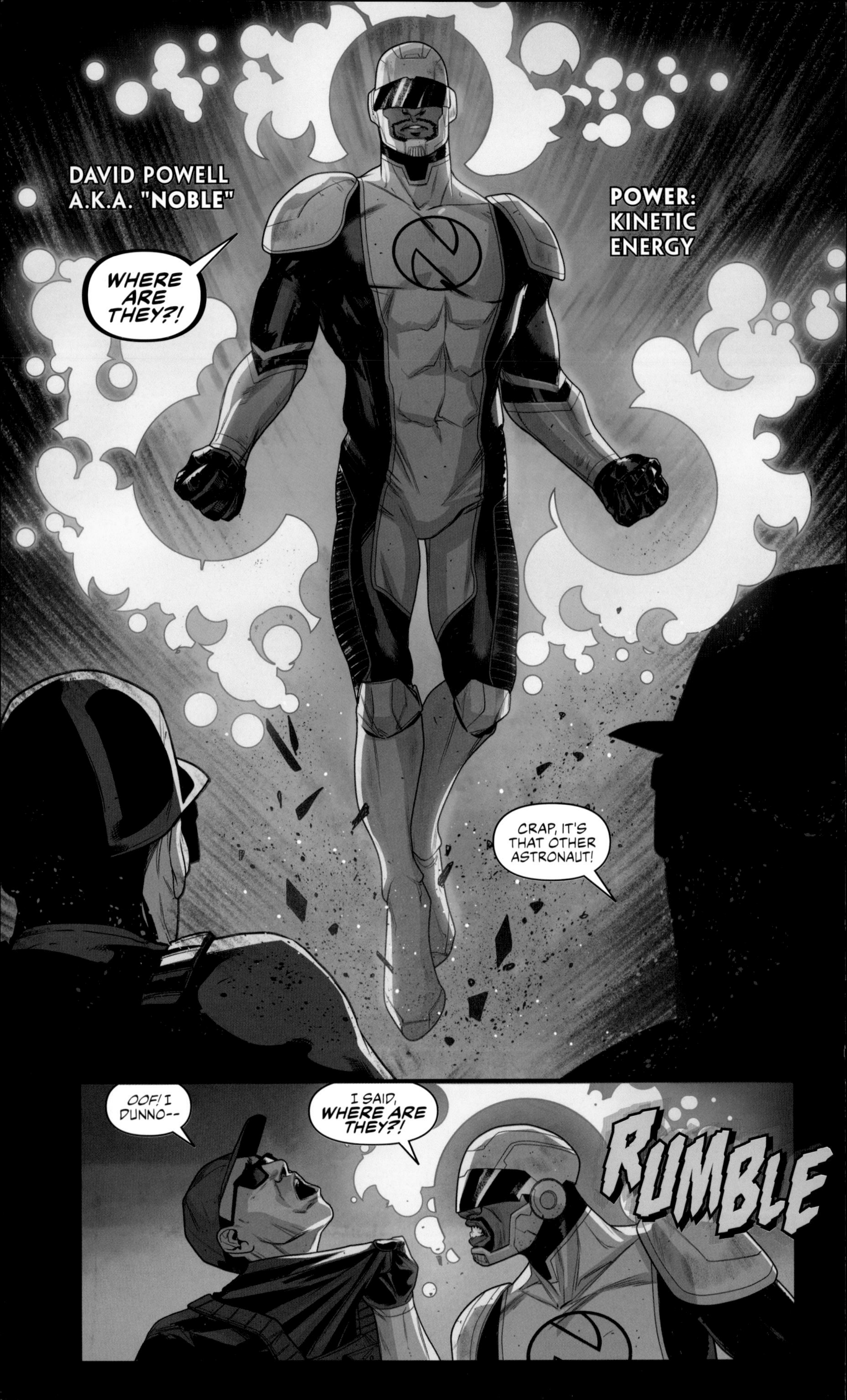
DAVID POWELL
A.K.A. "NOBLE"
POWER:
KINETIC
ENERGY
WHERE ARE THEY?!
CRAP, IT'S THAT OTHER ASTRONAUT!
OOF! I DUNNO--
I SAID, WHERE ARE THEY?!
RUMBLE

INSIDE THE WAREHOUSE--

NO!

RUMBLE

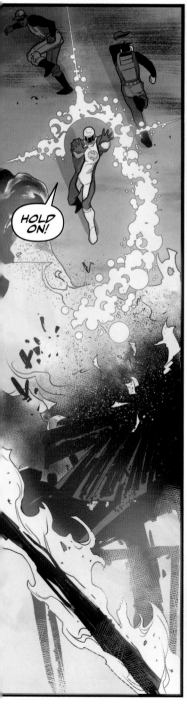

HOLD ON!

LOOK! IT'S NOBLE!

THANK YOU, DAVID.

STAND BACK! I'M MAKING AN EXIT FOR US!

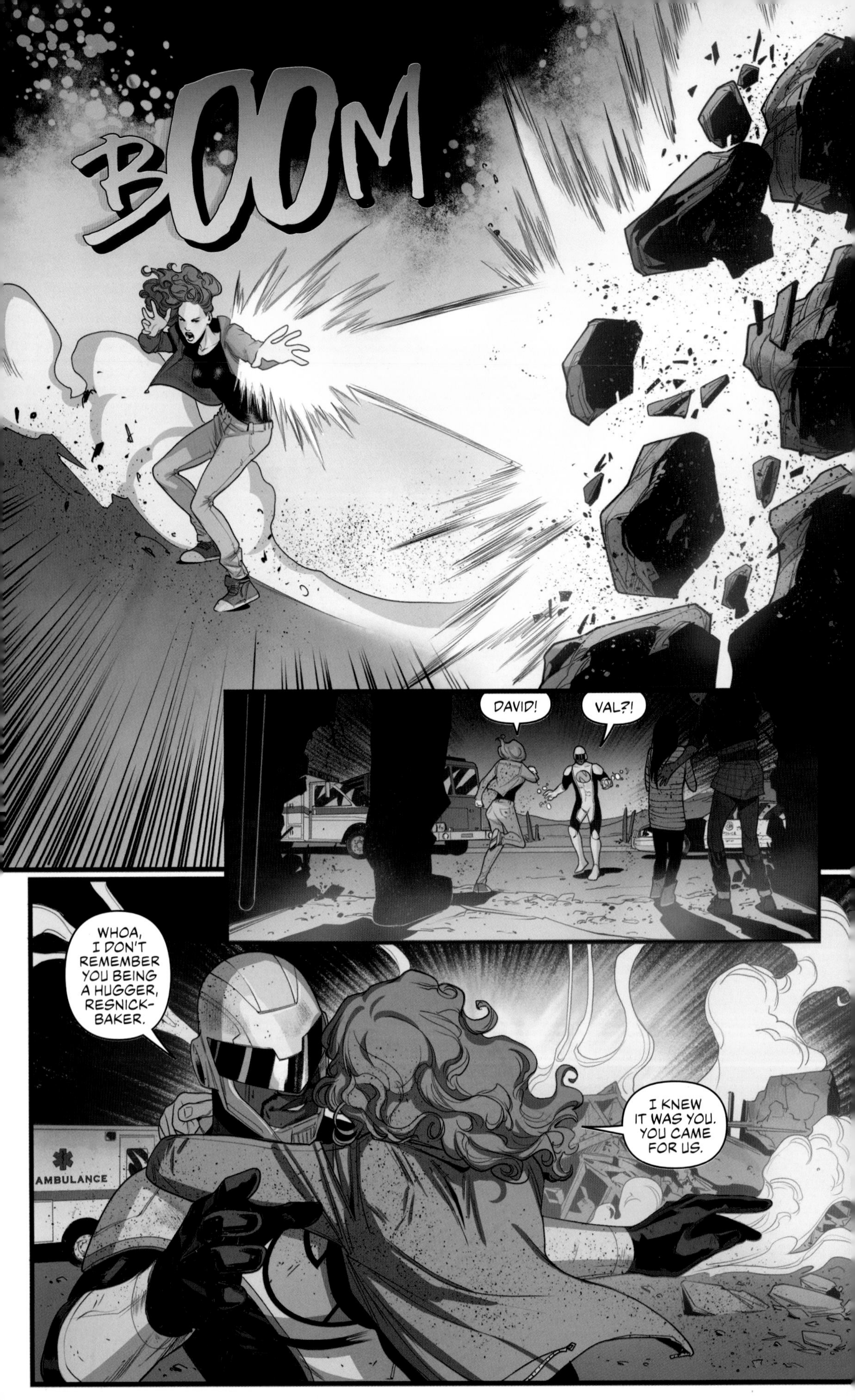
BOOM
DAVID!
VAL?!
WHOA, I DON'T REMEMBER YOU BEING A HUGGER, RESNICK-BAKER.
I KNEW IT WAS YOU. YOU CAME FOR US.
AMBULANCE

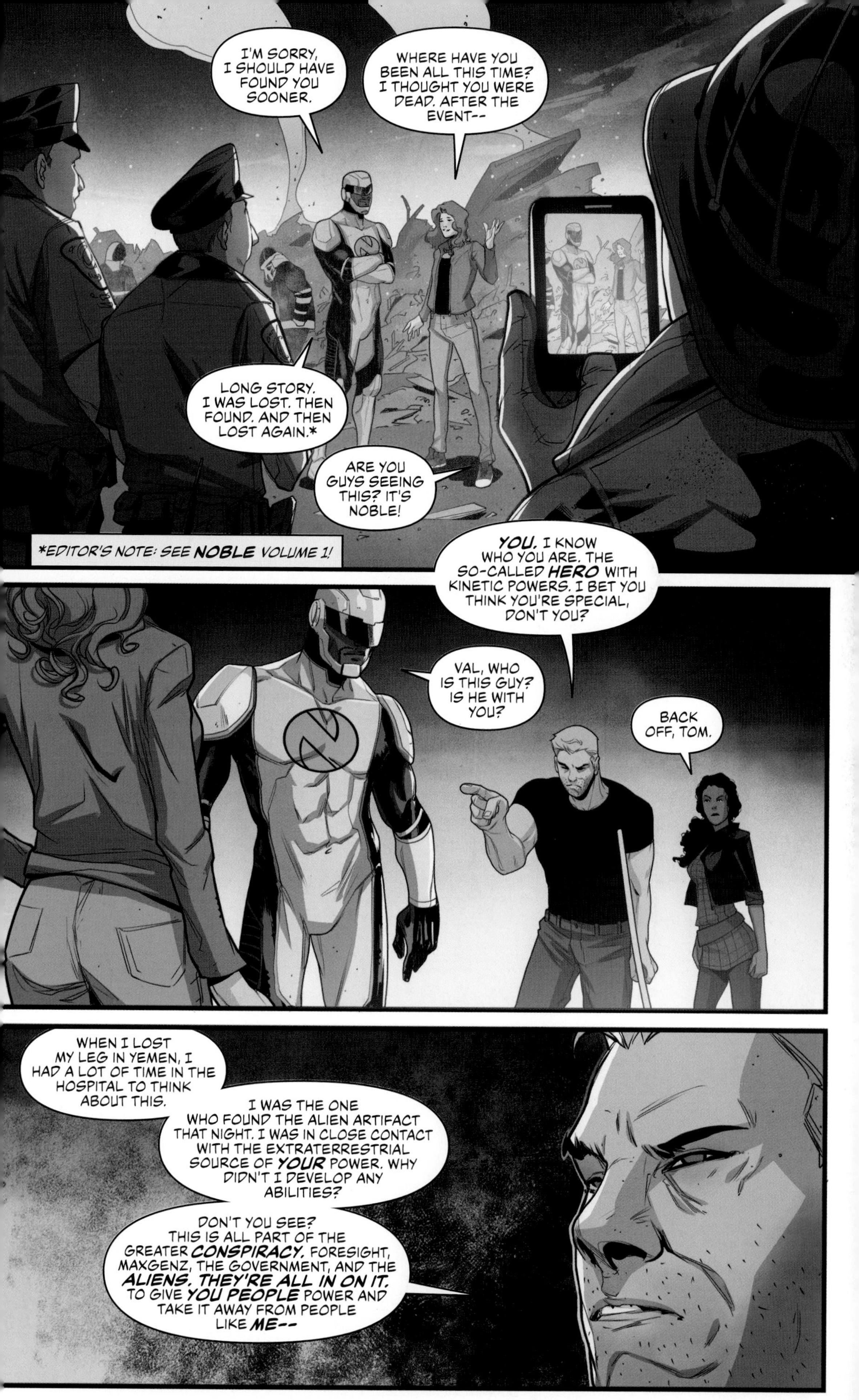
I'M SORRY, I SHOULD HAVE FOUND YOU SOONER.
WHERE HAVE YOU BEEN ALL THIS TIME? I THOUGHT YOU WERE DEAD. AFTER THE EVENT--
LONG STORY. I WAS LOST. THEN FOUND. AND THEN LOST AGAIN.*
ARE YOU GUYS SEEING THIS? IT'S NOBLE!
*EDITOR'S NOTE: SEE NOBLE VOLUME 1!
YOU. I KNOW WHO YOU ARE. THE SO-CALLED HERO WITH KINETIC POWERS. I BET YOU THINK YOU'RE SPECIAL, DON'T YOU?
VAL, WHO IS THIS GUY? IS HE WITH YOU?
BACK OFF, TOM.
WHEN I LOST MY LEG IN YEMEN, I HAD A LOT OF TIME IN THE HOSPITAL TO THINK ABOUT THIS.
I WAS THE ONE WHO FOUND THE ALIEN ARTIFACT THAT NIGHT. I WAS IN CLOSE CONTACT WITH THE EXTRATERRESTRIAL SOURCE OF YOUR POWER. WHY DIDN'T I DEVELOP ANY ABILITIES?
DON'T YOU SEE? THIS IS ALL PART OF THE GREATER CONSPIRACY. FORESIGHT, MAXGENZ, THE GOVERNMENT, AND THE ALIENS. THEY'RE ALL IN ON IT. TO GIVE YOU PEOPLE POWER AND TAKE IT AWAY FROM PEOPLE LIKE ME--

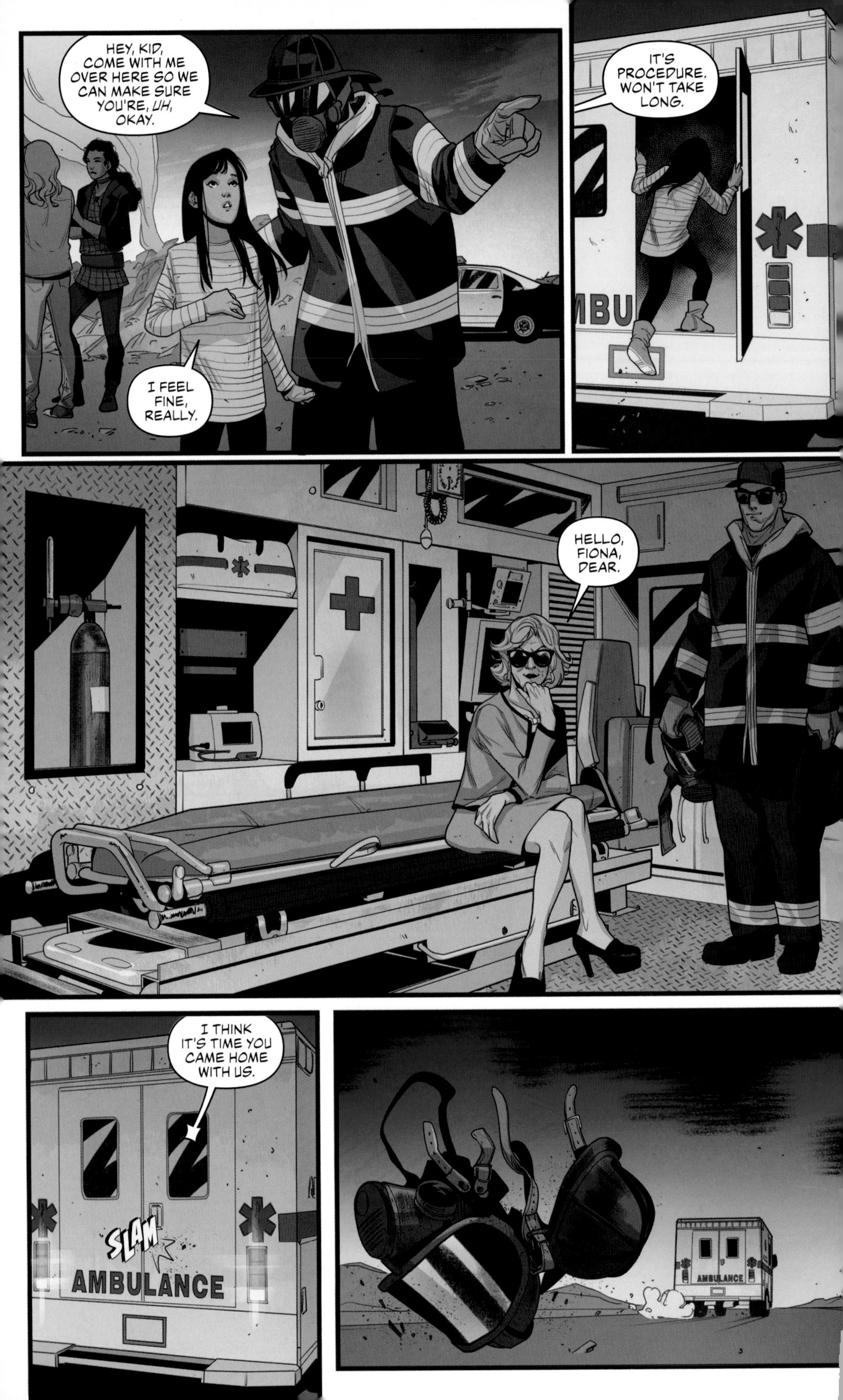

HEY, KID, COME WITH ME OVER HERE SO WE CAN MAKE SURE YOU'RE, *UH,* OKAY.
I FEEL FINE, REALLY.
IT'S PROCEDURE. WON'T TAKE LONG.
MBU
HELLO, FIONA, DEAR.
I THINK IT'S TIME YOU CAME HOME WITH US.
SLAM
AMBULANCE
AMBULANCE

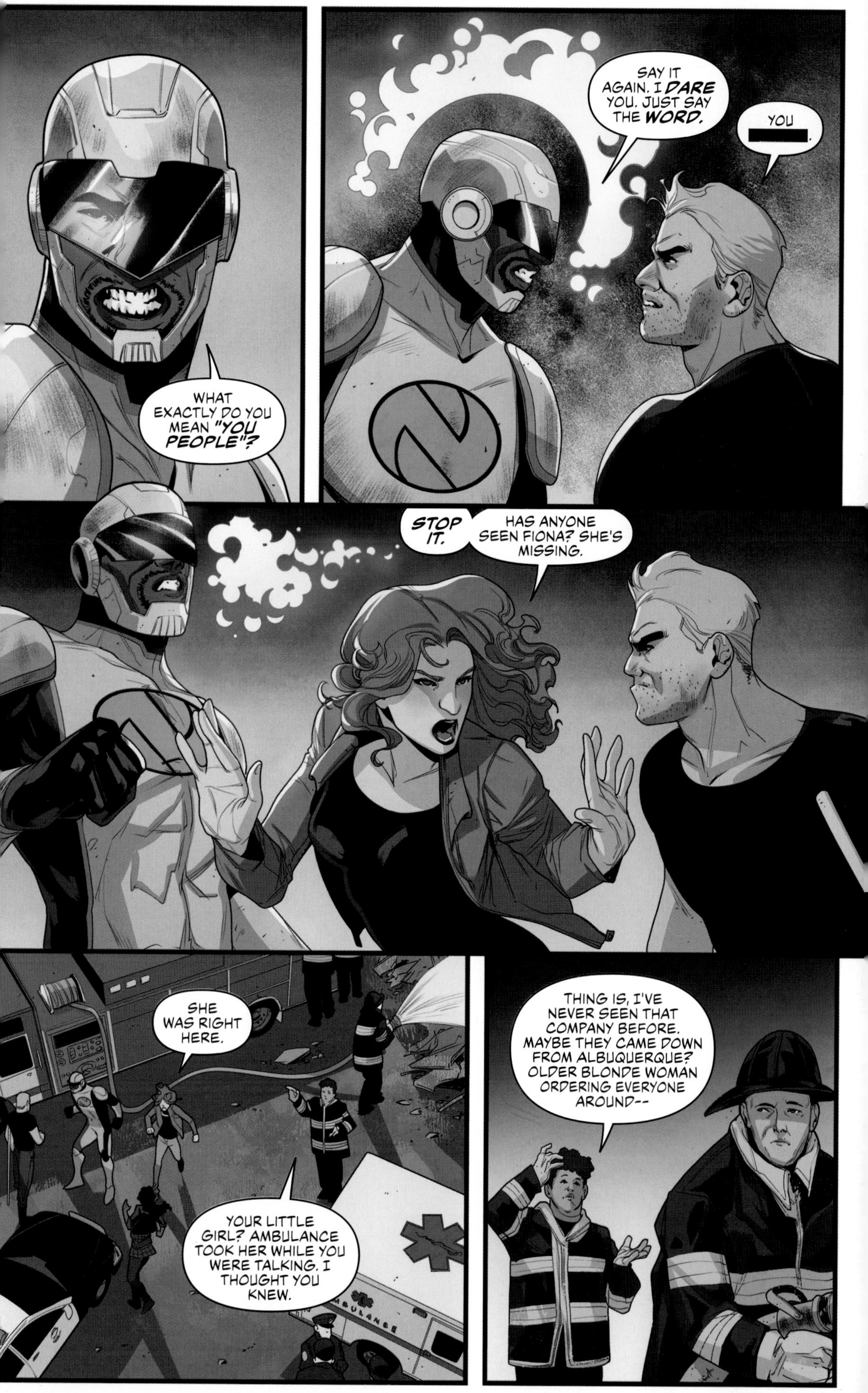
WHAT EXACTLY DO YOU MEAN "YOU PEOPLE"?
SAY IT AGAIN. I DARE YOU. JUST SAY THE WORD.
YOU [redacted].
STOP IT.
HAS ANYONE SEEN FIONA? SHE'S MISSING.
SHE WAS RIGHT HERE.
YOUR LITTLE GIRL? AMBULANCE TOOK HER WHILE YOU WERE TALKING. I THOUGHT YOU KNEW.
THING IS, I'VE NEVER SEEN THAT COMPANY BEFORE. MAYBE THEY CAME DOWN FROM ALBUQUERQUE? OLDER BLONDE WOMAN ORDERING EVERYONE AROUND--

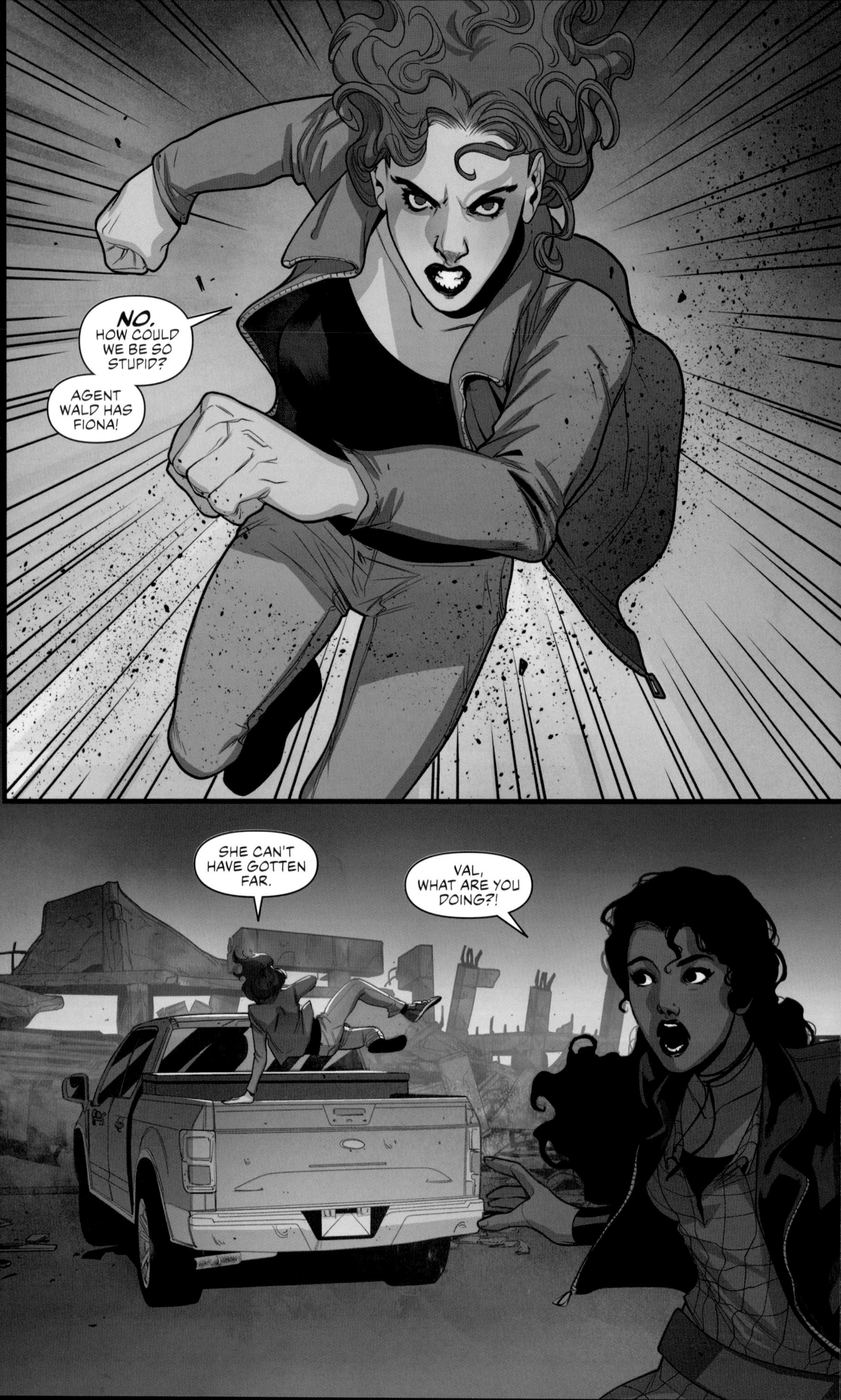
NO. HOW COULD WE BE SO STUPID?
AGENT WALD HAS FIONA!
SHE CAN'T HAVE GOTTEN FAR.
VAL, WHAT ARE YOU DOING?!

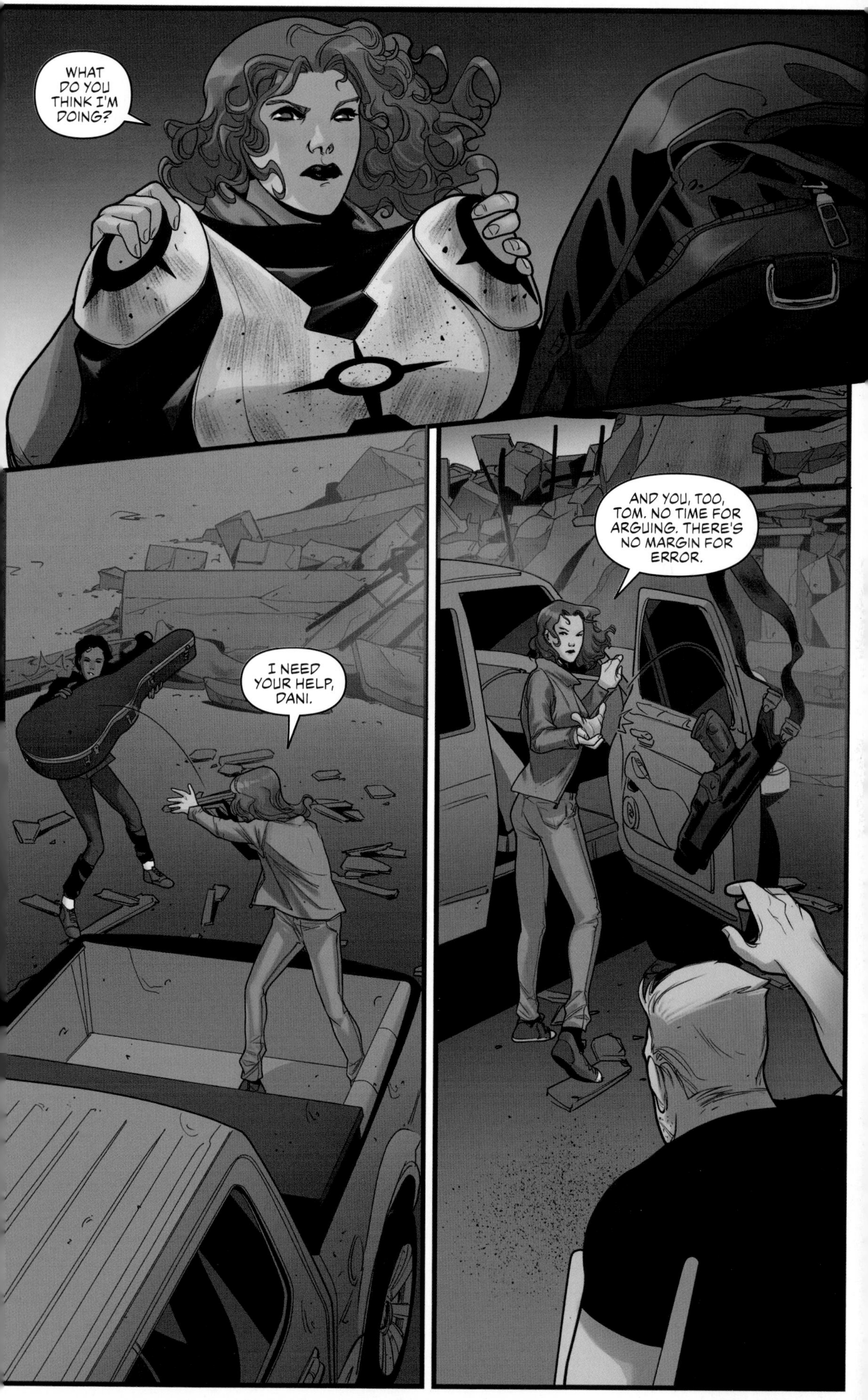
WHAT DO YOU THINK I'M DOING?
I NEED YOUR HELP, DANI.
AND YOU, TOO, TOM. NO TIME FOR ARGUING. THERE'S NO MARGIN FOR ERROR.

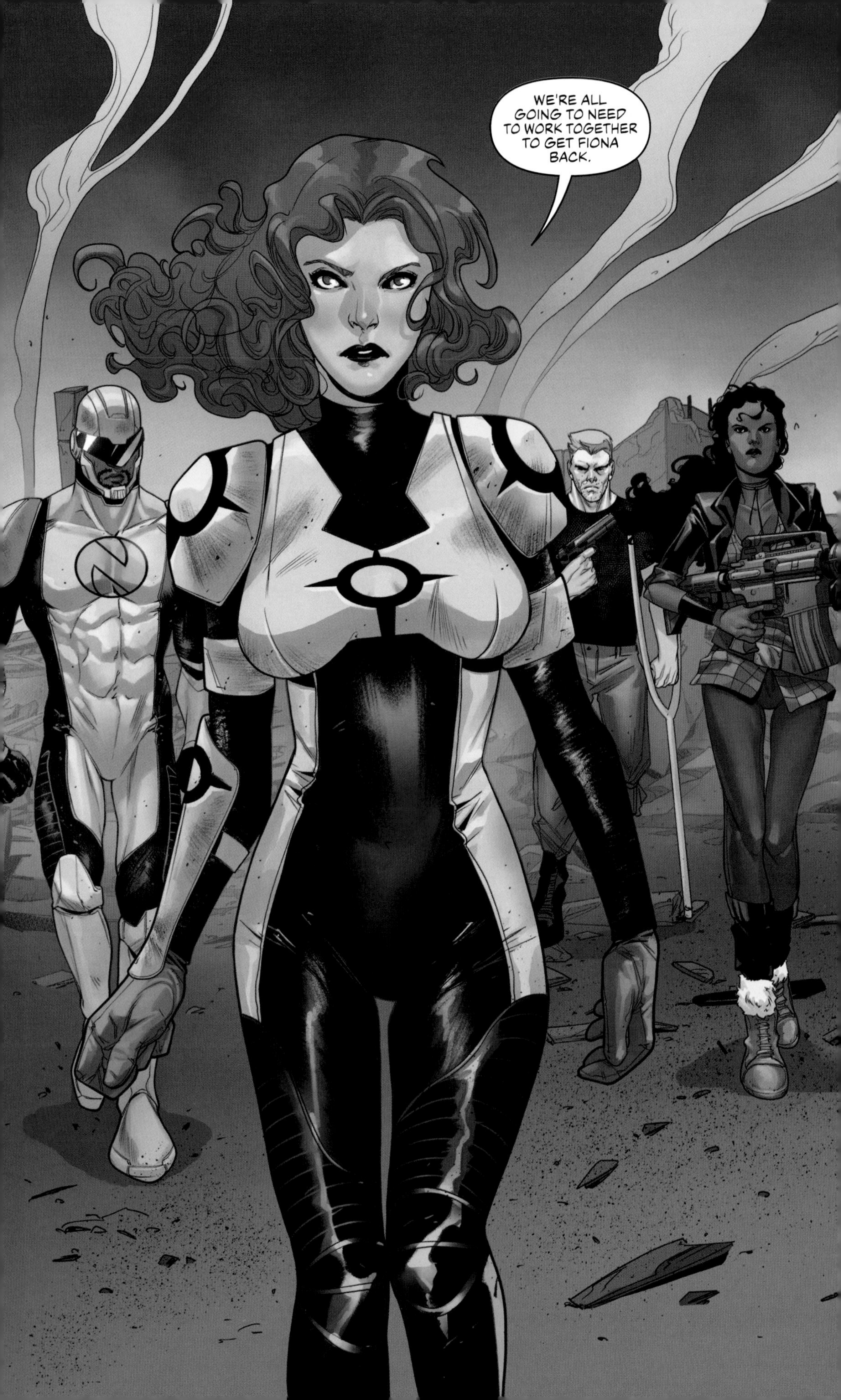
WE'RE ALL GOING TO NEED TO WORK TOGETHER TO GET FIONA BACK.

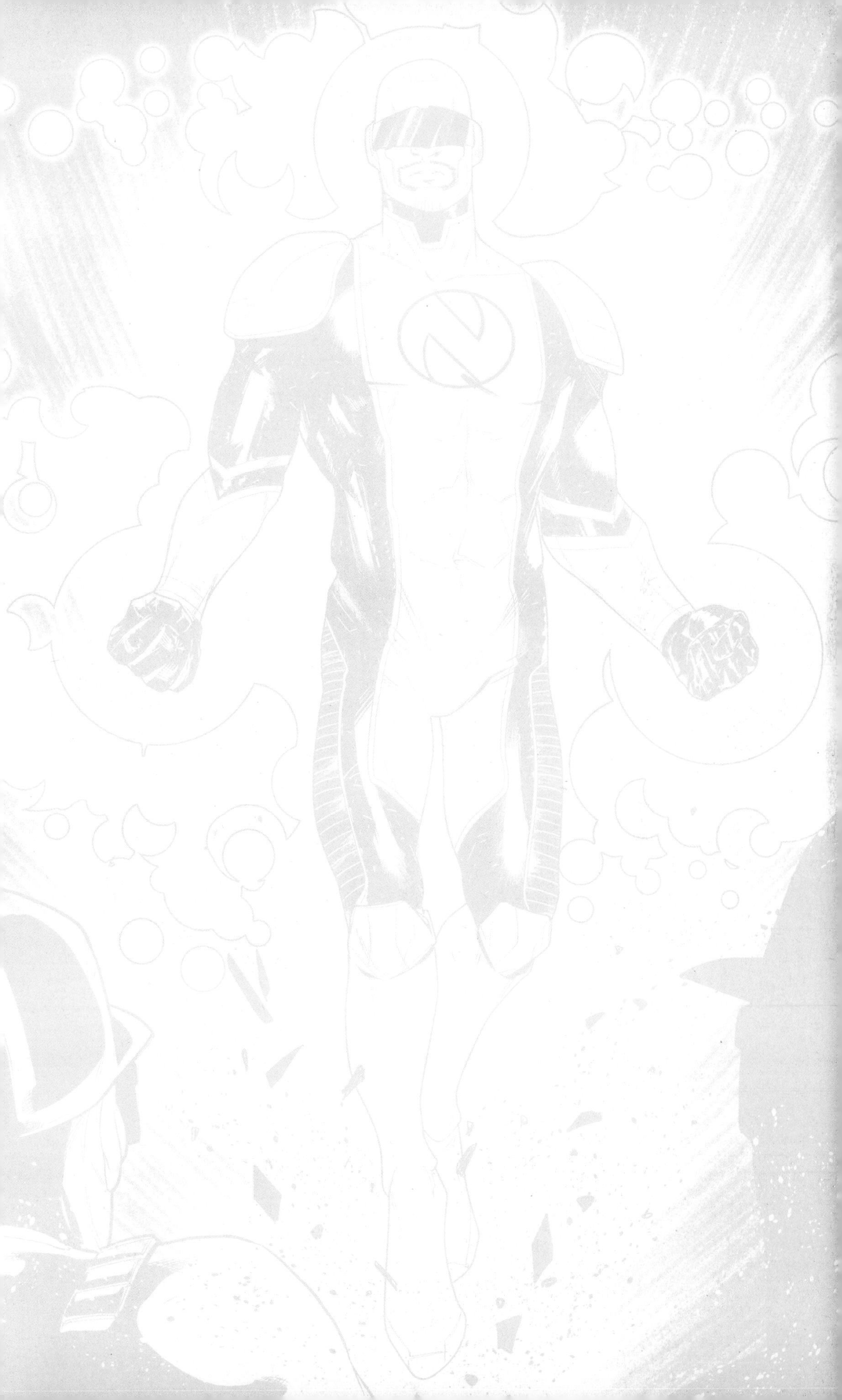

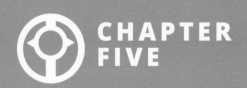

CHAPTER FIVE

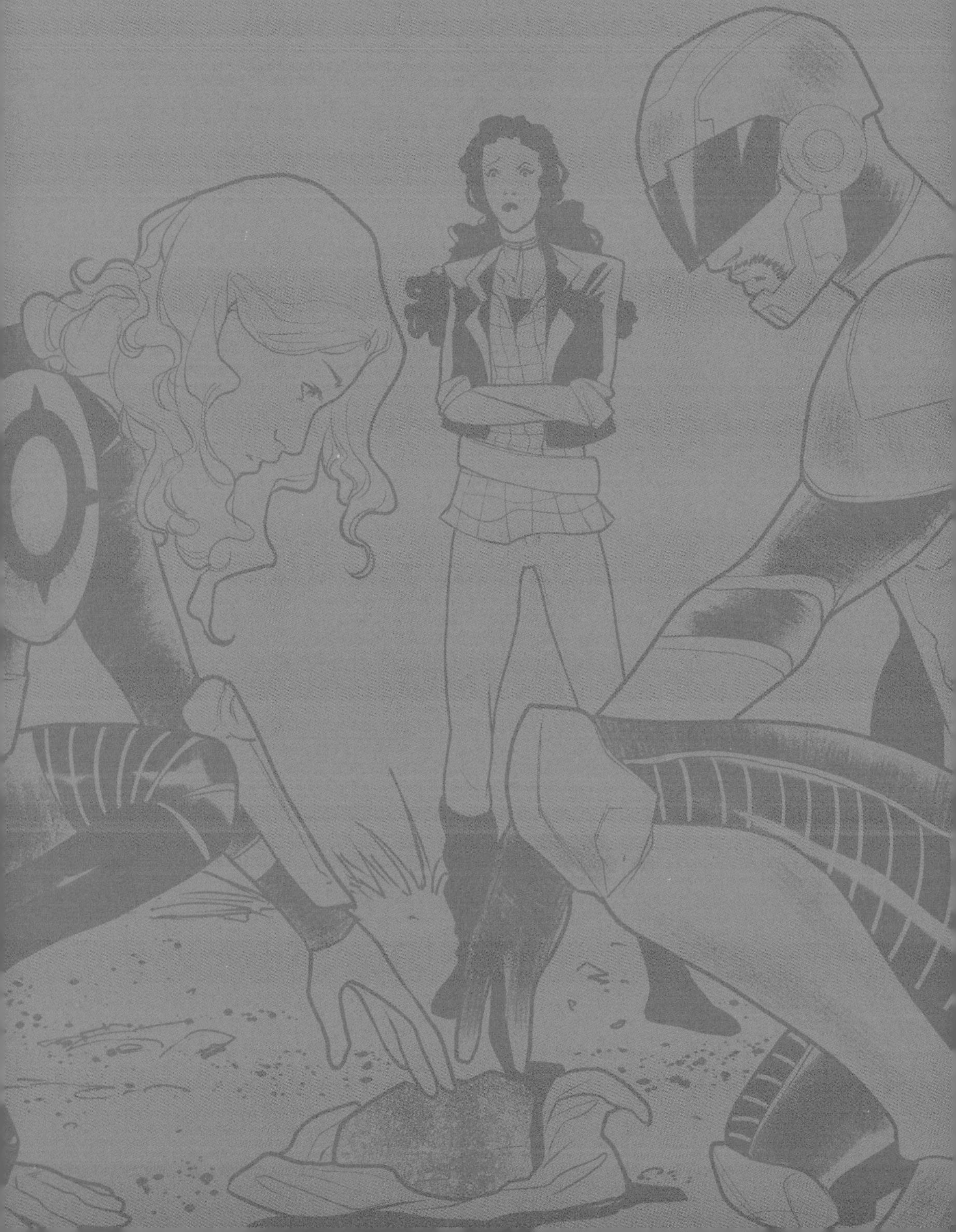

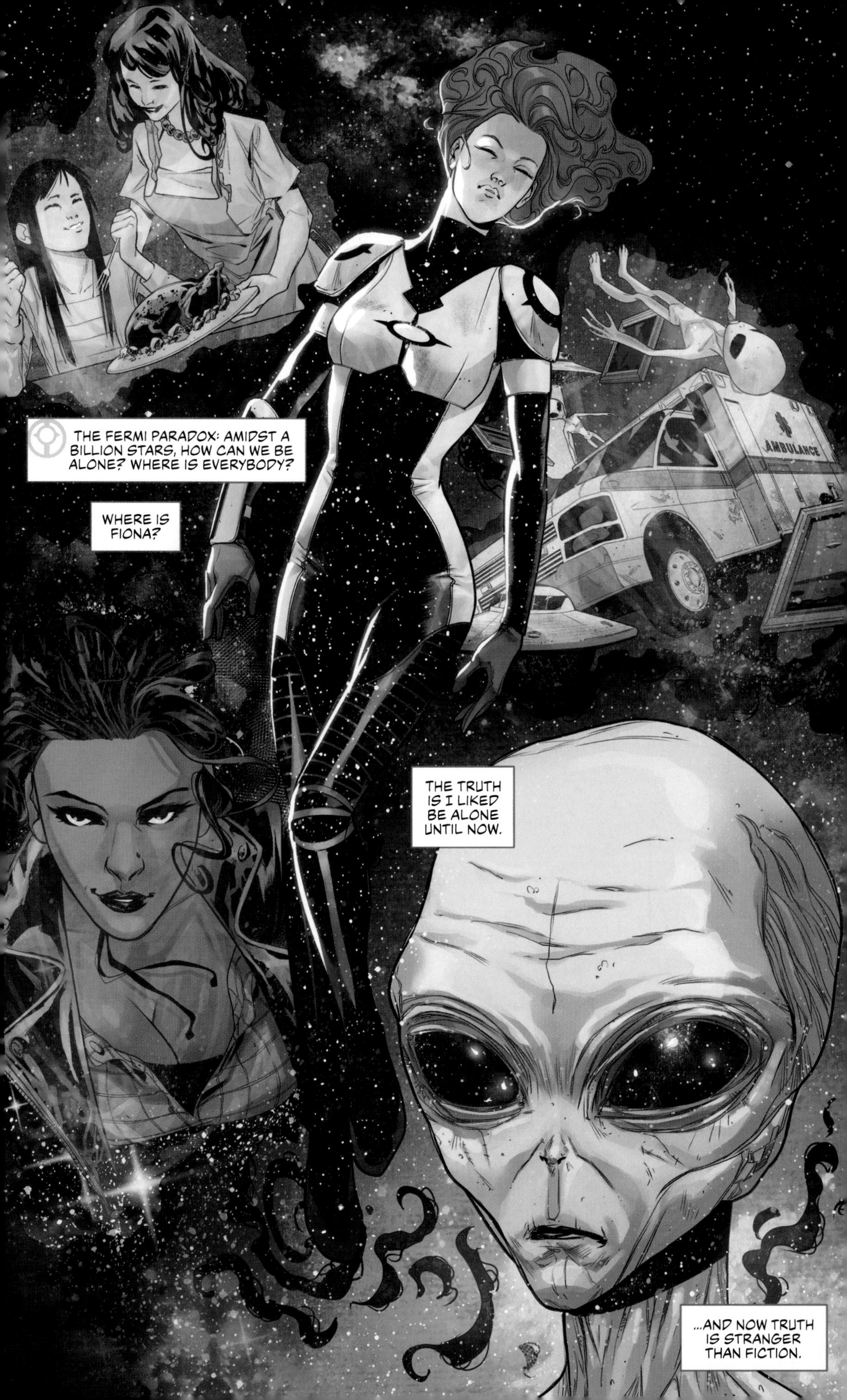
THE FERMI PARADOX: AMIDST A BILLION STARS, HOW CAN WE BE ALONE? WHERE IS EVERYBODY?
WHERE IS FIONA?
THE TRUTH IS I LIKED BE ALONE UNTIL NOW.
...AND NOW TRUTH IS STRANGER THAN FICTION.
AMBULANCE

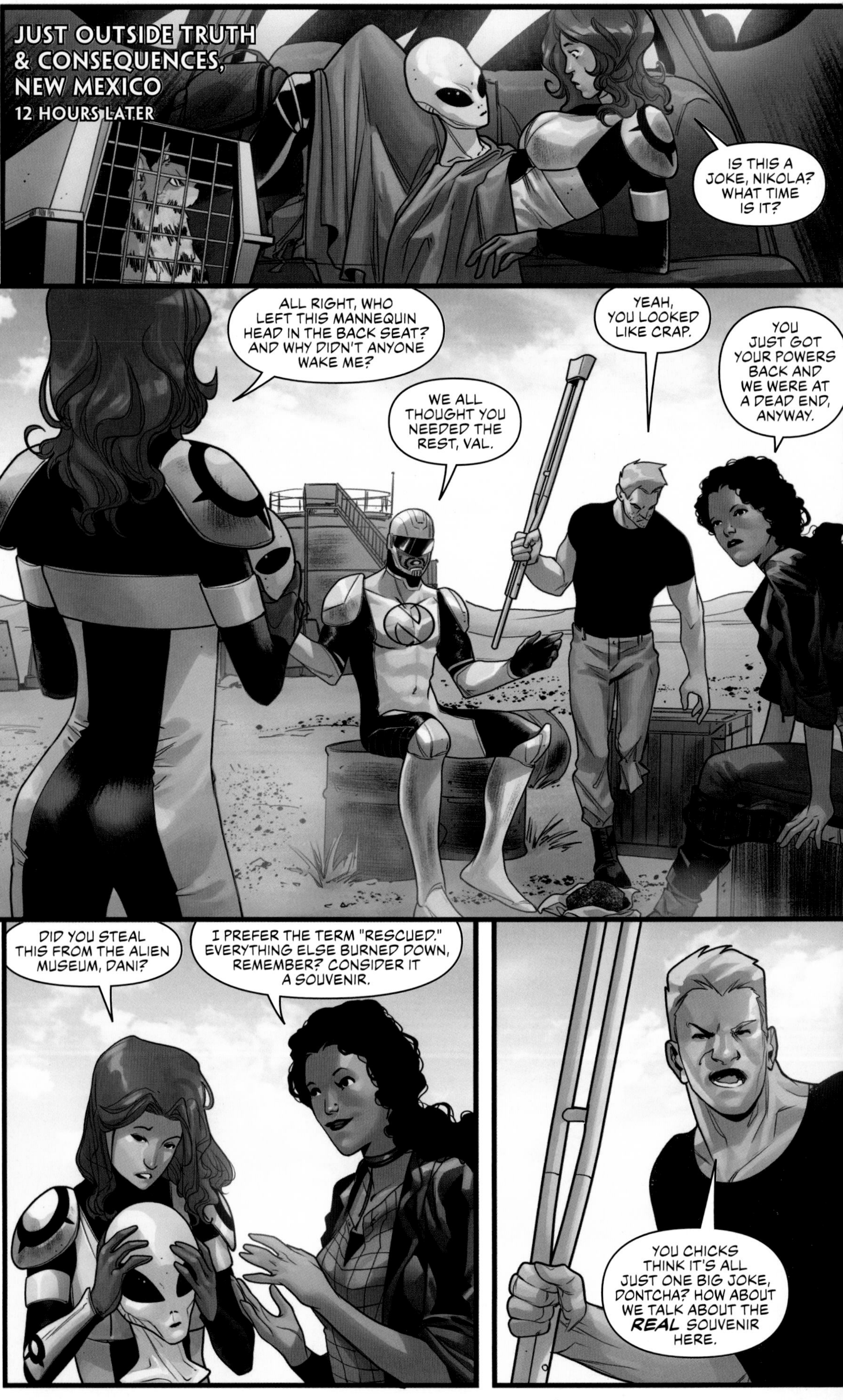
JUST OUTSIDE TRUTH & CONSEQUENCES, NEW MEXICO
12 HOURS LATER
IS THIS A JOKE, NIKOLA? WHAT TIME IS IT?
ALL RIGHT, WHO LEFT THIS MANNEQUIN HEAD IN THE BACK SEAT? AND WHY DIDN'T ANYONE WAKE ME?
WE ALL THOUGHT YOU NEEDED THE REST, VAL.
YEAH, YOU LOOKED LIKE CRAP.
YOU JUST GOT YOUR POWERS BACK AND WE WERE AT A DEAD END, ANYWAY.
DID YOU STEAL THIS FROM THE ALIEN MUSEUM, DANI?
I PREFER THE TERM "RESCUED." EVERYTHING ELSE BURNED DOWN, REMEMBER? CONSIDER IT A SOUVENIR.
YOU CHICKS THINK IT'S ALL JUST ONE BIG JOKE, DONTCHA? HOW ABOUT WE TALK ABOUT THE *REAL* SOUVENIR HERE.

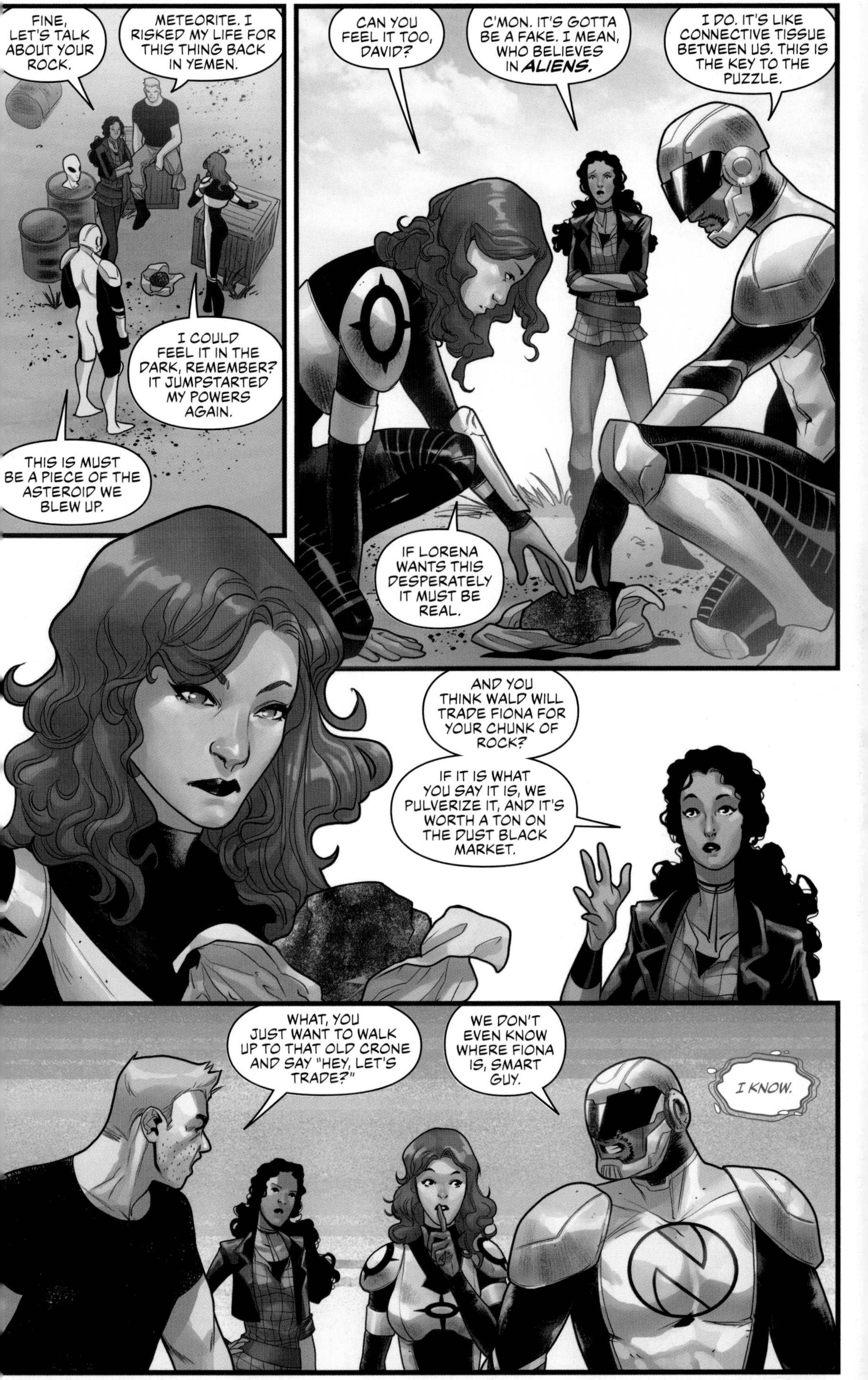
FINE, LET'S TALK ABOUT YOUR ROCK.
METEORITE. I RISKED MY LIFE FOR THIS THING BACK IN YEMEN.
I COULD FEEL IT IN THE DARK, REMEMBER? IT JUMPSTARTED MY POWERS AGAIN.
THIS IS MUST BE A PIECE OF THE ASTEROID WE BLEW UP.
CAN YOU FEEL IT TOO, DAVID?
C'MON. IT'S GOTTA BE A FAKE. I MEAN, WHO BELIEVES IN ALIENS.
I DO. IT'S LIKE CONNECTIVE TISSUE BETWEEN US. THIS IS THE KEY TO THE PUZZLE.
IF LORENA WANTS THIS DESPERATELY IT MUST BE REAL.
AND YOU THINK WALD WILL TRADE FIONA FOR YOUR CHUNK OF ROCK?
IF IT IS WHAT YOU SAY IT IS, WE PULVERIZE IT, AND IT'S WORTH A TON ON THE DUST BLACK MARKET.
WHAT, YOU JUST WANT TO WALK UP TO THAT OLD CRONE AND SAY "HEY, LET'S TRADE?"
WE DON'T EVEN KNOW WHERE FIONA IS, SMART GUY.
I KNOW.

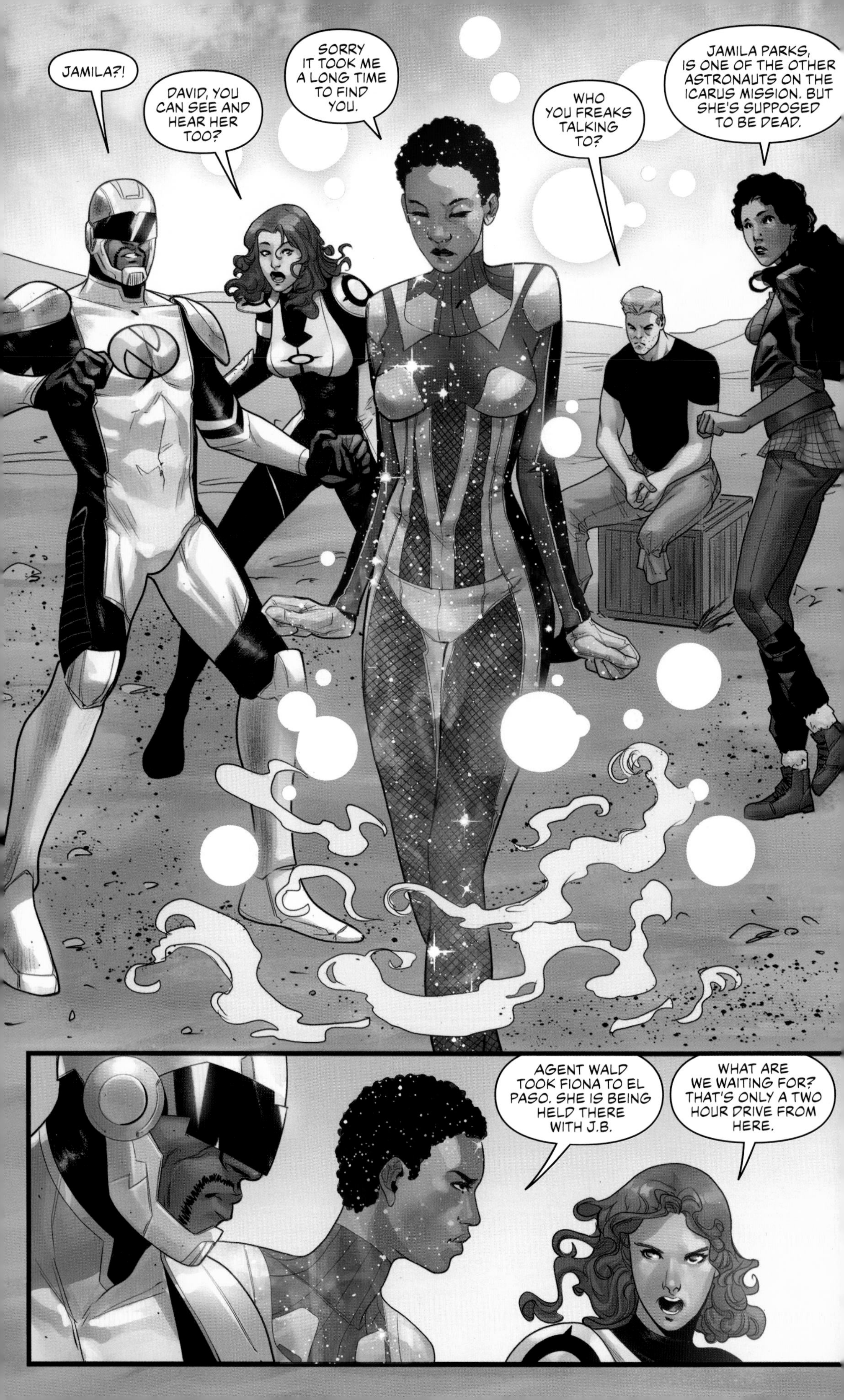
JAMILA?!
DAVID, YOU CAN SEE AND HEAR HER TOO?
SORRY IT TOOK ME A LONG TIME TO FIND YOU.
WHO YOU FREAKS TALKING TO?
JAMILA PARKS, IS ONE OF THE OTHER ASTRONAUTS ON THE ICARUS MISSION. BUT SHE'S SUPPOSED TO BE DEAD.
AGENT WALD TOOK FIONA TO EL PASO. SHE IS BEING HELD THERE WITH J.B.
WHAT ARE WE WAITING FOR? THAT'S ONLY A TWO HOUR DRIVE FROM HERE.

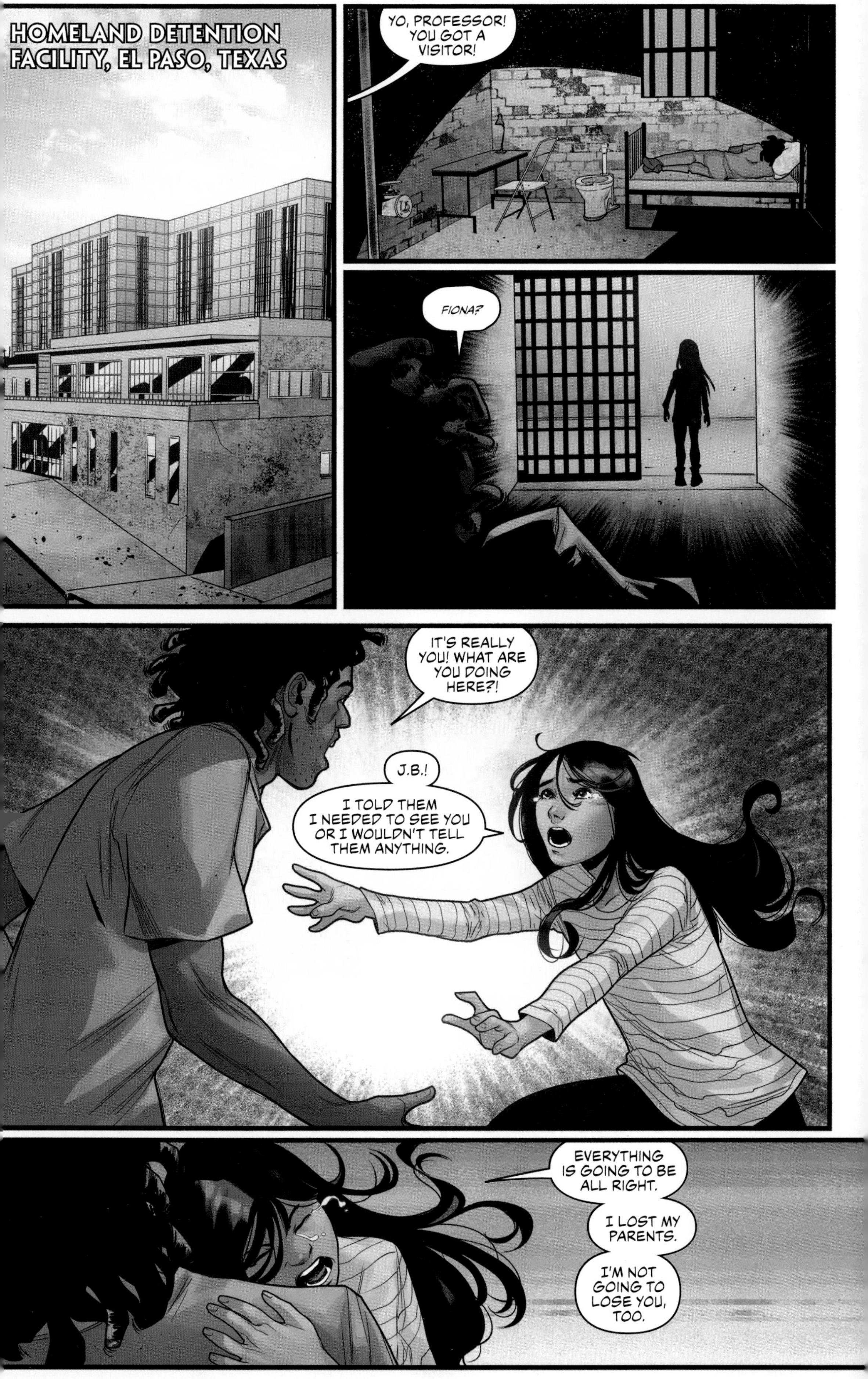
HOMELAND DETENTION FACILITY, EL PASO, TEXAS
YO, PROFESSOR! YOU GOT A VISITOR!
FIONA?
IT'S REALLY YOU! WHAT ARE YOU DOING HERE?!
J.B.!
I TOLD THEM I NEEDED TO SEE YOU OR I WOULDN'T TELL THEM ANYTHING.
EVERYTHING IS GOING TO BE ALL RIGHT.
I LOST MY PARENTS.
I'M NOT GOING TO LOSE YOU, TOO.

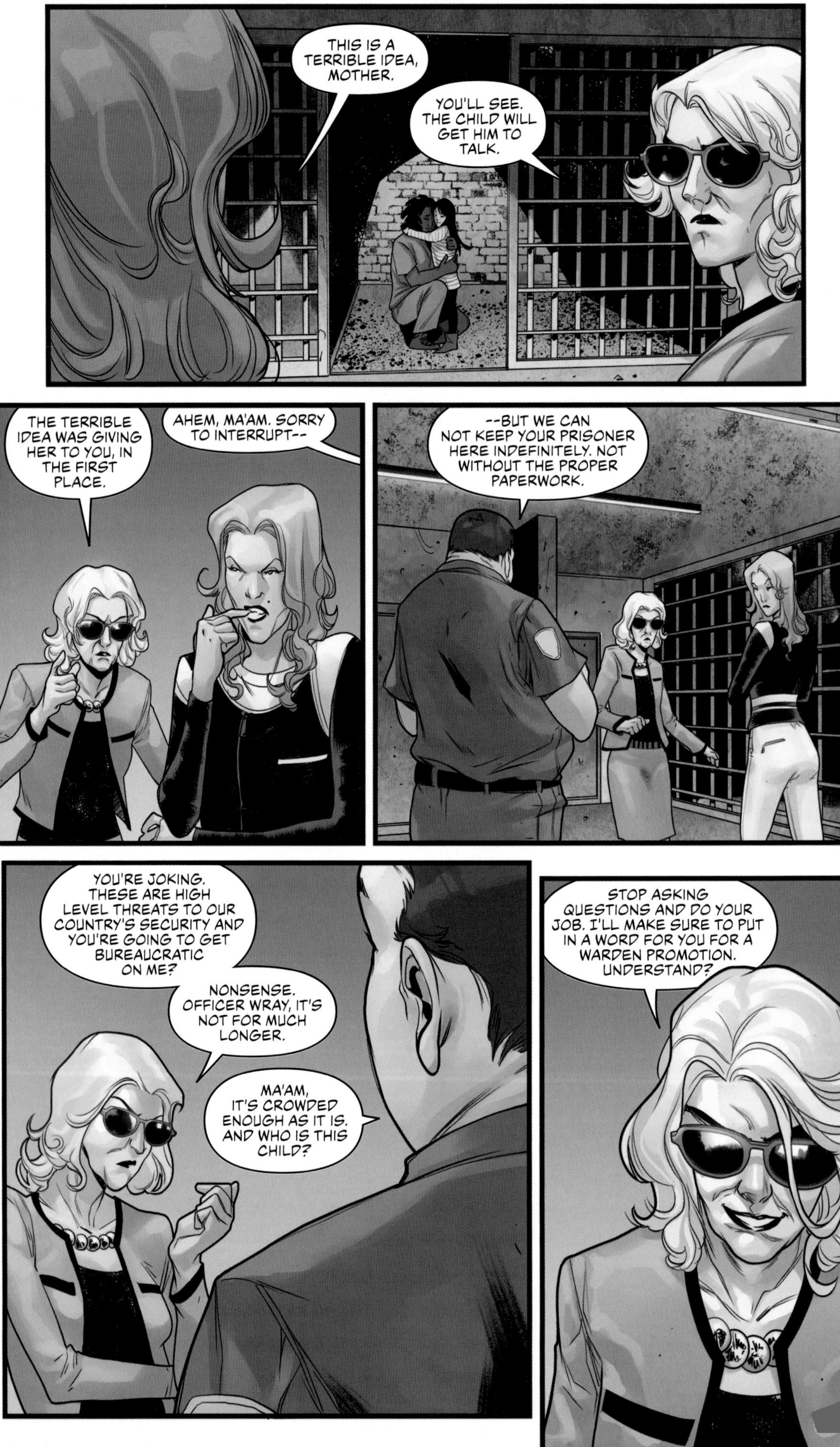
THIS IS A TERRIBLE IDEA, MOTHER.
YOU'LL SEE. THE CHILD WILL GET HIM TO TALK.
THE TERRIBLE IDEA WAS GIVING HER TO YOU, IN THE FIRST PLACE.
AHEM, MA'AM. SORRY TO INTERRUPT--
--BUT WE CAN NOT KEEP YOUR PRISONER HERE INDEFINITELY. NOT WITHOUT THE PROPER PAPERWORK.
YOU'RE JOKING. THESE ARE HIGH LEVEL THREATS TO OUR COUNTRY'S SECURITY AND YOU'RE GOING TO GET BUREAUCRATIC ON ME?
NONSENSE. OFFICER WRAY, IT'S NOT FOR MUCH LONGER.
MA'AM, IT'S CROWDED ENOUGH AS IT IS. AND WHO IS THIS CHILD?
STOP ASKING QUESTIONS AND DO YOUR JOB. I'LL MAKE SURE TO PUT IN A WORD FOR YOU FOR A WARDEN PROMOTION. UNDERSTAND?

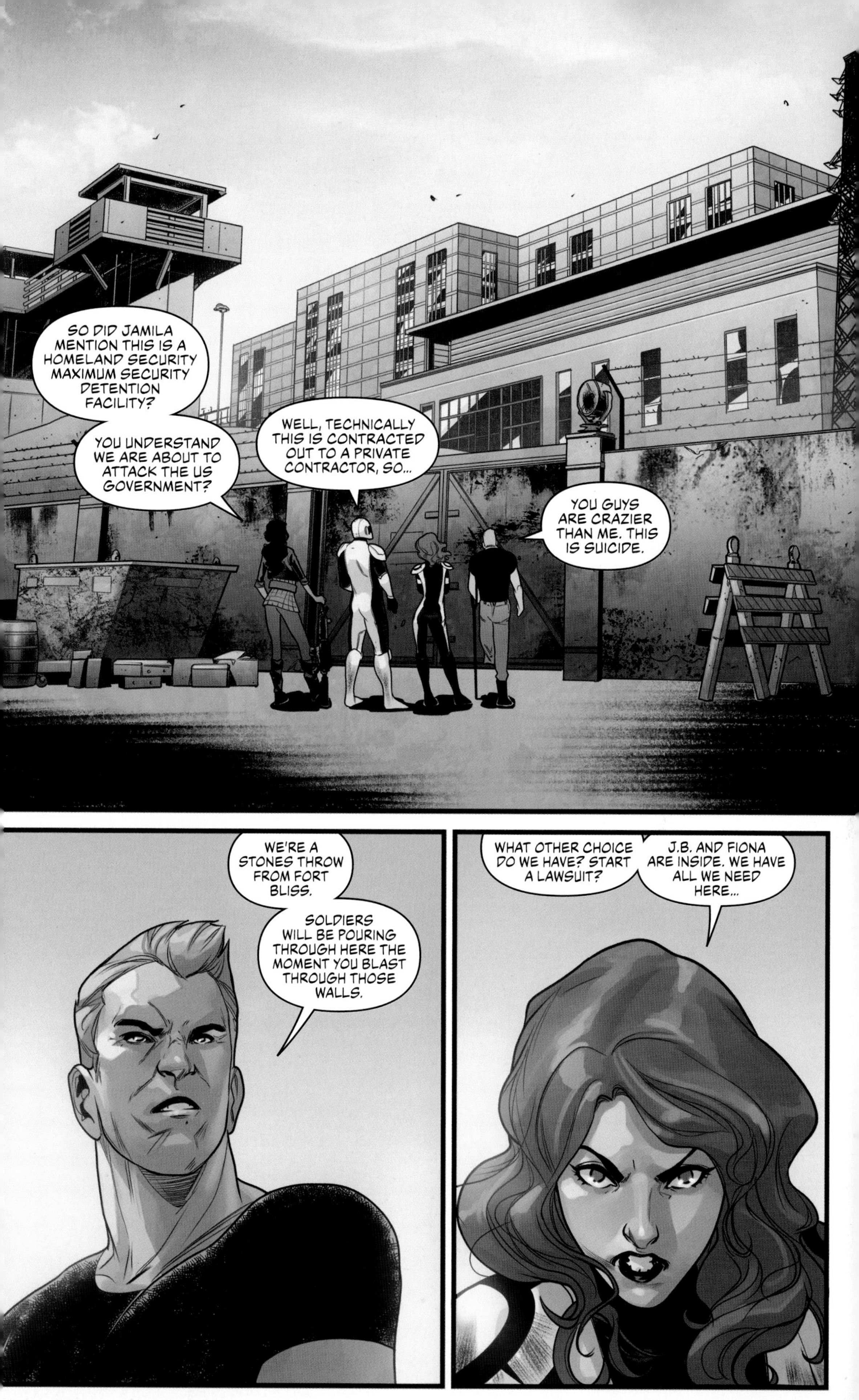
SO DID JAMILA MENTION THIS IS A HOMELAND SECURITY MAXIMUM SECURITY DETENTION FACILITY?
YOU UNDERSTAND WE ARE ABOUT TO ATTACK THE US GOVERNMENT?
WELL, TECHNICALLY THIS IS CONTRACTED OUT TO A PRIVATE CONTRACTOR, SO...
YOU GUYS ARE CRAZIER THAN ME. THIS IS SUICIDE.
WE'RE A STONES THROW FROM FORT BLISS.
SOLDIERS WILL BE POURING THROUGH HERE THE MOMENT YOU BLAST THROUGH THOSE WALLS.
WHAT OTHER CHOICE DO WE HAVE? START A LAWSUIT?
J.B. AND FIONA ARE INSIDE. WE HAVE ALL WE NEED HERE...

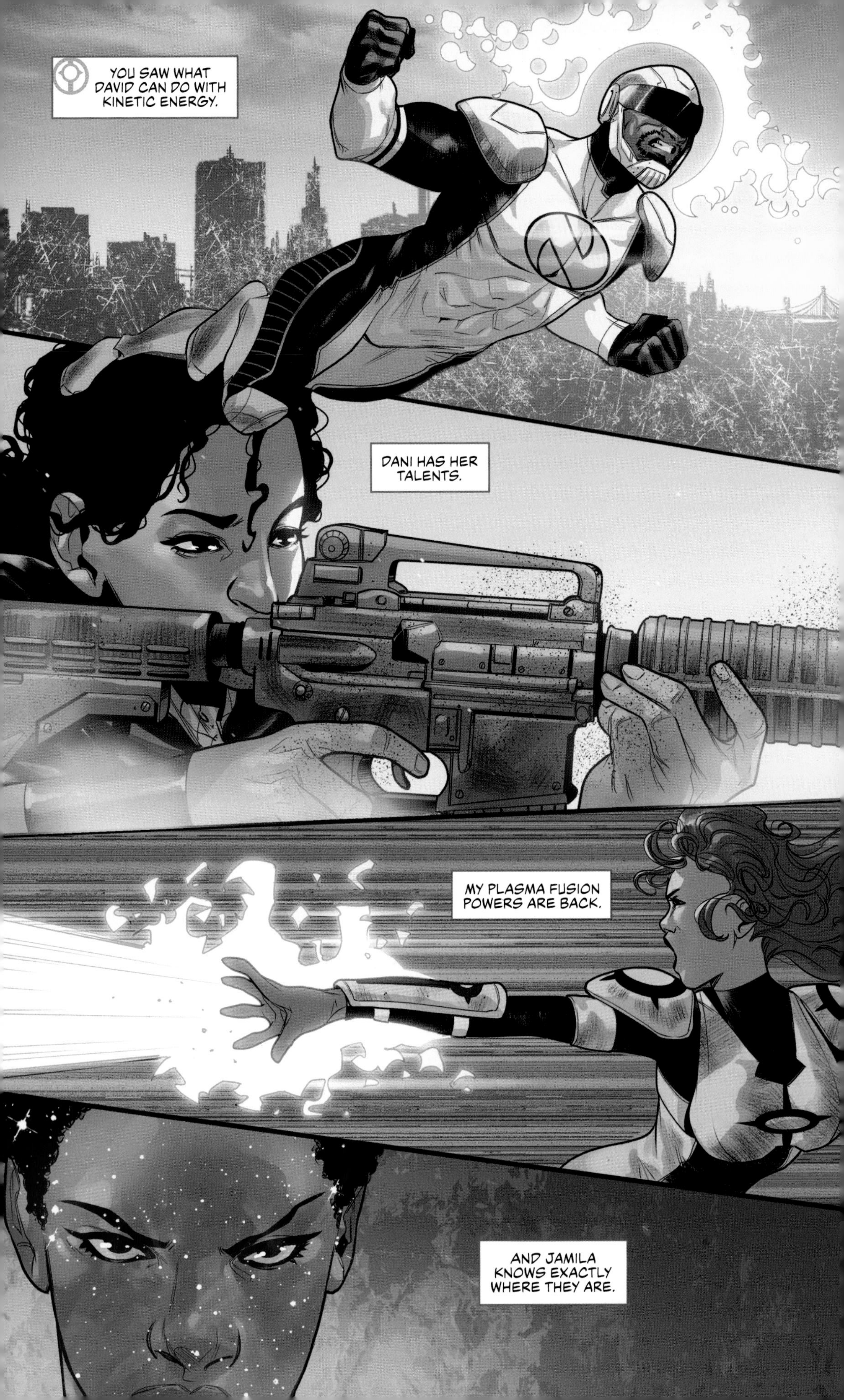
YOU SAW WHAT DAVID CAN DO WITH KINETIC ENERGY.
DANI HAS HER TALENTS.
MY PLASMA FUSION POWERS ARE BACK.
AND JAMILA KNOWS EXACTLY WHERE THEY ARE.

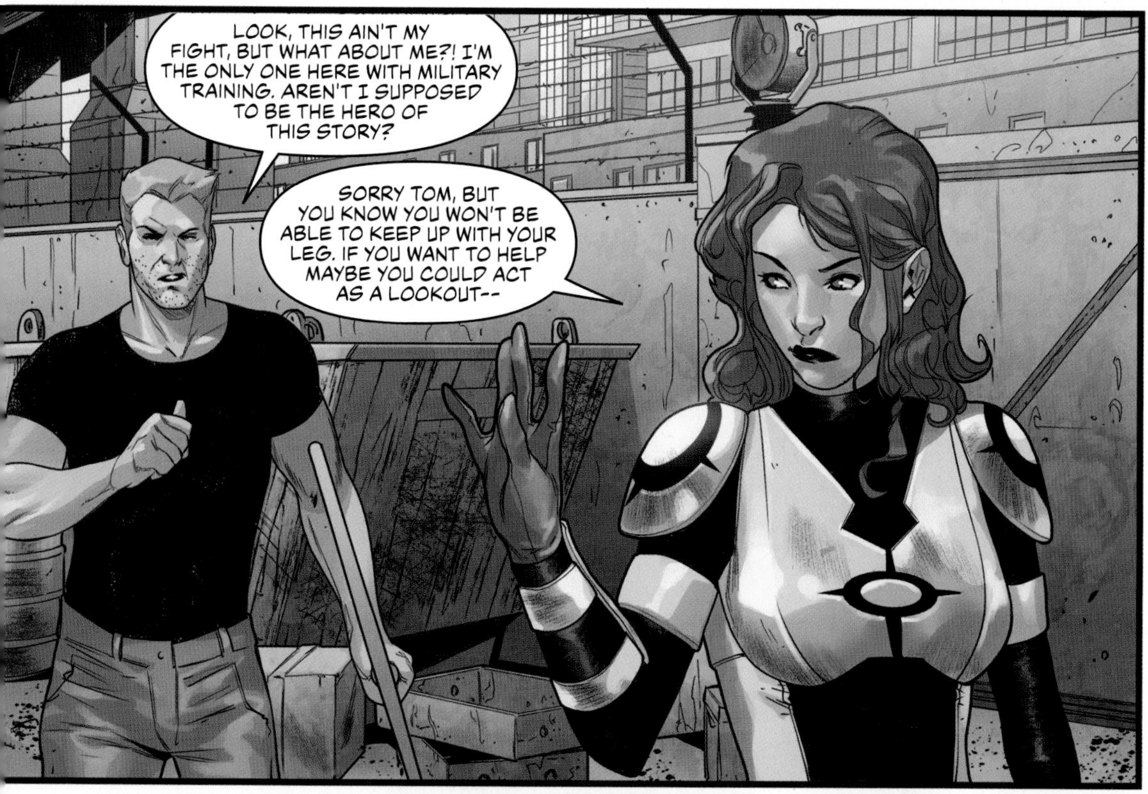
LOOK, THIS AIN'T MY FIGHT, BUT WHAT ABOUT ME?! I'M THE ONLY ONE HERE WITH MILITARY TRAINING. AREN'T I SUPPOSED TO BE THE HERO OF THIS STORY?
SORRY TOM, BUT YOU KNOW YOU WON'T BE ABLE TO KEEP UP WITH YOUR LEG. IF YOU WANT TO HELP MAYBE YOU COULD ACT AS A LOOKOUT--

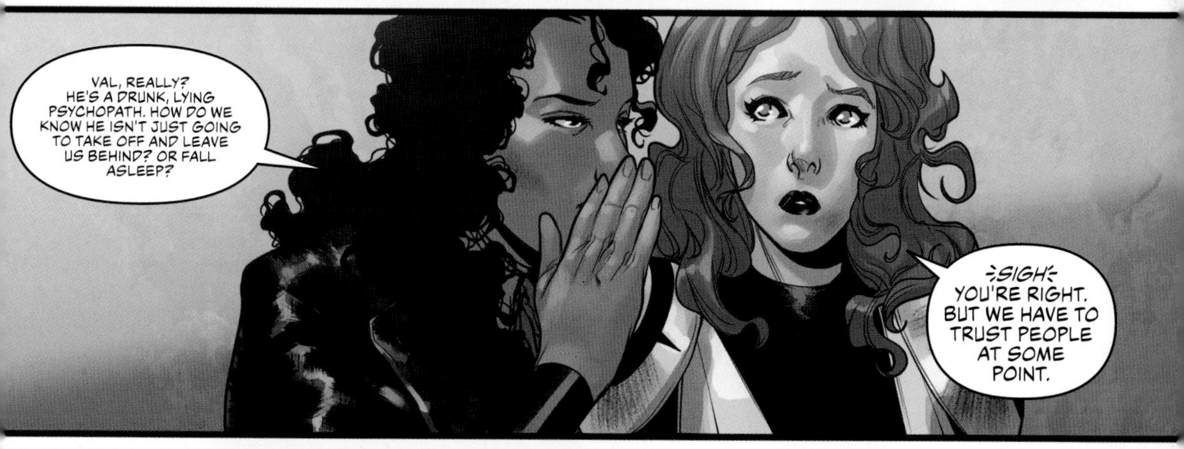
VAL, REALLY? HE'S A DRUNK, LYING PSYCHOPATH. HOW DO WE KNOW HE ISN'T JUST GOING TO TAKE OFF AND LEAVE US BEHIND? OR FALL ASLEEP?
SIGH
YOU'RE RIGHT. BUT WE HAVE TO TRUST PEOPLE AT SOME POINT.

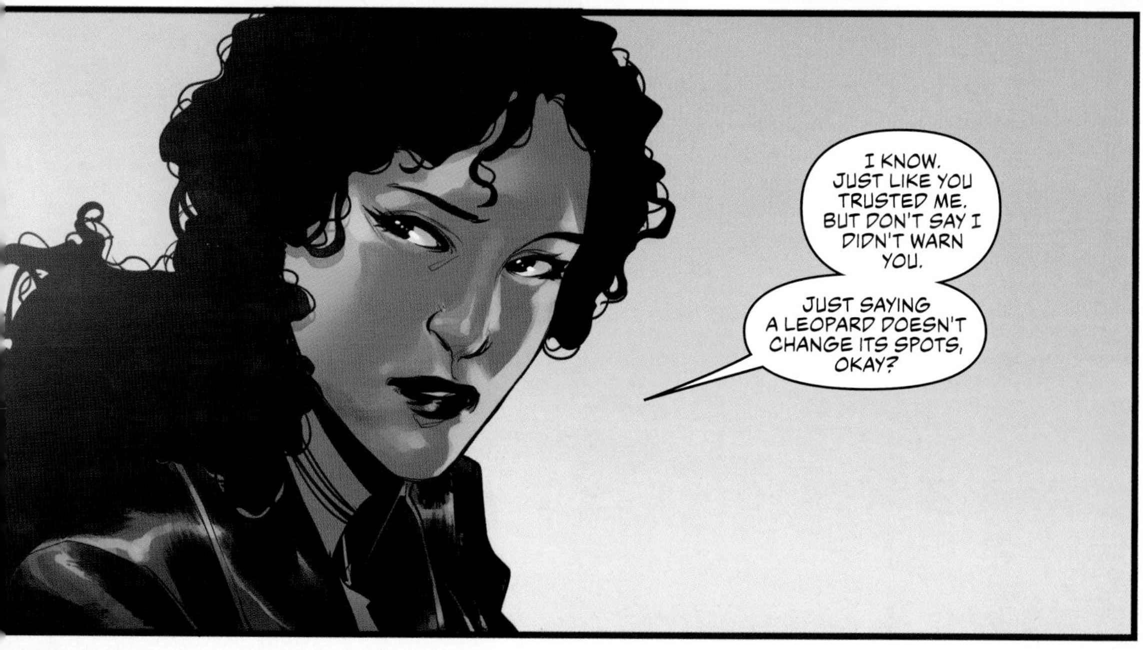
I KNOW. JUST LIKE YOU TRUSTED ME. BUT DON'T SAY I DIDN'T WARN YOU.
JUST SAYING A LEOPARD DOESN'T CHANGE ITS SPOTS, OKAY?

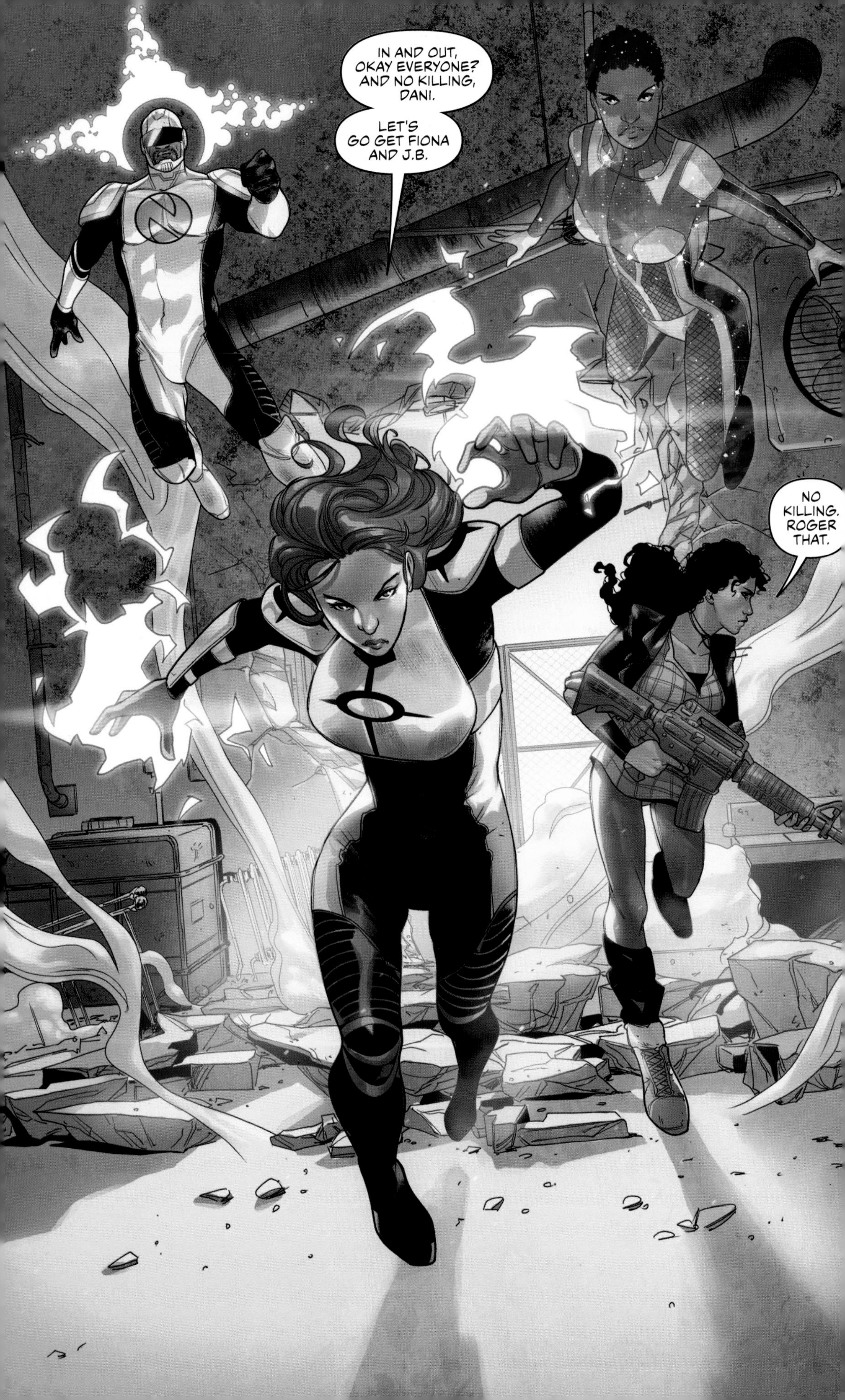
IN AND OUT, OKAY EVERYONE? AND NO KILLING, DANI.
LET'S GO GET FIONA AND J.B.
NO KILLING. ROGER THAT.

OKAY, BIG GUY. SLEEPY TIME.

ONE DOWN, THREE HUNDRED OR MORE TO GO.

≷HRKK≷

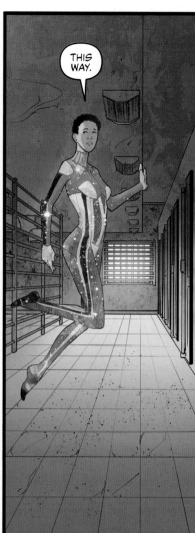

THIS WAY.

WE NEED TO GO UP.

WHAT'S WRONG, JAMILA?! YOU'RE FADING!

SOMETHING IS INTERFERING WITH MY SIGNAL. IT'S TAKING TOO MUCH ENERGY TO STAY WITH YOU. I'M LOSING MYSELF--

I'M SORRY! I CAN'T HELP YOU MORE--

JAMILA?! COME BACK! WE NEED YOU!

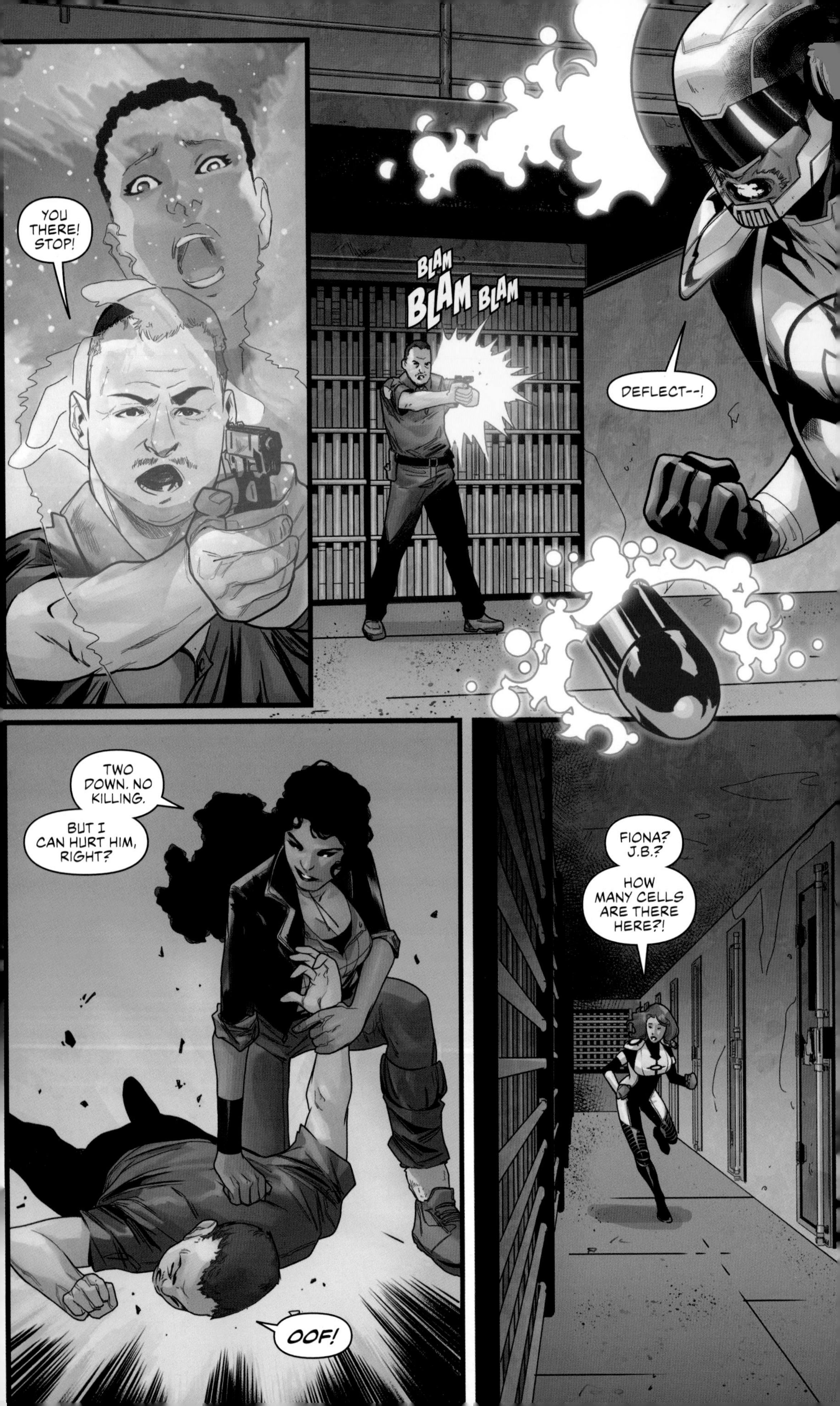

YOU THERE! STOP!
BLAM
BLAM BLAM
DEFLECT--!
TWO DOWN. NO KILLING.
BUT I CAN HURT HIM, RIGHT?
OOF!
FIONA? J.B.?
HOW MANY CELLS ARE THERE HERE?!

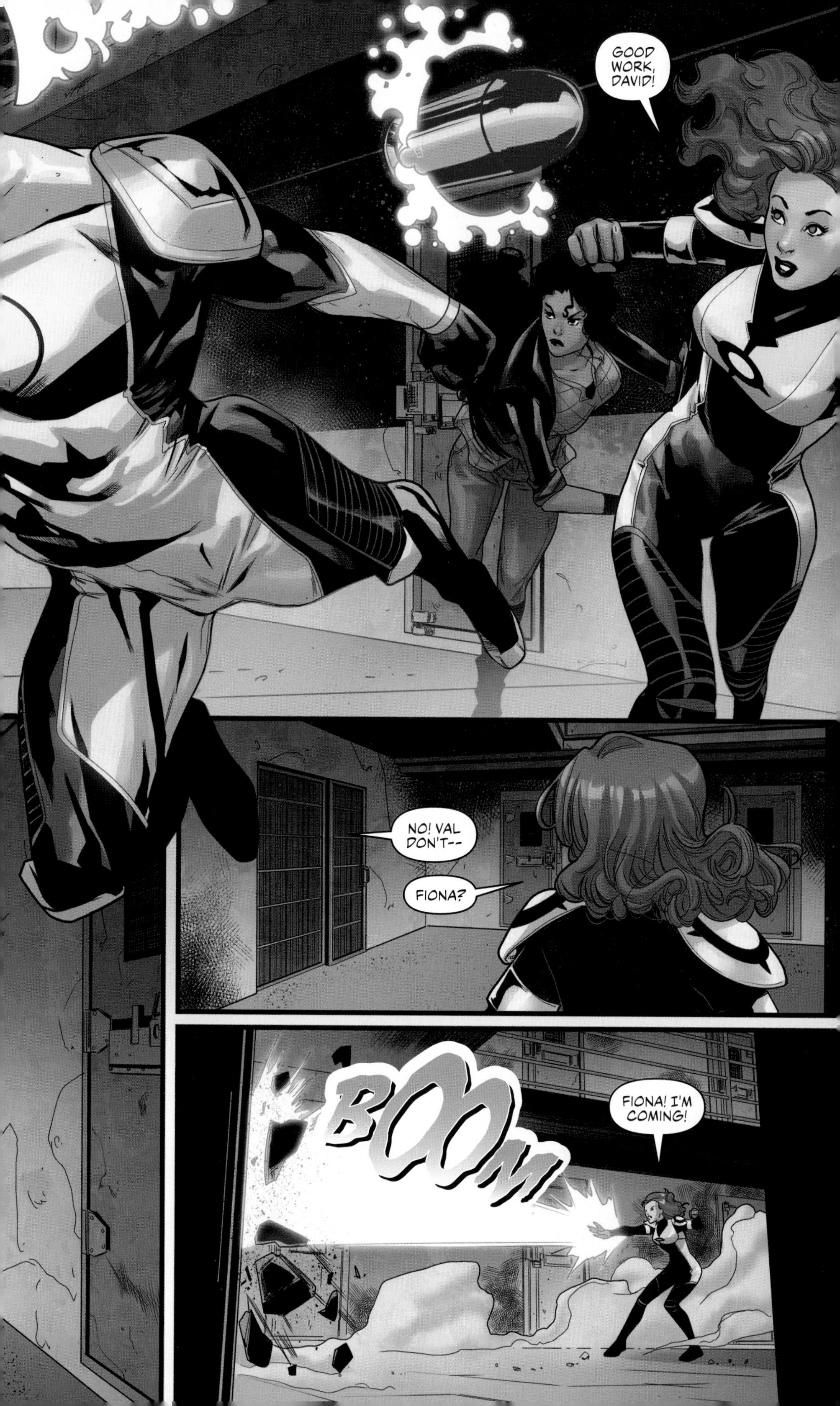
GOOD WORK, DAVID!
NO! VAL DON'T--
FIONA?
BOOM
FIONA! I'M COMING!

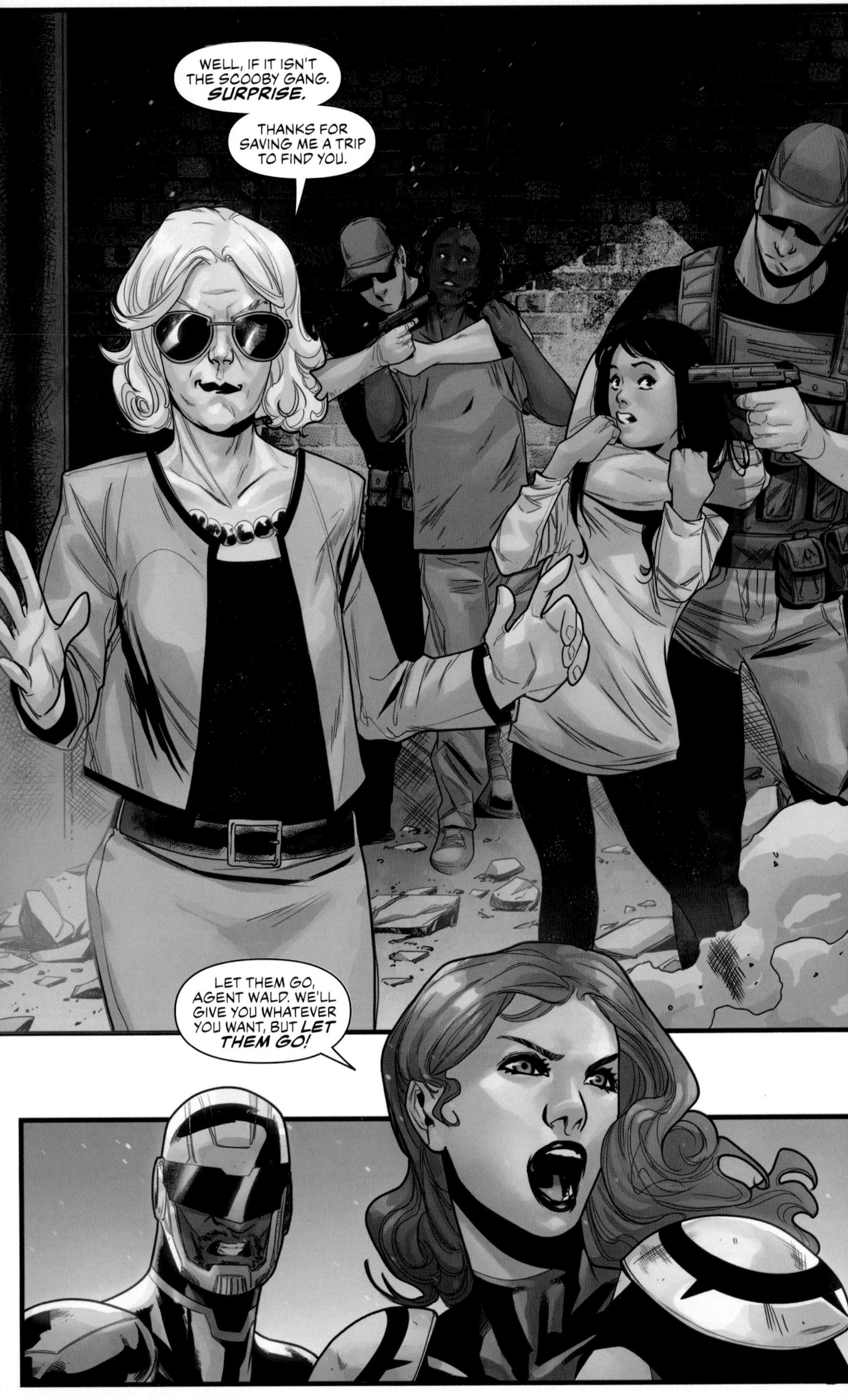
WELL, IF IT ISN'T THE SCOOBY GANG. SURPRISE.
THANKS FOR SAVING ME A TRIP TO FIND YOU.
LET THEM GO, AGENT WALD. WE'LL GIVE YOU WHATEVER YOU WANT, BUT LET THEM GO!

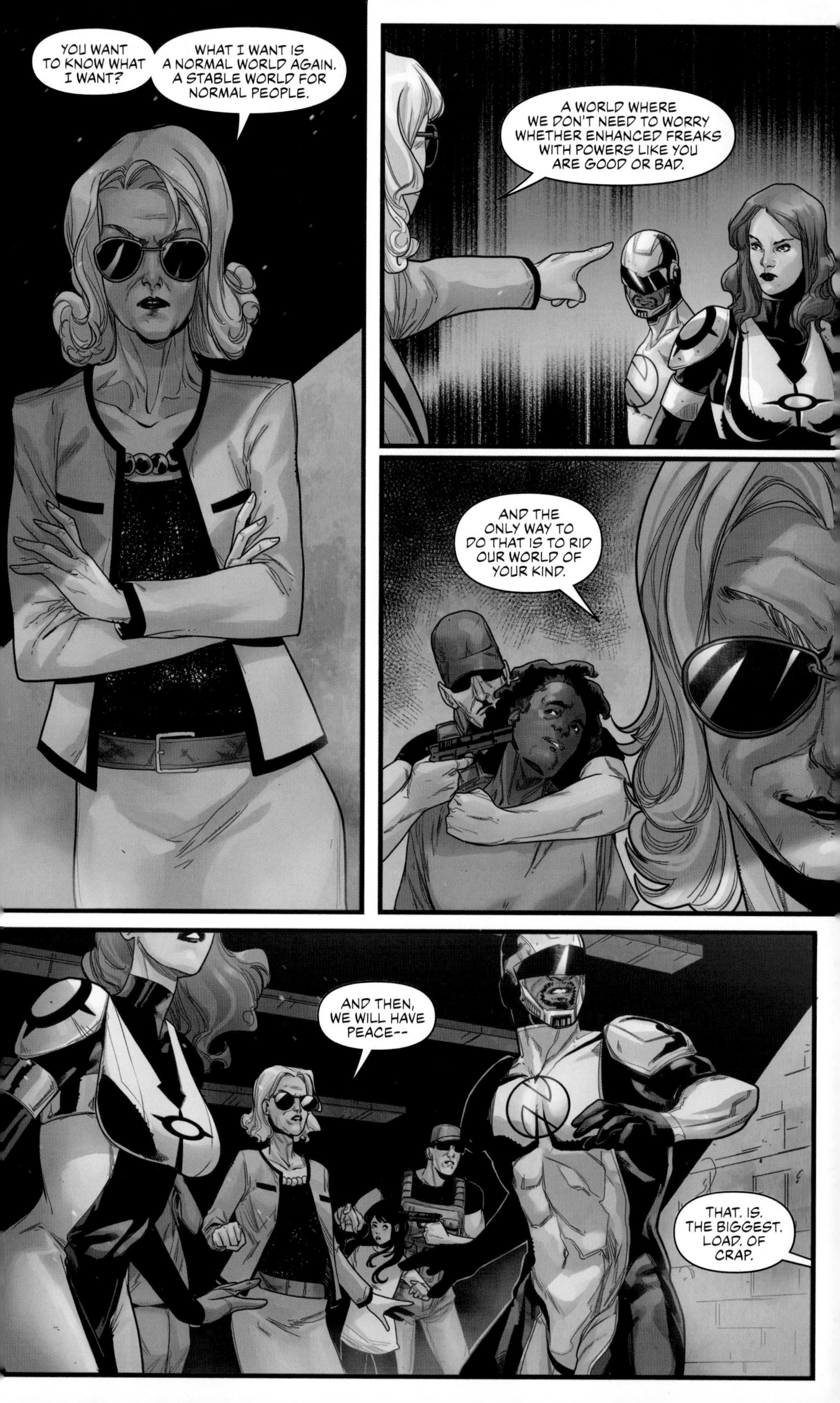

YOU WANT TO KNOW WHAT I WANT?
WHAT I WANT IS A NORMAL WORLD AGAIN. A STABLE WORLD FOR NORMAL PEOPLE.
A WORLD WHERE WE DON'T NEED TO WORRY WHETHER ENHANCED FREAKS WITH POWERS LIKE YOU ARE GOOD OR BAD.
AND THE ONLY WAY TO DO THAT IS TO RID OUR WORLD OF YOUR KIND.
AND THEN, WE WILL HAVE PEACE--
THAT. IS. THE BIGGEST. LOAD. OF CRAP.

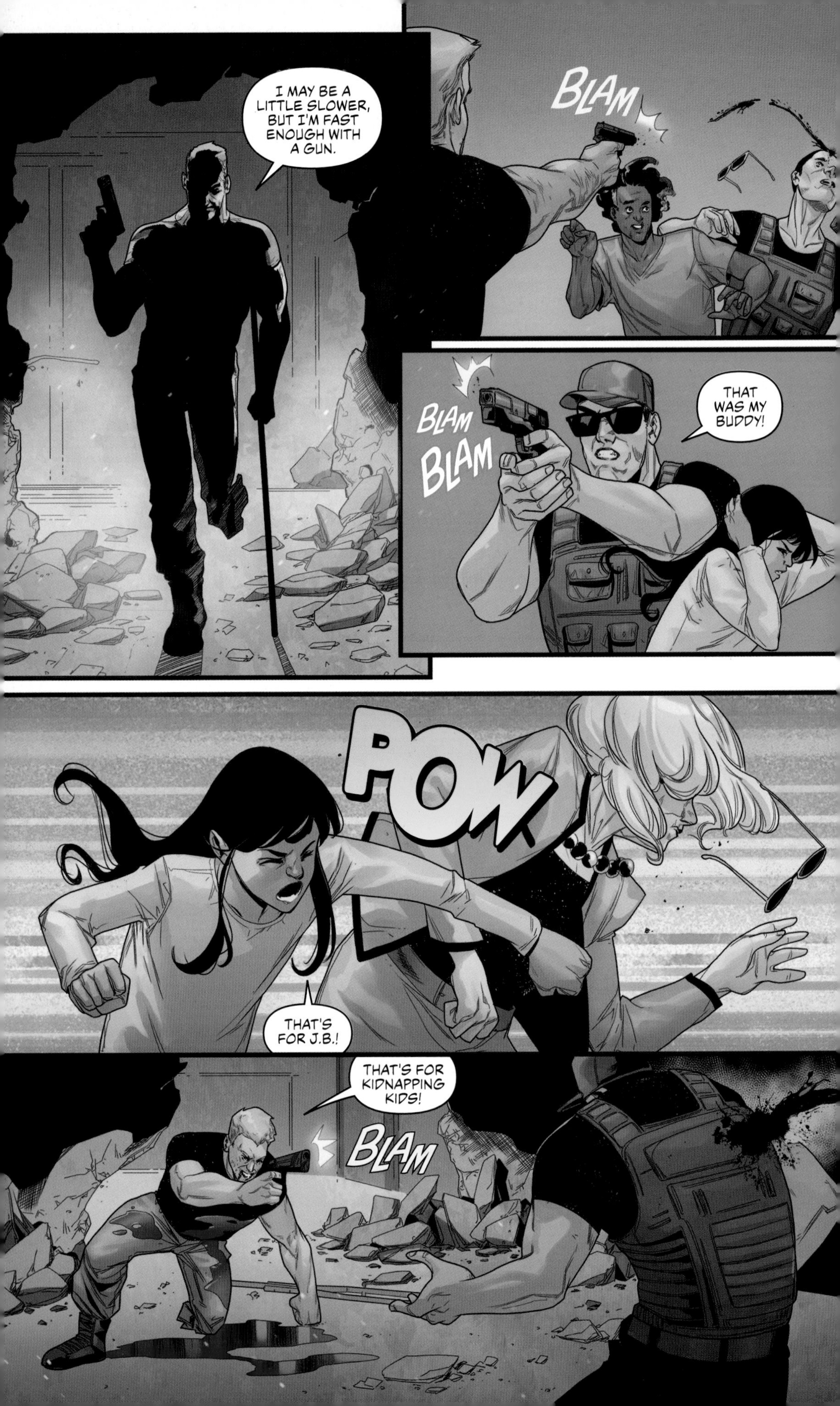
I MAY BE A LITTLE SLOWER, BUT I'M FAST ENOUGH WITH A GUN.
BLAM
BLAM
BLAM
THAT WAS MY BUDDY!
POW
THAT'S FOR J.B.!
THAT'S FOR KIDNAPPING KIDS!
BLAM

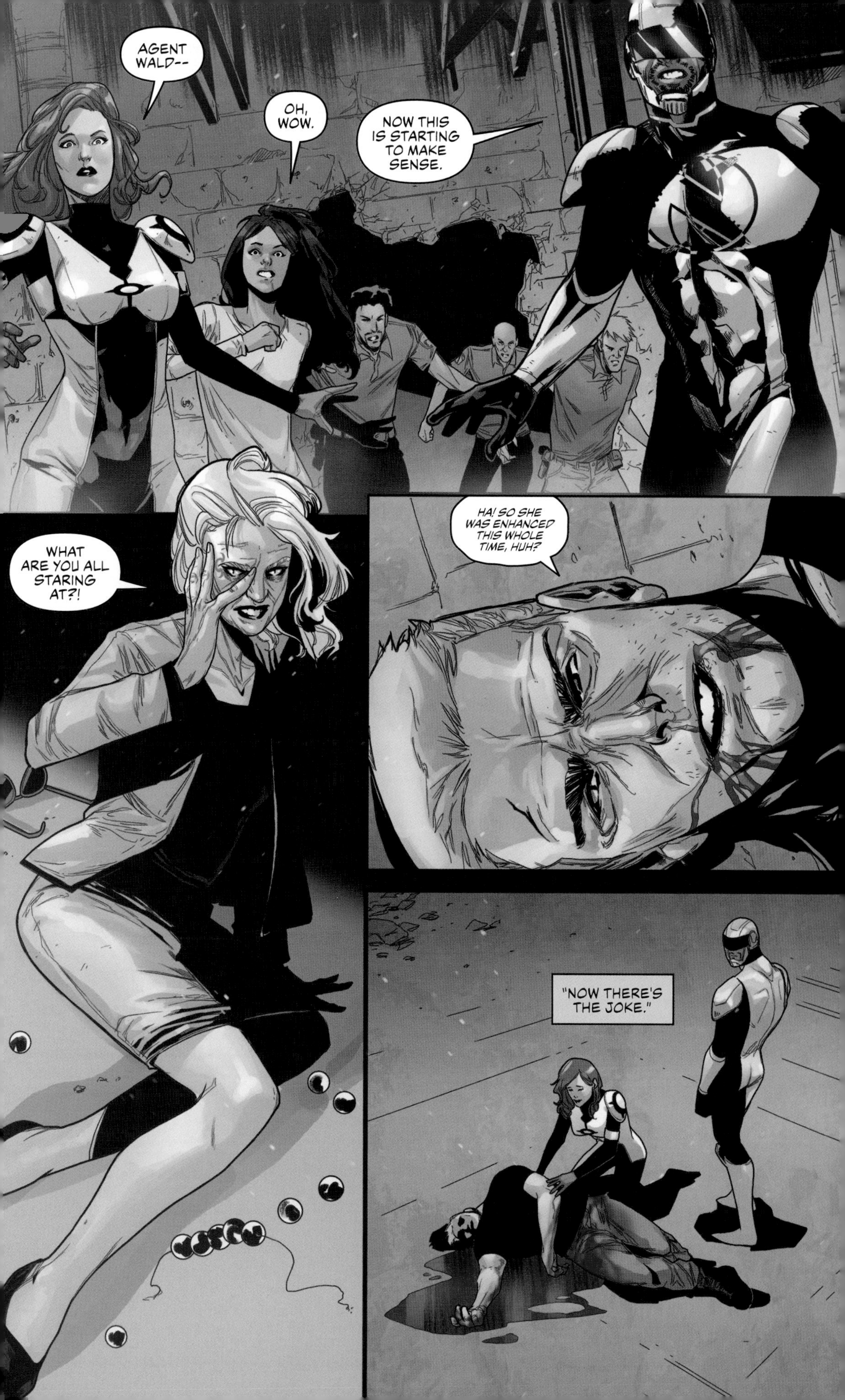
AGENT WALD--
OH, WOW.
NOW THIS IS STARTING TO MAKE SENSE.
WHAT ARE YOU ALL STARING AT?!
HA! SO SHE WAS ENHANCED THIS WHOLE TIME, HUH?
"NOW THERE'S THE JOKE."

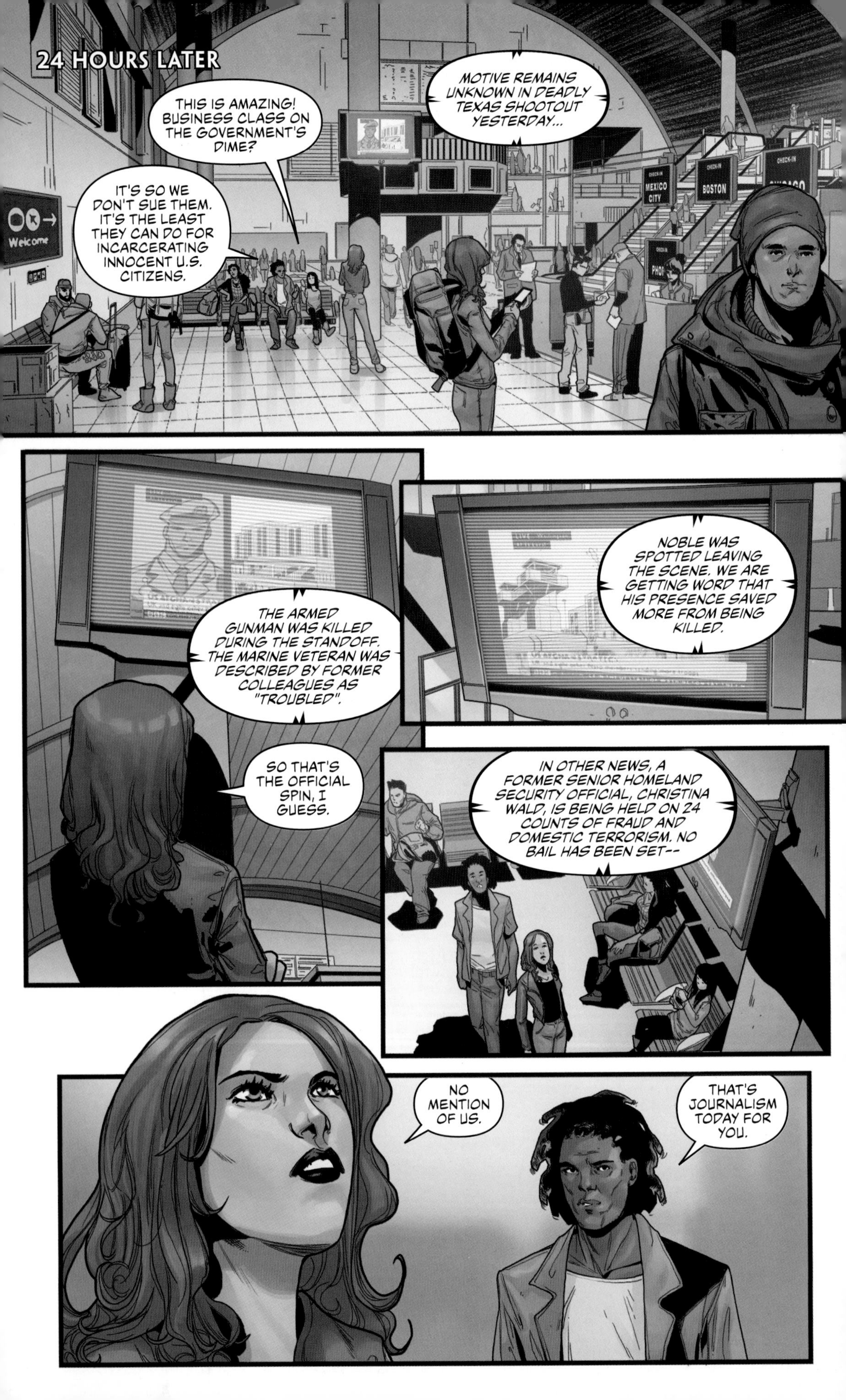
24 HOURS LATER
THIS IS AMAZING! BUSINESS CLASS ON THE GOVERNMENT'S DIME?
MOTIVE REMAINS UNKNOWN IN DEADLY TEXAS SHOOTOUT YESTERDAY...
IT'S SO WE DON'T SUE THEM. IT'S THE LEAST THEY CAN DO FOR INCARCERATING INNOCENT U.S. CITIZENS.
Welcome
CHECK-IN MEXICO CITY
CHECK-IN BOSTON
CHECK-IN
THE ARMED GUNMAN WAS KILLED DURING THE STANDOFF. THE MARINE VETERAN WAS DESCRIBED BY FORMER COLLEAGUES AS "TROUBLED".
NOBLE WAS SPOTTED LEAVING THE SCENE. WE ARE GETTING WORD THAT HIS PRESENCE SAVED MORE FROM BEING KILLED.
SO THAT'S THE OFFICIAL SPIN, I GUESS.
IN OTHER NEWS, A FORMER SENIOR HOMELAND SECURITY OFFICIAL, CHRISTINA WALD, IS BEING HELD ON 24 COUNTS OF FRAUD AND DOMESTIC TERRORISM. NO BAIL HAS BEEN SET--
NO MENTION OF US.
THAT'S JOURNALISM TODAY FOR YOU.

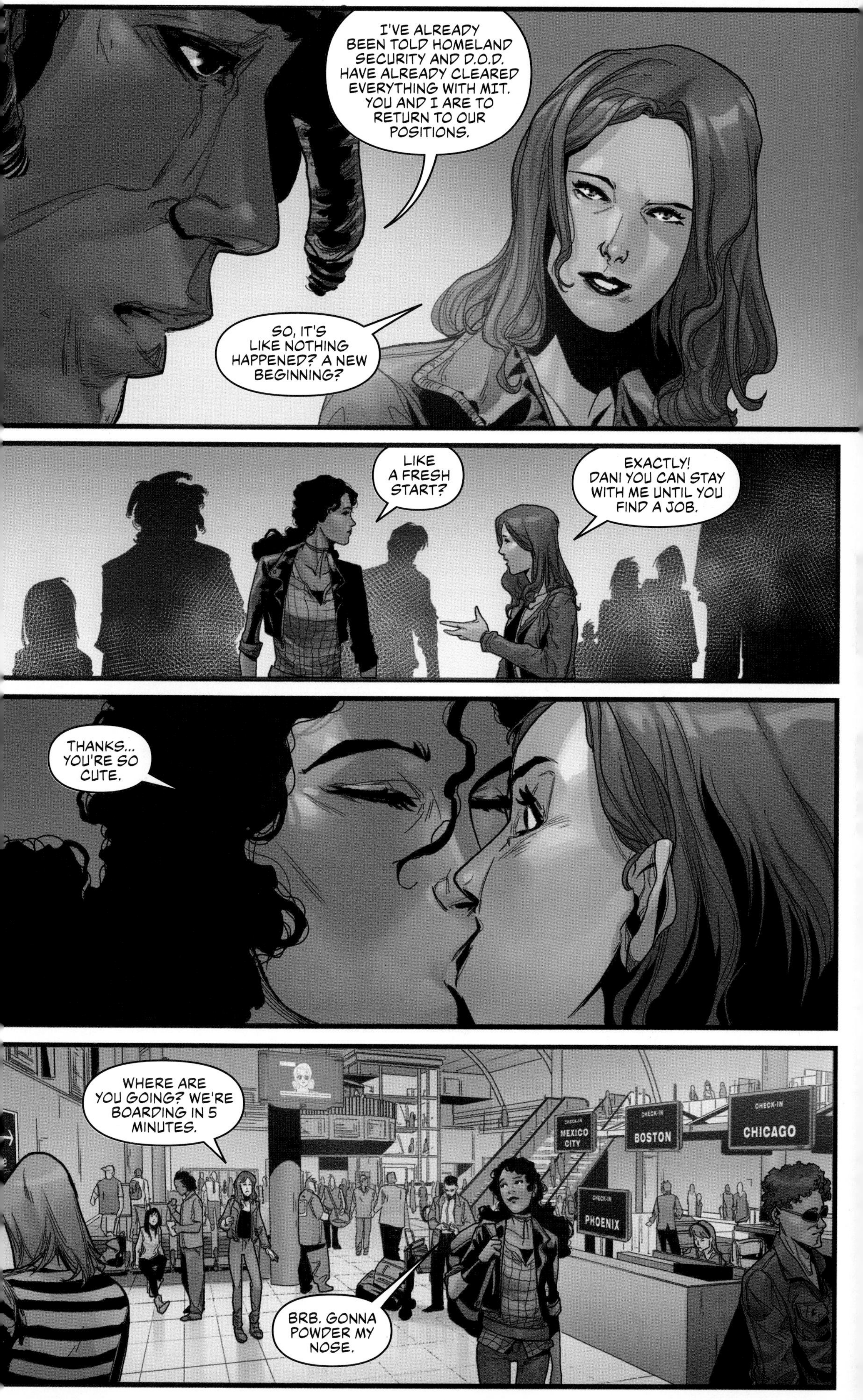
I'VE ALREADY BEEN TOLD HOMELAND SECURITY AND D.O.D. HAVE ALREADY CLEARED EVERYTHING WITH MIT. YOU AND I ARE TO RETURN TO OUR POSITIONS.
SO, IT'S LIKE NOTHING HAPPENED? A NEW BEGINNING?
LIKE A FRESH START?
EXACTLY! DANI YOU CAN STAY WITH ME UNTIL YOU FIND A JOB.
THANKS... YOU'RE SO CUTE.
WHERE ARE YOU GOING? WE'RE BOARDING IN 5 MINUTES.
CHECK-IN
MEXICO CITY
CHECK-IN
BOSTON
CHECK-IN
CHICAGO
CHECK-IN
PHOENIX
BRB. GONNA POWDER MY NOSE.

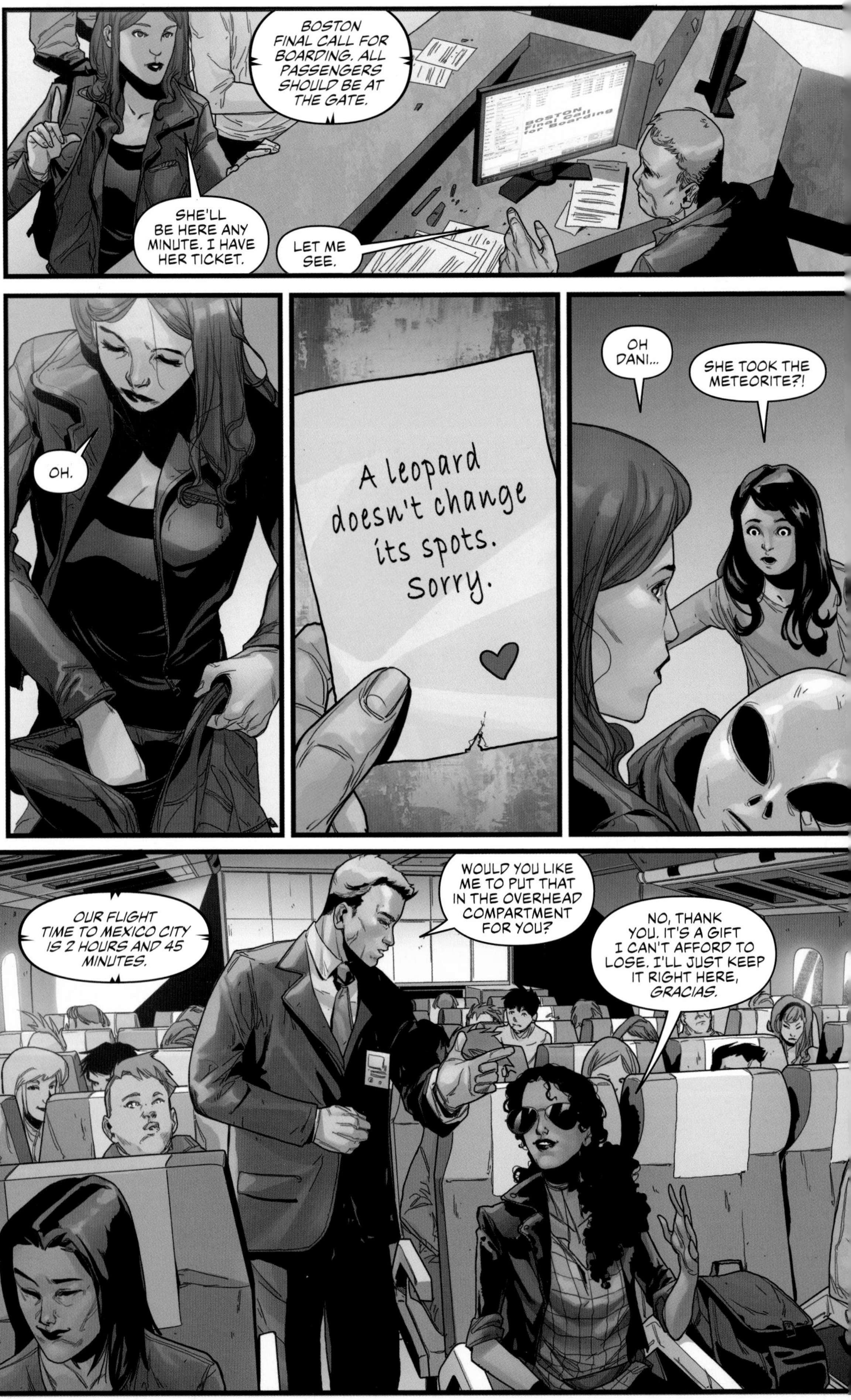
BOSTON FINAL CALL FOR BOARDING. ALL PASSENGERS SHOULD BE AT THE GATE.
BOSTON Final Call for Boarding
SHE'LL BE HERE ANY MINUTE. I HAVE HER TICKET.
LET ME SEE.
OH.
A leopard doesn't change its spots. Sorry.
OH DANI...
SHE TOOK THE METEORITE?!
OUR FLIGHT TIME TO MEXICO CITY IS 2 HOURS AND 45 MINUTES.
WOULD YOU LIKE ME TO PUT THAT IN THE OVERHEAD COMPARTMENT FOR YOU?
NO, THANK YOU. IT'S A GIFT I CAN'T AFFORD TO LOSE. I'LL JUST KEEP IT RIGHT HERE, GRACIAS.

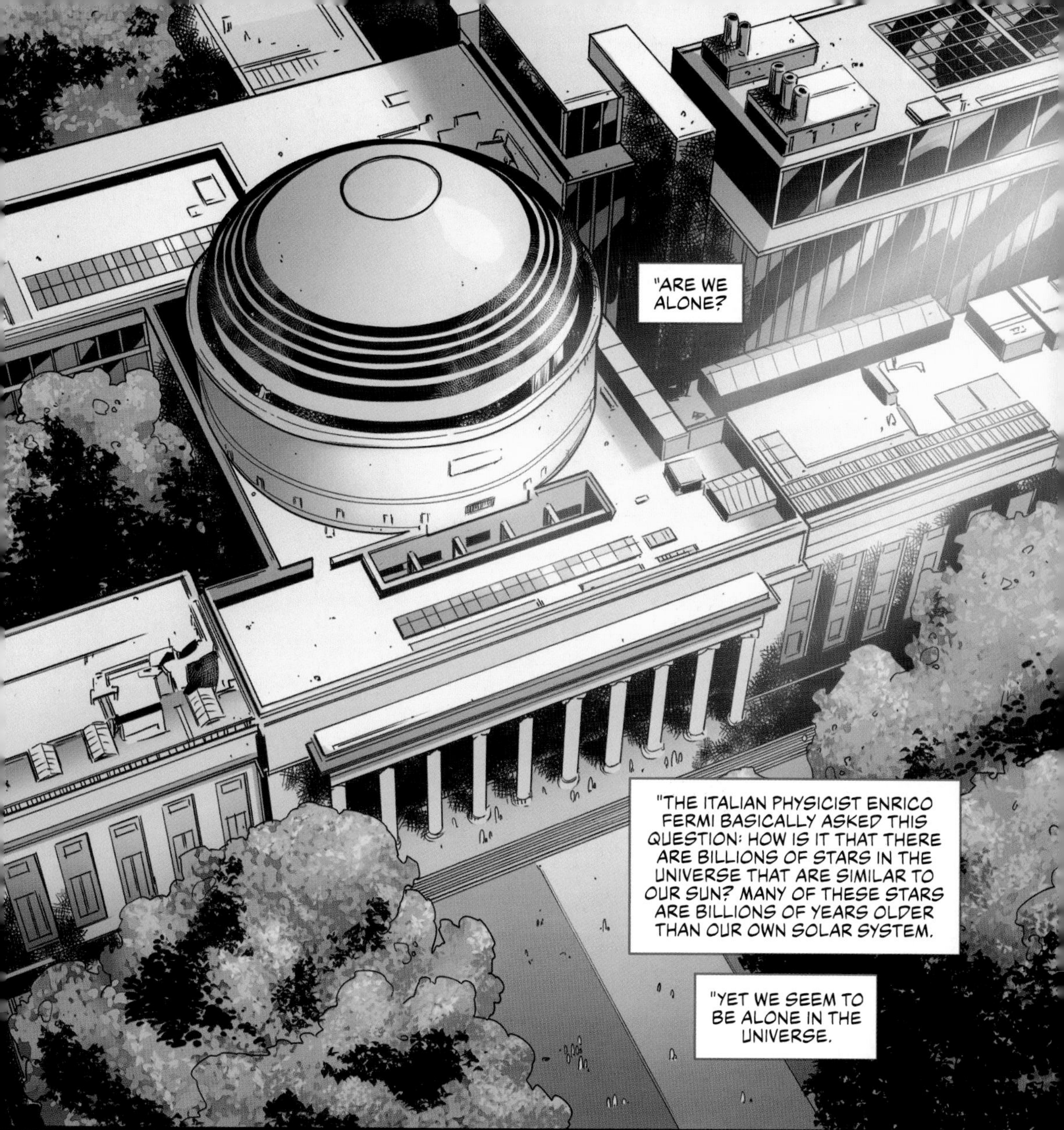
"ARE WE ALONE?
"THE ITALIAN PHYSICIST ENRICO FERMI BASICALLY ASKED THIS QUESTION: HOW IS IT THAT THERE ARE BILLIONS OF STARS IN THE UNIVERSE THAT ARE SIMILAR TO OUR SUN? MANY OF THESE STARS ARE BILLIONS OF YEARS OLDER THAN OUR OWN SOLAR SYSTEM.
"YET WE SEEM TO BE ALONE IN THE UNIVERSE.

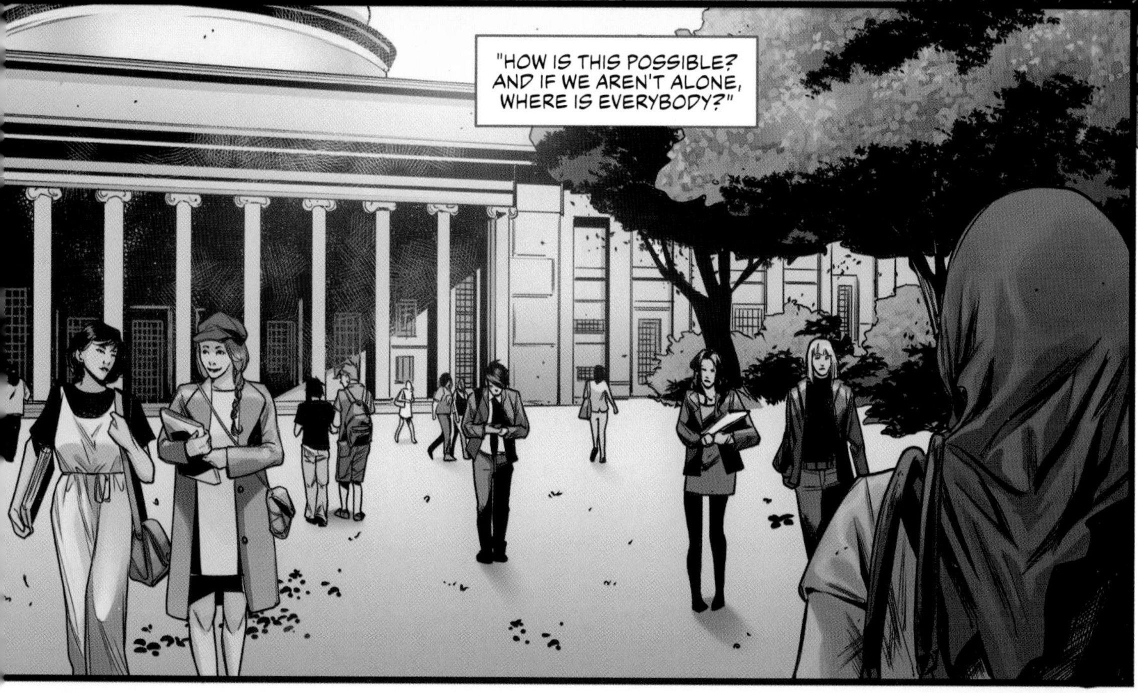
"HOW IS THIS POSSIBLE? AND IF WE AREN'T ALONE, WHERE IS EVERYBODY?"

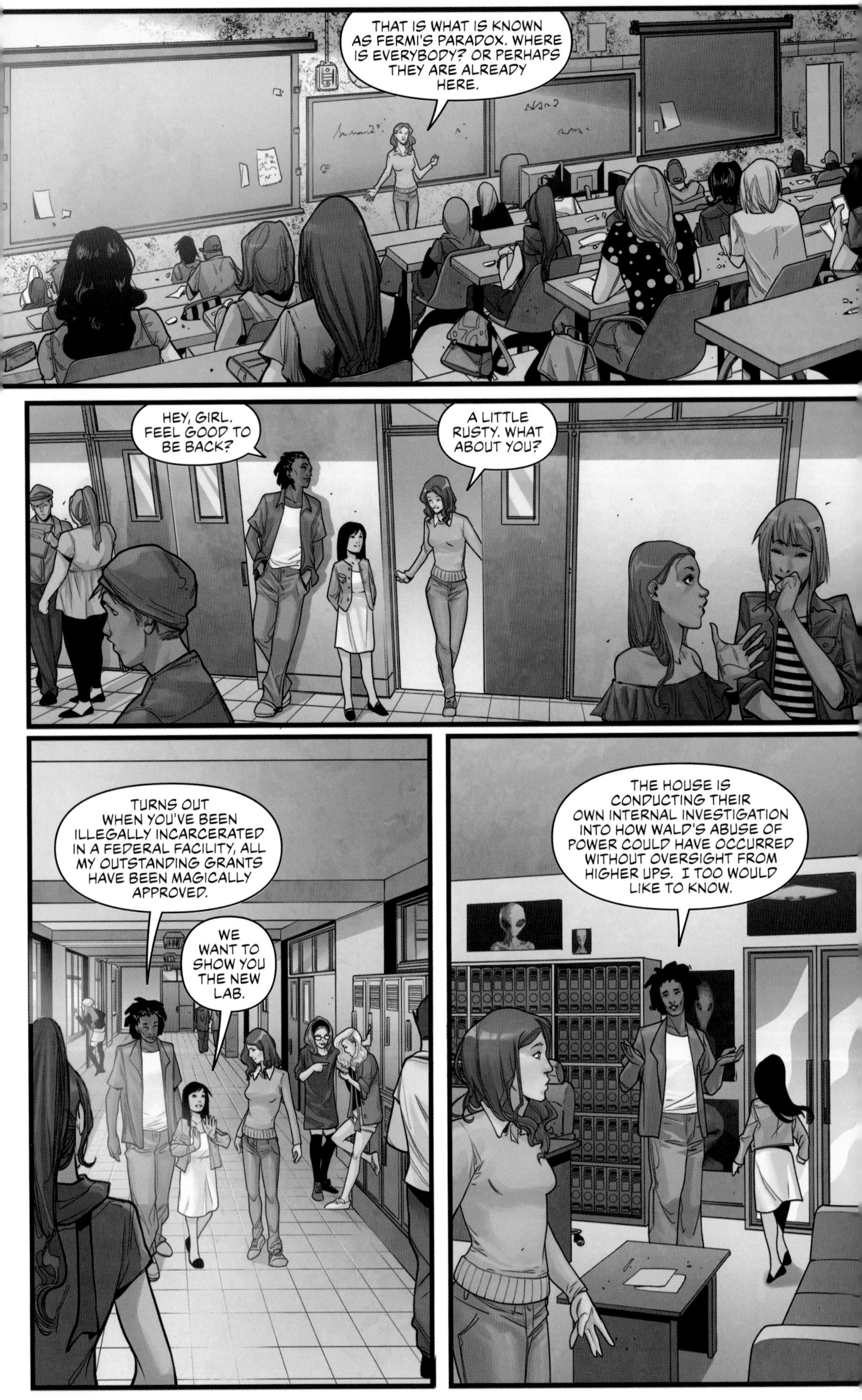
THAT IS WHAT IS KNOWN AS FERMI'S PARADOX. WHERE IS EVERYBODY? OR PERHAPS THEY ARE ALREADY HERE.
HEY, GIRL. FEEL GOOD TO BE BACK?
A LITTLE RUSTY. WHAT ABOUT YOU?
TURNS OUT WHEN YOU'VE BEEN ILLEGALLY INCARCERATED IN A FEDERAL FACILITY, ALL MY OUTSTANDING GRANTS HAVE BEEN MAGICALLY APPROVED.
WE WANT TO SHOW YOU THE NEW LAB.
THE HOUSE IS CONDUCTING THEIR OWN INTERNAL INVESTIGATION INTO HOW WALD'S ABUSE OF POWER COULD HAVE OCCURRED WITHOUT OVERSIGHT FROM HIGHER UPS. I TOO WOULD LIKE TO KNOW.

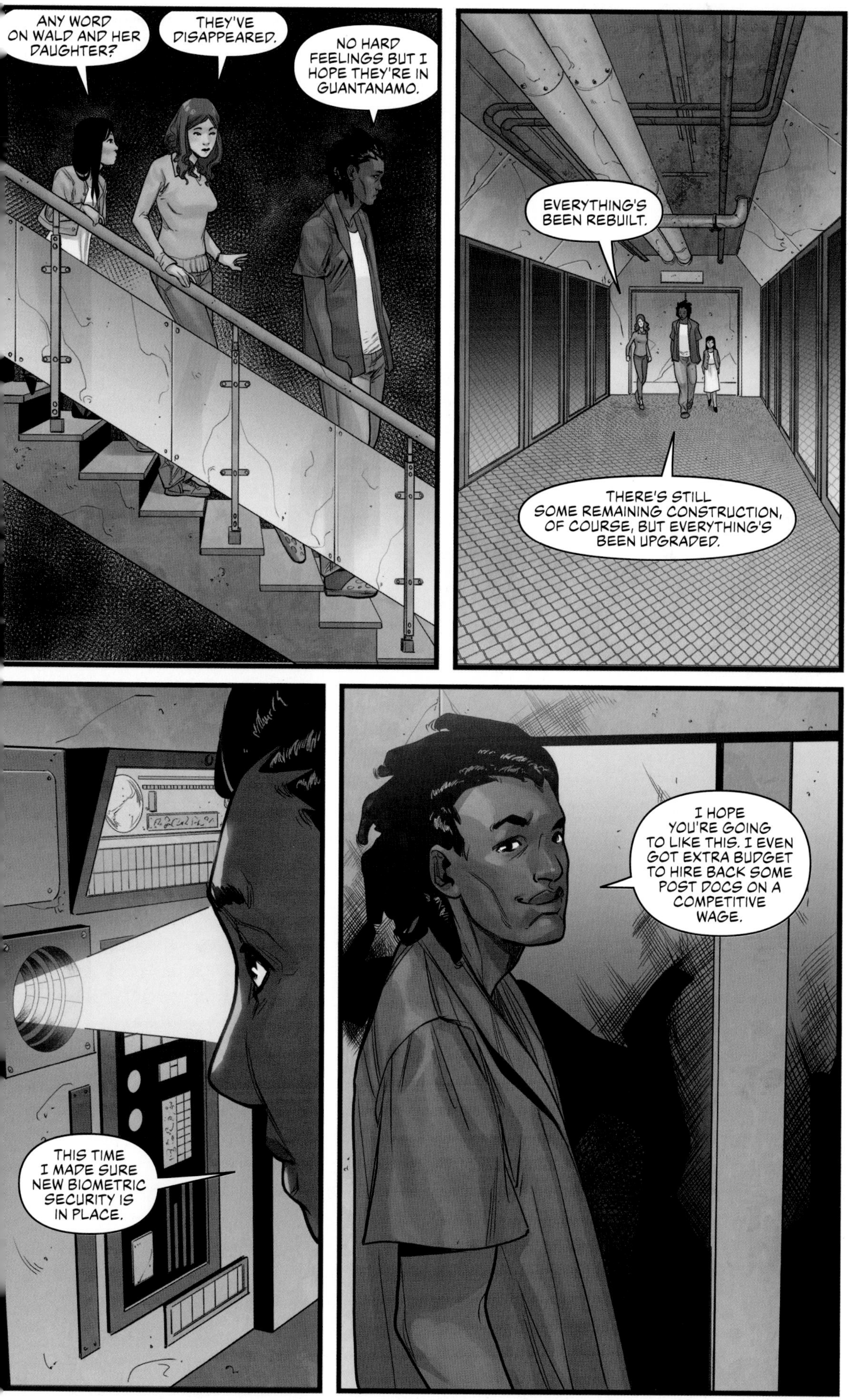
ANY WORD ON WALD AND HER DAUGHTER?
THEY'VE DISAPPEARED.
NO HARD FEELINGS BUT I HOPE THEY'RE IN GUANTANAMO.
EVERYTHING'S BEEN REBUILT.
THERE'S STILL SOME REMAINING CONSTRUCTION, OF COURSE, BUT EVERYTHING'S BEEN UPGRADED.
THIS TIME I MADE SURE NEW BIOMETRIC SECURITY IS IN PLACE.
I HOPE YOU'RE GOING TO LIKE THIS. I EVEN GOT EXTRA BUDGET TO HIRE BACK SOME POST DOCS ON A COMPETITIVE WAGE.

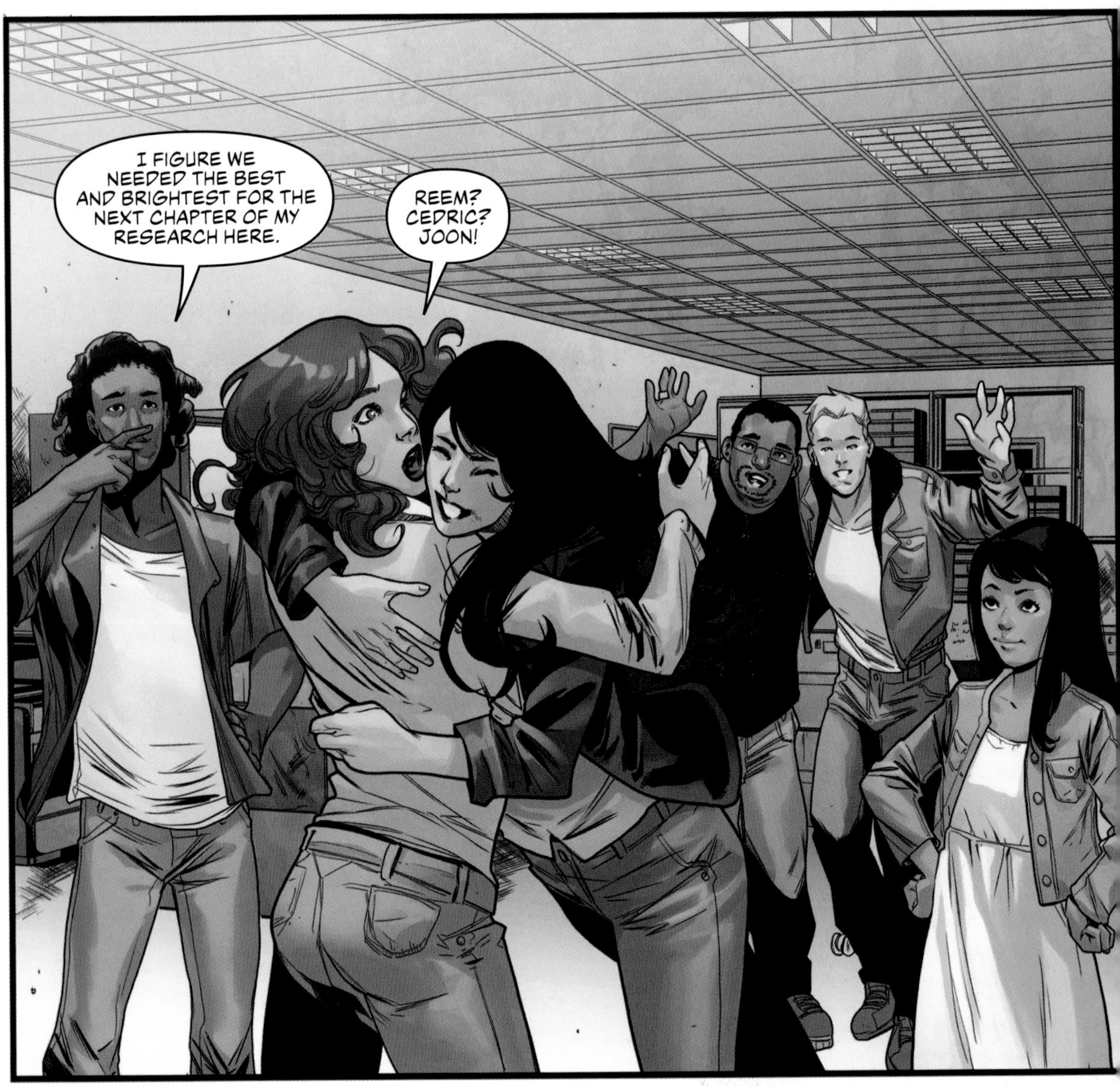
I FIGURE WE NEEDED THE BEST AND BRIGHTEST FOR THE NEXT CHAPTER OF MY RESEARCH HERE.
REEM? CEDRIC? JOON!

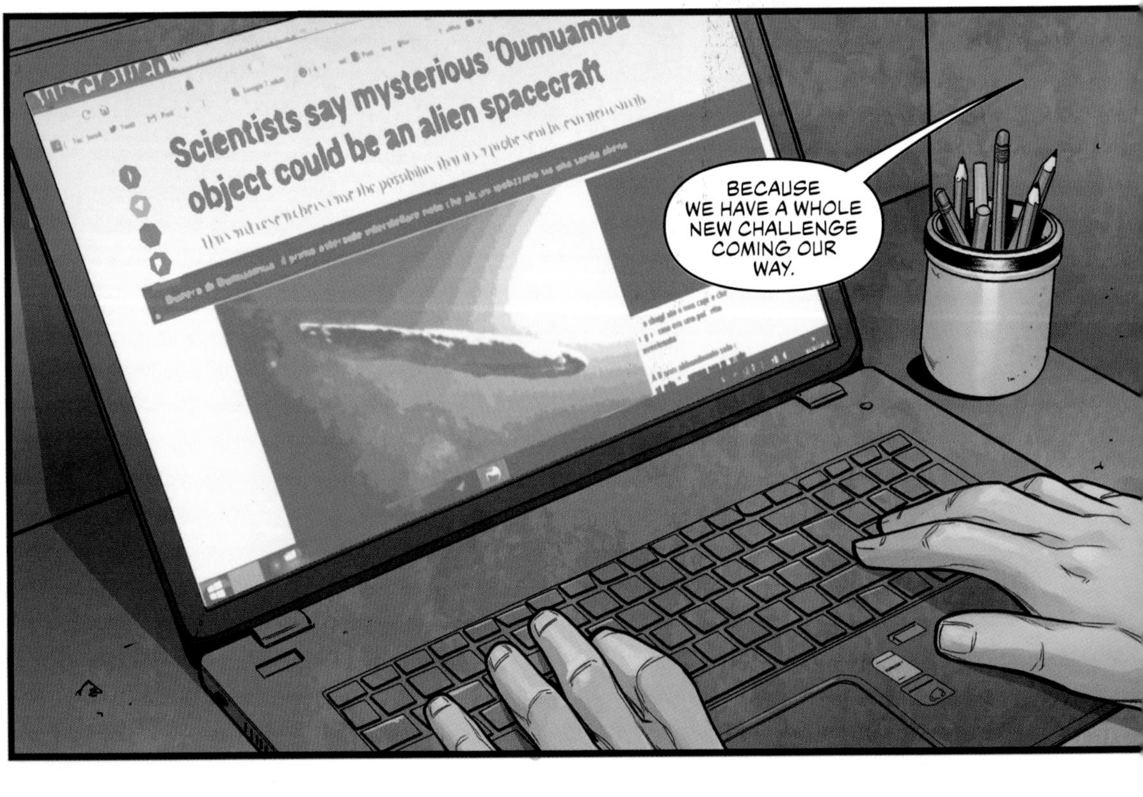
Scientists say mysterious 'Oumuamua object could be an alien spacecraft
BECAUSE WE HAVE A WHOLE NEW CHALLENGE COMING OUR WAY.

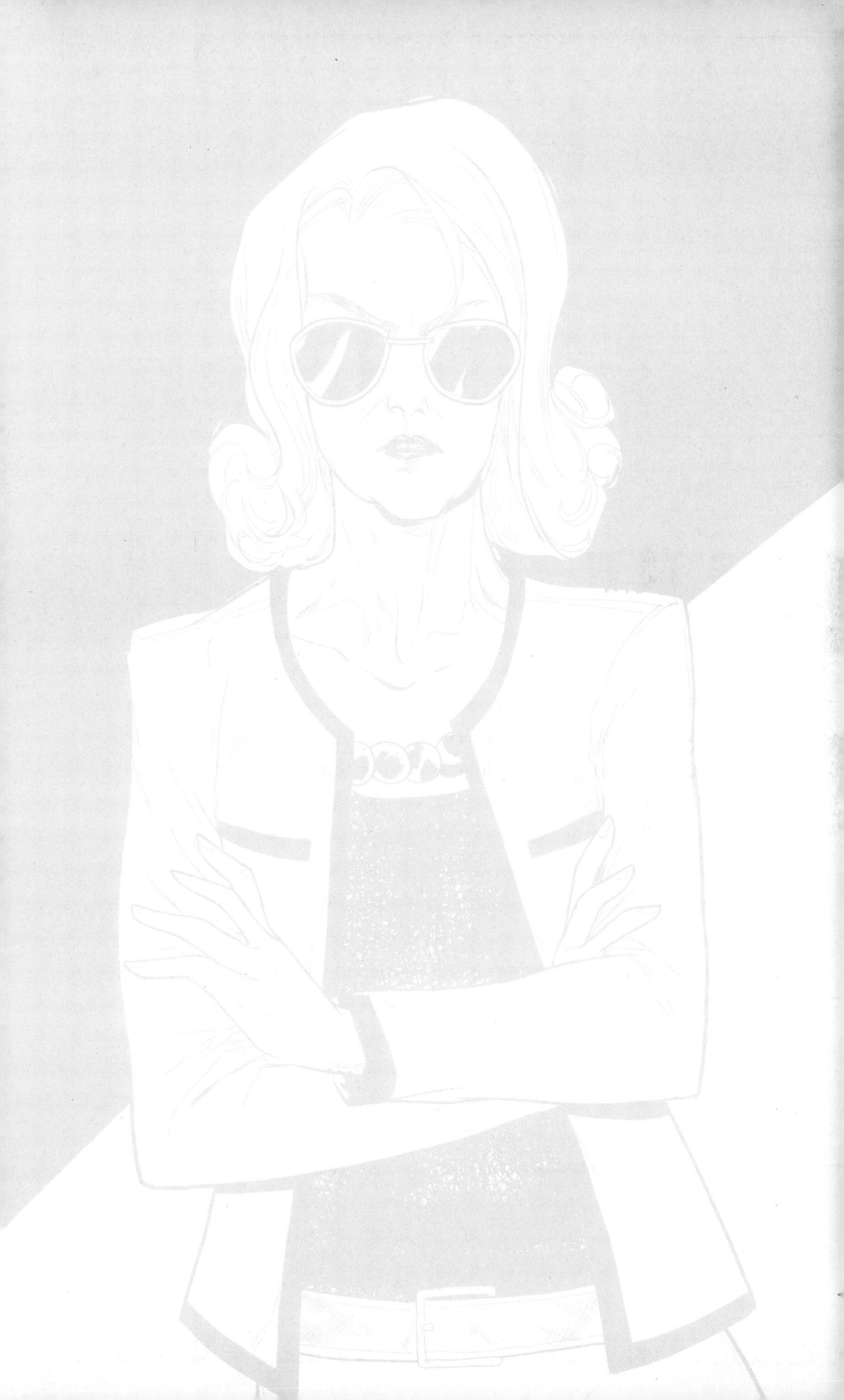

COVER GALLERY

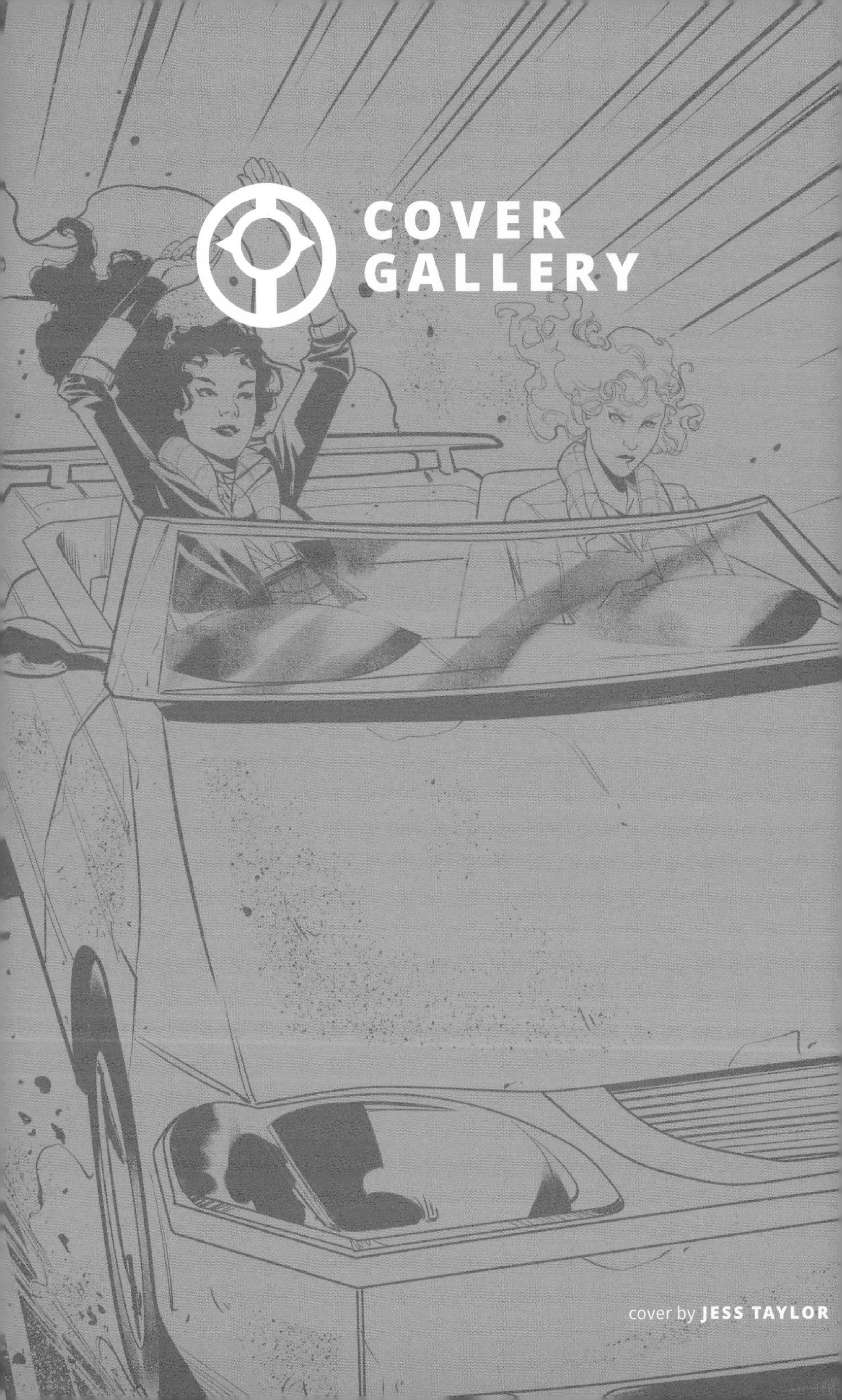

cover by **JESS TAYLOR**

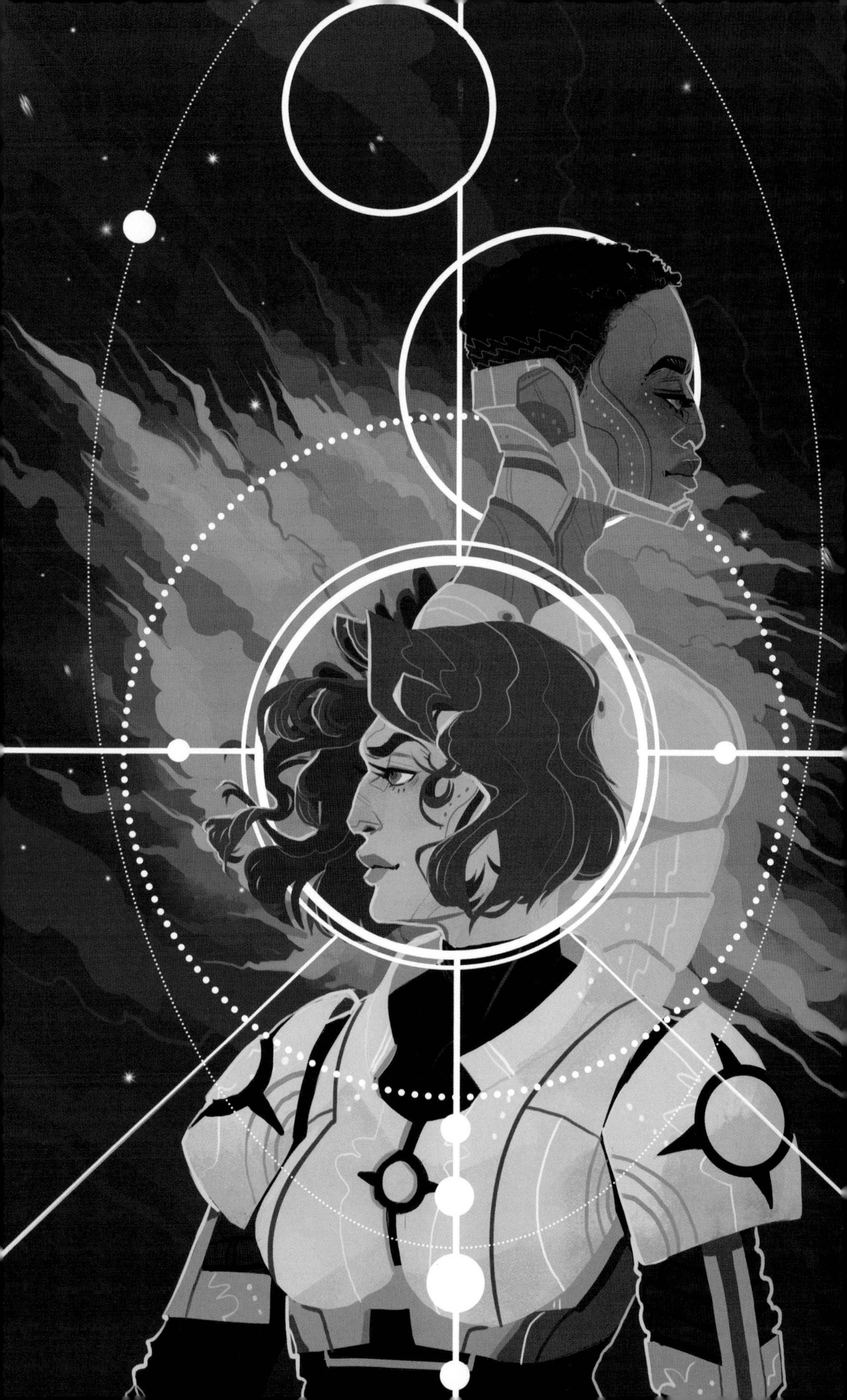

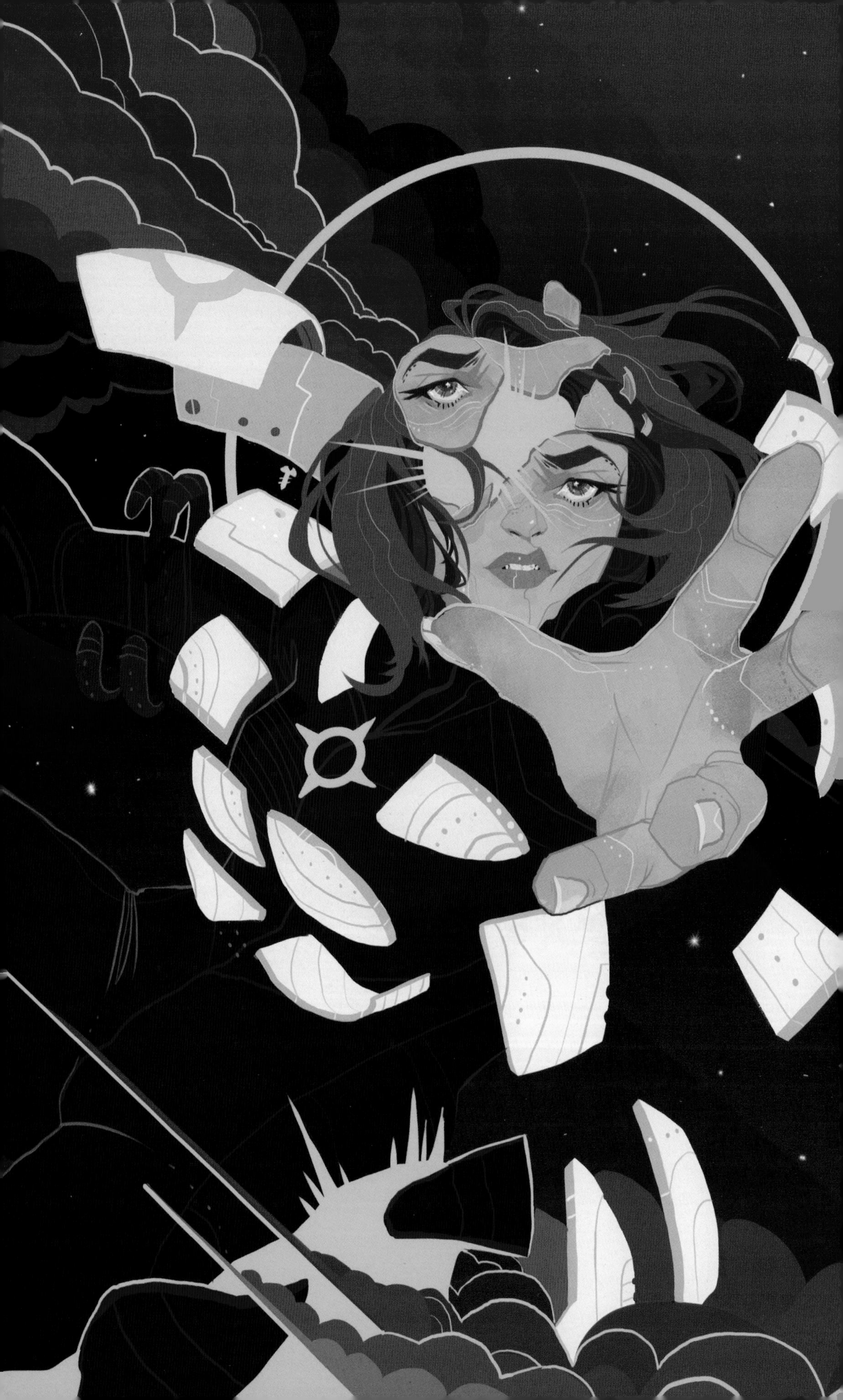

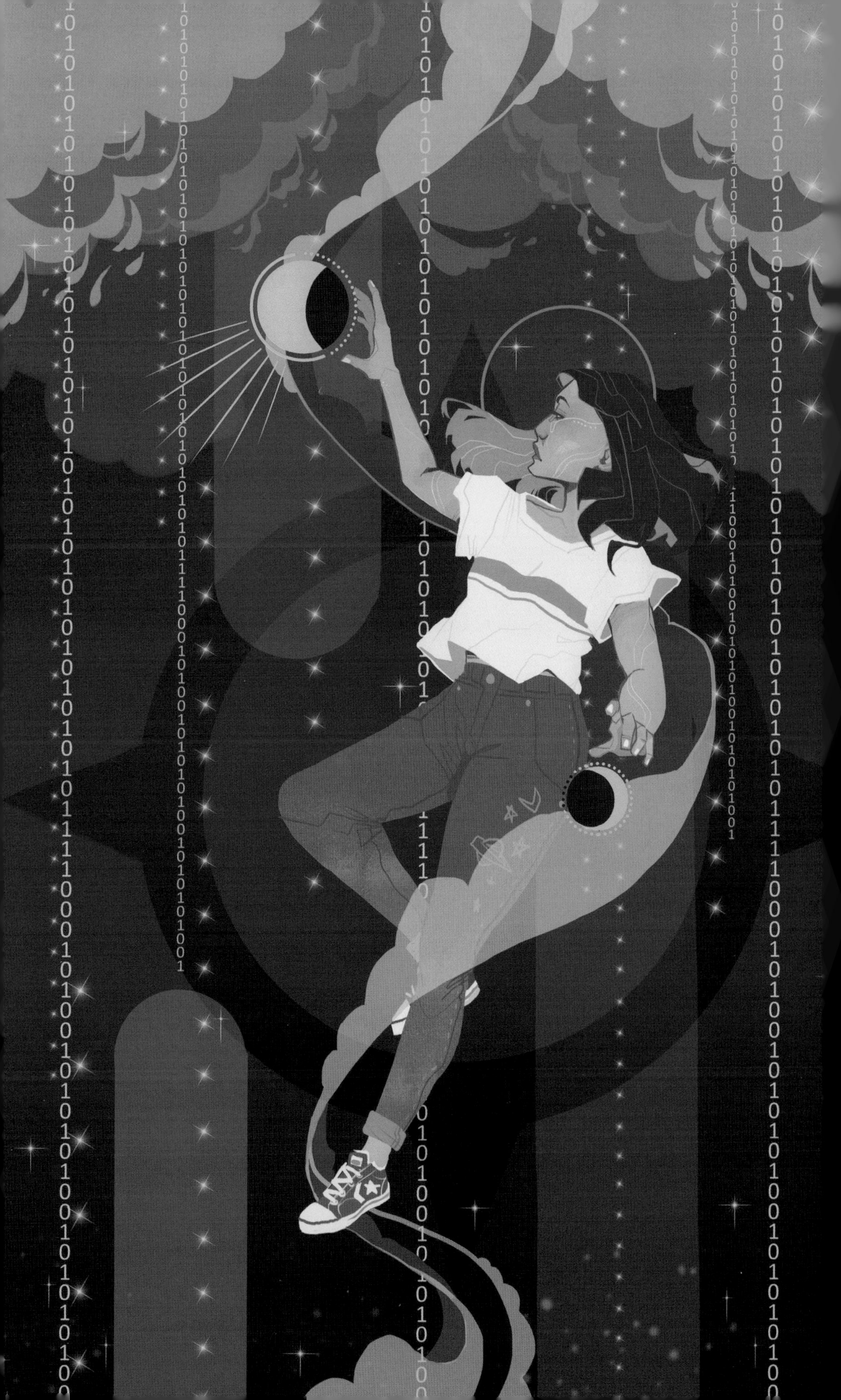

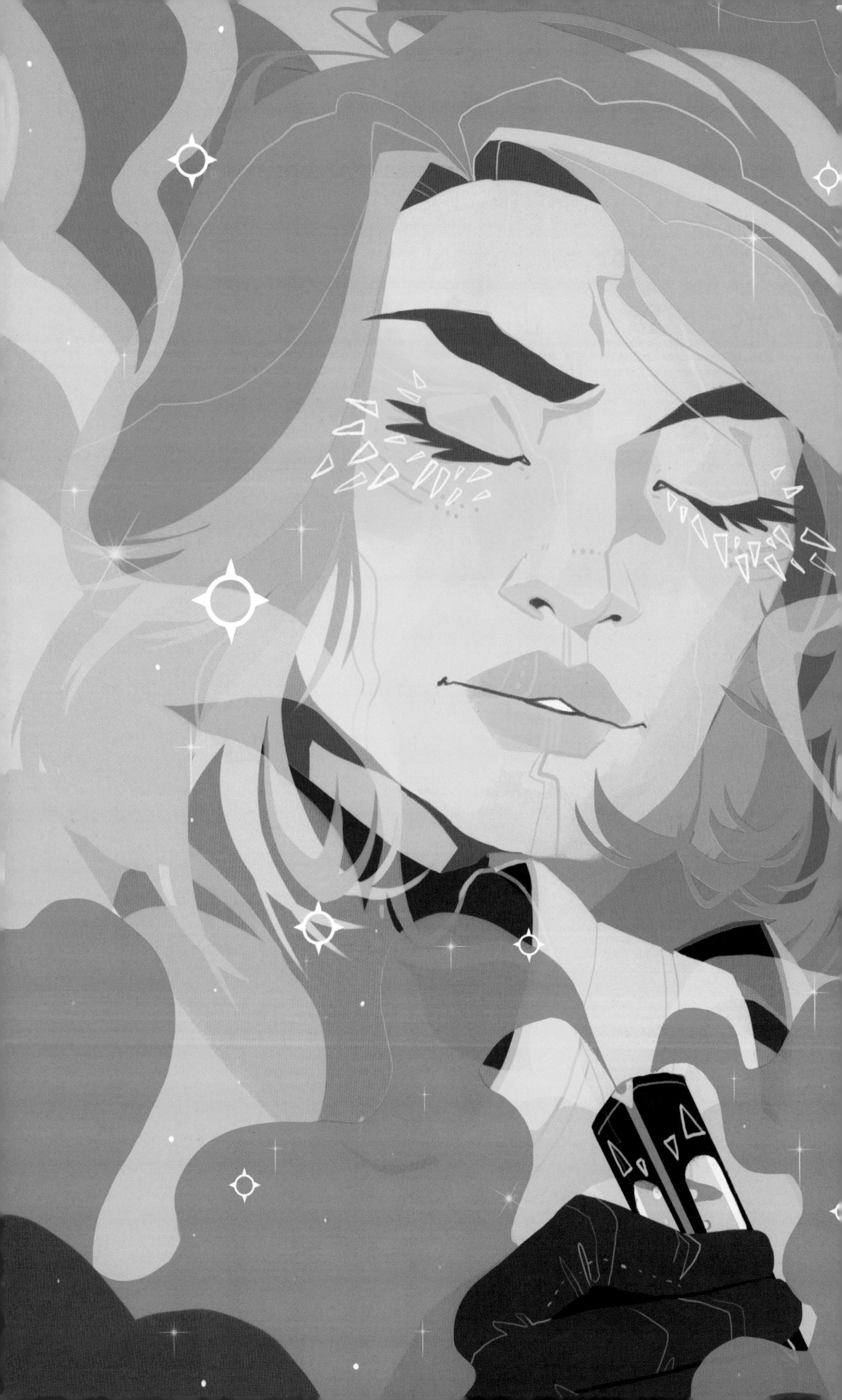

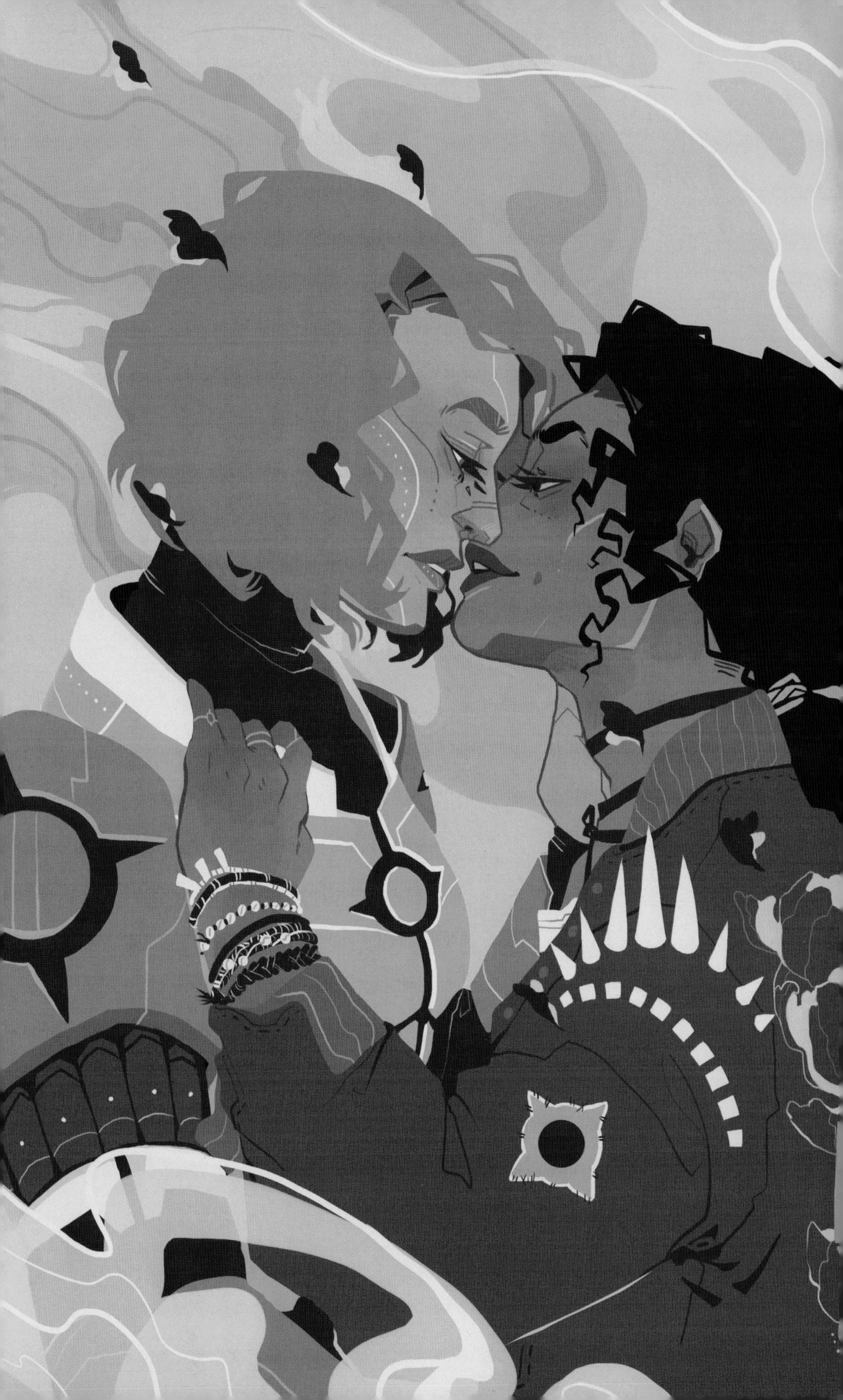

EDITORS NOTE

When the developmental discussions for Summit volume three began, we knew we wanted to introduce a new love interest for Val. It had been nine issues of mourning for her previous girlfriend Kay who died during The Event (see the Free Comic Book Day one shot), and it just felt like the time.

When it was discussed Amy Chu came up with a great description for the character, "Somewhere in between Lisa Bonet/Janelle Monae/Zoe Washburn; gorgeous but not pretty, natural curly hair, rocker chick look late '20s, '30s maybe. Wears aviators, leather jacket, boots, probably rides a motorcycle". To sum up, Dani was meant to look "cool" channeling the attitude of Zoe Washburn, with a James Dean aesthetic.

Who better to bring back a little bit of romance to Val's life than her opposite in so many ways. Marika Cresta took the description and came up with a fantastic design for the character. Dani has resonated with readers, and we hope to see her character included in future issues of Summit!

BOOK Summit ISSUE # 11 ARTIST Marika Cresta

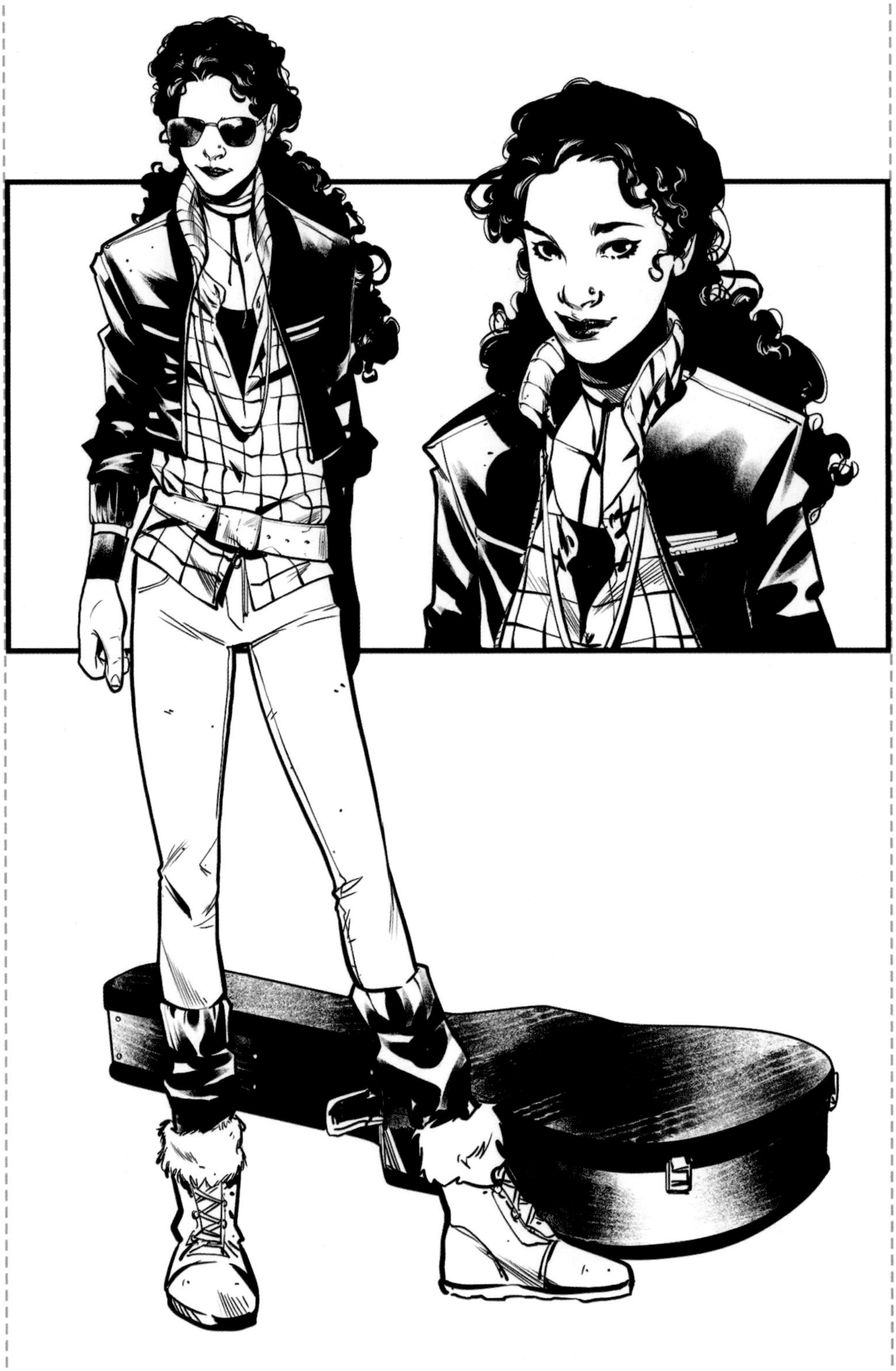

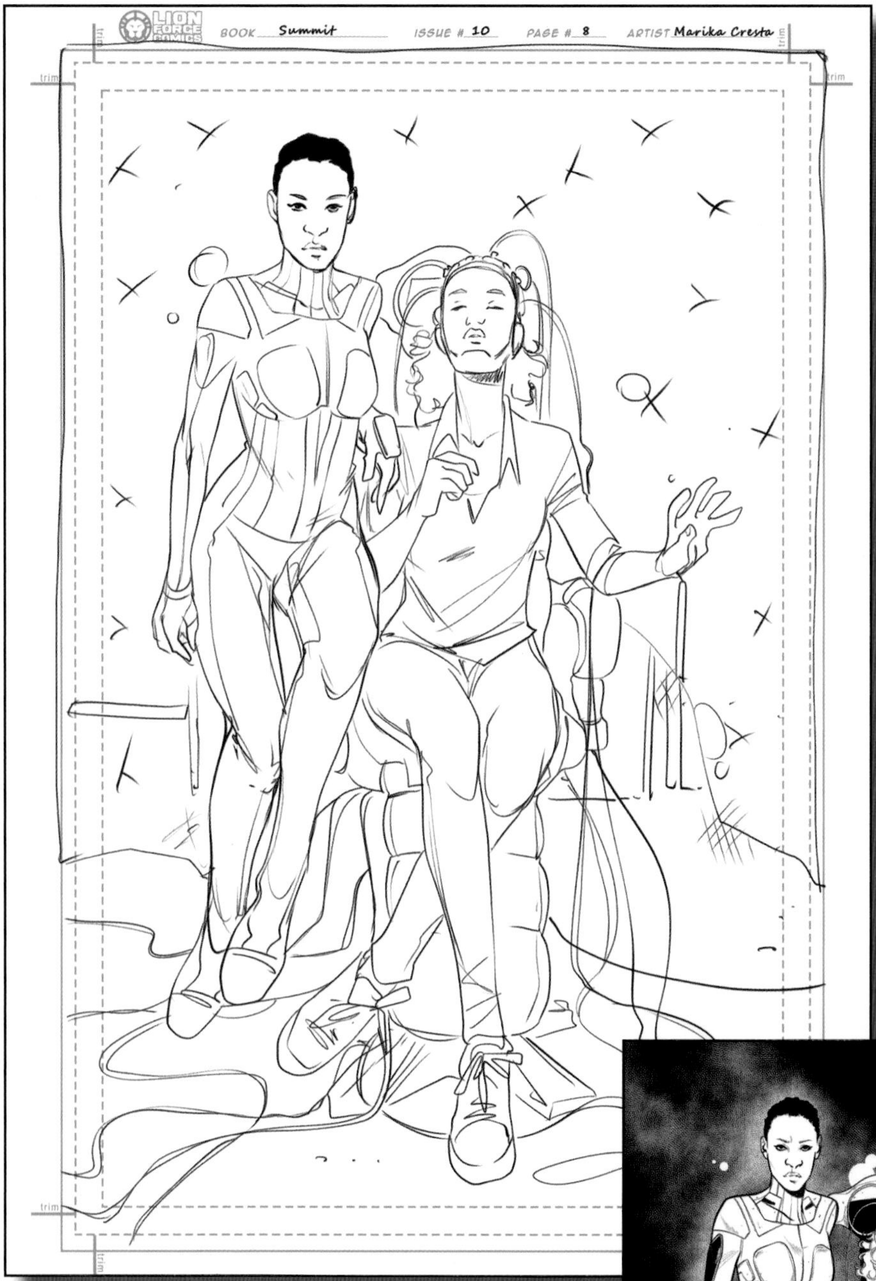
LION FORCE COMICS
BOOK Summit ISSUE # 10 PAGE # 8 ARTIST Marika Cresta
trim

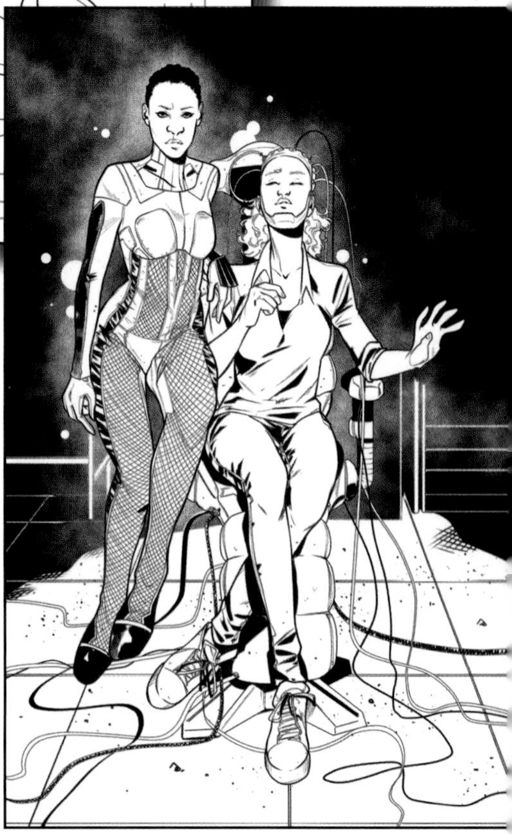

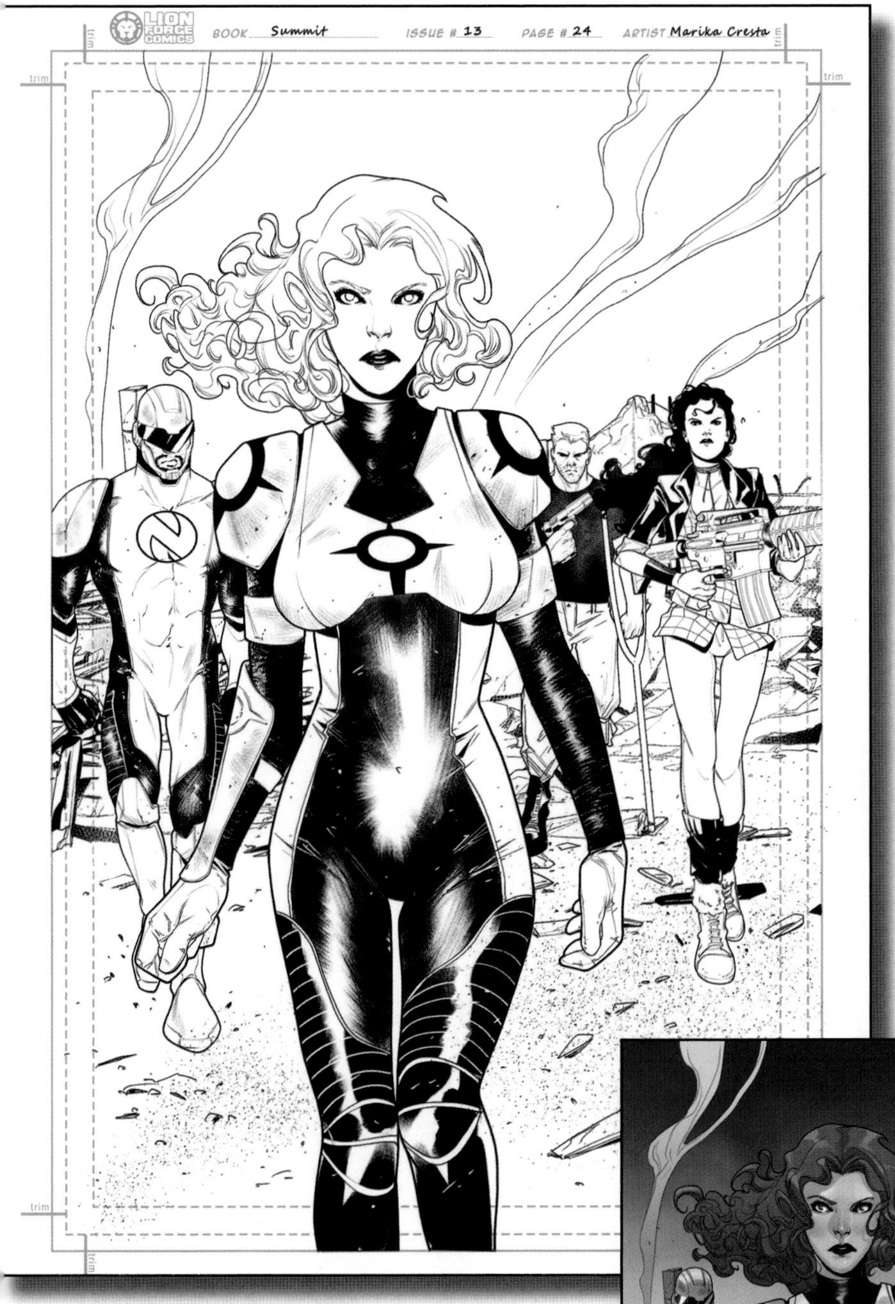
LION FORCE COMICS
BOOK Summit
ISSUE # 13
PAGE # 24
ARTIST Marika Cresta

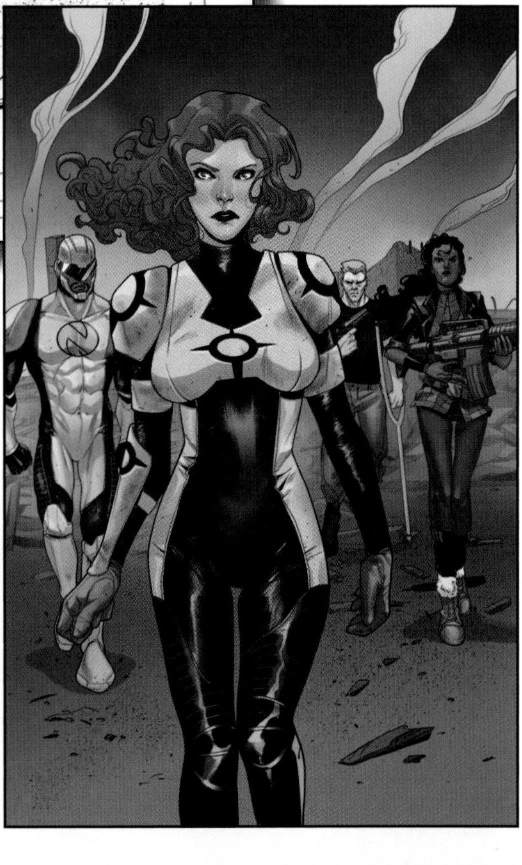

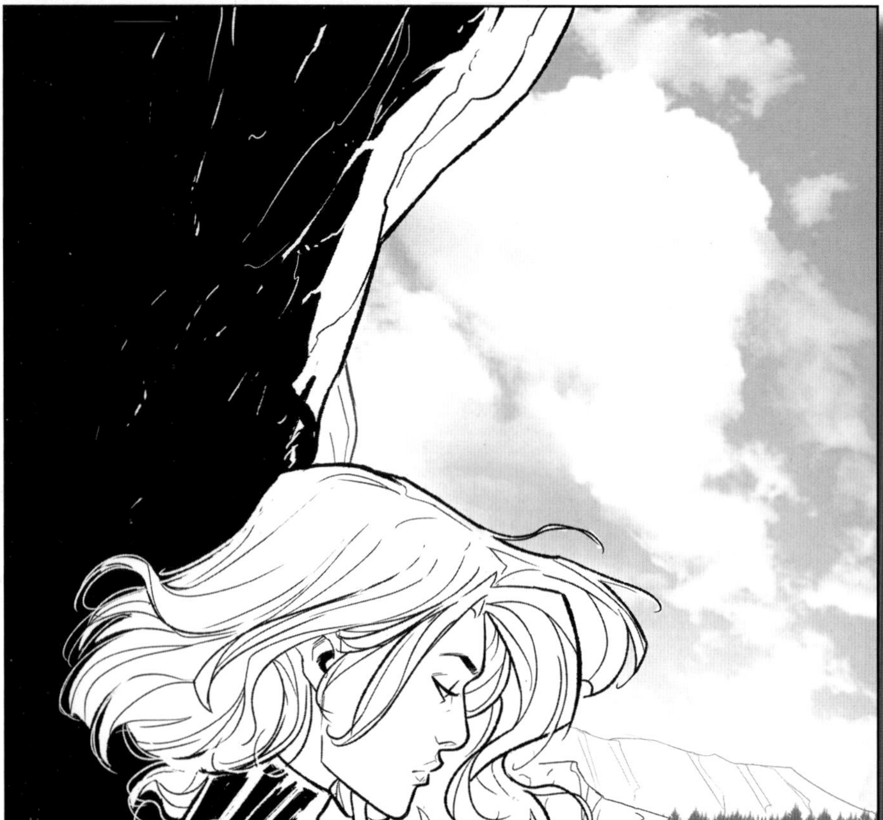

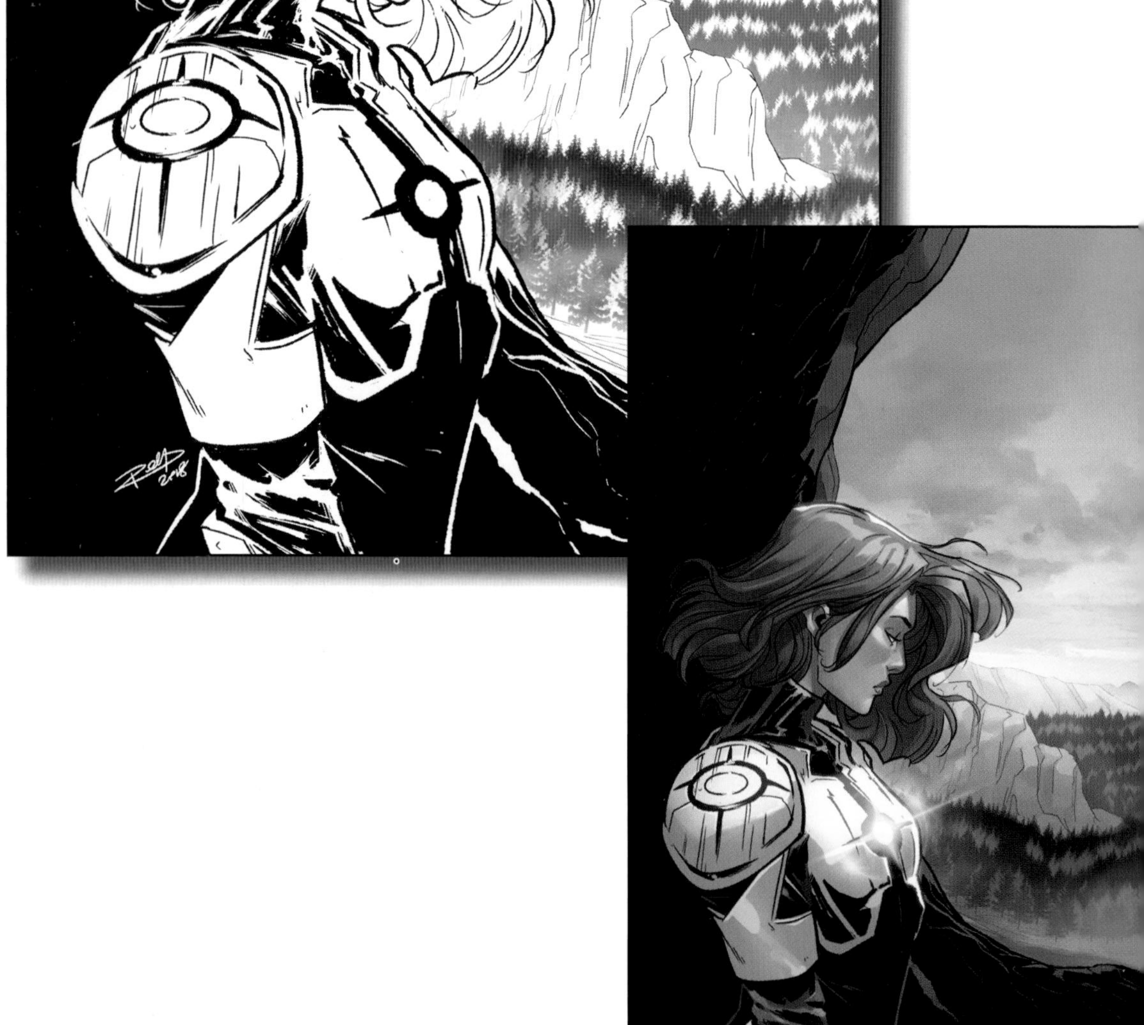